Essential Japanese

Written by
Mamori Sugita Hughes

Edited by
Suzanne McQuade

Content in this program has been modified and enhanced from *Starting Out in Japanese*, published in 2010.

Living Language and colophon are registered trademarks of Random House, Inc.

Published in the United States by Living Language, an imprint of Random House, Inc.

www.livinglanguage.com

Editor: Suzanne McQuade
Production Editor: Ciara Robinson
Production Manager: Tom Marshall
Interior Design: Sophie Chin
Illustrations: Sophie Chin

First Edition

ISBN: 978-0-307-97189-0

Library of Congress Cataloging-in-Publication Data

Hughes, Mamori.
  Essential Japanese / written by Mamori Hughes ; edited by Suzanne McQuade. -- 1st ed.
    p. cm.
  Text in English and Japanese.
  Includes bibliographical references and index.
  ISBN 978-0-307-97189-0 (alk. paper)
  1. Japanese language--Textbooks for foreign speakers--English. 2. Japanese language--Grammar. 3. Japanese language--Spoken Japanese. I. McQuade, Suzanne. II. Title.
  PL539.5.E5H84 2011
  495.6'82421--dc23
                          2011043120

This book is available at special discounts for bulk purchases for sales promotions or premiums. Special editions, including personalized covers, excerpts of existing books, and corporate imprints, can be created in large quantities for special needs. For more information, write to Special Markets/ Premium Sales, 1745 Broadway, MD 3-1, New York, New York 10019 or e-mail specialmarkets@ randomhouse.com.

PRINTED IN THE UNITED STATES OF AMERICA

10 9 8 7 6 5

Acknowledgments

Thanks to the Living Language team: Amanda D'Acierno, Christopher Warnasch, Suzanne McQuade, Laura Riggio, Erin Quirk, Amanda Munoz, Fabrizio LaRocca, Siobhan O'Hare, Sophie Chin, Sue Daulton, Alison Skrabek, Carolyn Roth, Ciara Robinson, and Tom Marshall.

How to Use This Course **6**

COURSE

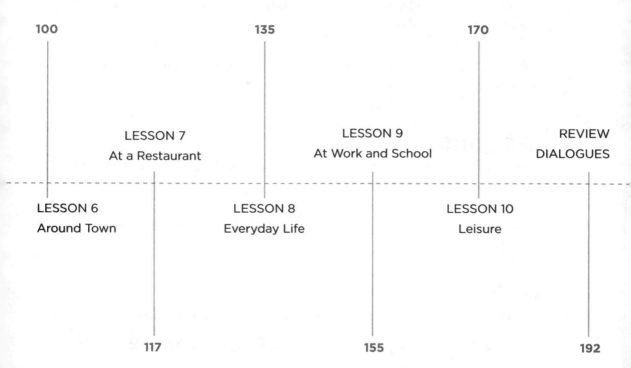
OUTLINE

How to Use This Course

Konnichi wa !

Welcome to *Living Language Essential Japanese*! Ready to learn how to speak, read, and write Japanese?

Before we begin, let's go over what you'll see in this course. It's very easy to use, but this section will help you get started.

LESSONS

There are 10 lessons in this course. Each lesson is divided into three parts and has the following components:

Welcome at the beginning outlining what you will cover in each of the three parts of the lesson.

PART 1

- **Vocabulary Builder 1** listing the key words and phrases for that lesson.

- **Vocabulary Practice 1** to practice what you learned in Vocabulary Builder 1.

- **Grammar Builder 1** to guide you through the structure of the Japanese language (how to form sentences, questions, and so on).

PART 2

- **Vocabulary Builder 2** listing more key words and phrases.

- **Vocabulary Practice 2** to practice what you learned in Vocabulary Builder 2.

- **Grammar Builder 2** for more information on language structure.

- **Work Out 1** for a comprehensive practice of what you've learned so far.

PART 3

- **Bring It All Together** to put what you've learned in a conversational context through a dialogue, monologue, description, or other similar text.

- **Work Out 2** for another helpful practice exercise.

- **Drive It Home** to ingrain Japanese particles and other vocabulary and structure for the long term.

- **Parting Words** outlining what you learned in the lesson.

TAKE IT FURTHER

- **Take It Further** sections scattered throughout the lesson to introduce elements of the Japanese script or provide extra information about the new vocabulary you just saw, expand on some grammar points, and introduce additional words and phrases.

WORD RECALL

Word Recall sections appear in between lessons. They review important vocabulary and grammar from previous lessons, including the one you just finished. These sections will reinforce what you've learned so far in the course, and help you retain the information for the long term.

QUIZZES

This course contains two quizzes: **Quiz 1** is halfway through the course (after Lesson 5), and **Quiz 2** appears after the last lesson (Lesson 10). The quizzes are self-graded so it's easy for you to test your progress and see what you might need to go back and review.

REVIEW DIALOGUES

There are five **Review Dialogues** at the end of the course, after Quiz 2. These everyday dialogues review what you learned in Lessons 1-10, introduce some new vocabulary and structures, and allow you to become more familiar with conversational Japanese. Each dialogue is followed by comprehension questions that serve as the course's final review.

PROGRESS BAR

You will see a **Progress Bar** on almost every page that has course material. It indicates your current position in the course and lets you know how much progress you're making. Each line in the bar represents a lesson, with the final line representing the Review Dialogues.

AUDIO

Look for this symbol ⊙ to help guide you through the audio as you're reading the book. It will tell you which track to listen to for each section that has audio. When you see the symbol, select the indicated track and start listening! If you don't see the symbol, then there isn't any audio for that section.

The audio can be used on its own—in other words, without the book—when you're on the go. Whether in your car or at the gym, you can listen to the audio to brush up on your pronunciation and review what you've learned in the book.

GLOSSARY

At the back of this book you will find an extensive Japanese-English and English-Japanese glossary, including all of the essential words from all three levels of this Japanese course, as well as some additional vocabulary.

GUIDE TO READING AND WRITING JAPANESE

Three different types of characters are used to write Japanese: ひらがな **hiragana**, カタカナ **katakana**, and かんじ **kanji** characters. You will learn about each type gradually through this book and in the *Guide to Reading and Writing Japanese* included with this course. You'll also see the Japanese sounds transcribed into the Roman alphabet (also called **romaji**) throughout this course.

FREE ONLINE TOOLS

Go to **www.livinglanguage.com/languagelab** to access your free online tools. The tools are organized around the lessons in this course, with audiovisual flashcards, as well as interactive games and quizzes for each lesson, plus a grammar summary for all three levels.. These tools will help you to review and practice the vocabulary and grammar that you've seen in the lessons, providing some extra words and phrases related to the lesson's topic as well.

Lesson 1: Essential Expression

Dai ikka: Hissu hyoogen

だいいっか: ひっすひょうげん

ようこそ！**Yookoso!** Welcome! By the end of this lesson, you'll be able to:

☐ Use basic expressions to greet someone

☐ Introduce yourself and ask someone for his or her name

☐ Use the particle は **wa**

☐ Ask someone how he or she is doing

☐ Say *I'm fine* in both polite and neutral tones

☐ Use courtesy expressions such as *thank you* and *I'm sorry*

☐ Use what you've learned when meeting people for the first time
Let's get started with some basic vocabulary. じゅんびはいいですか。**Junbi wa ii desu ka.** *Are you ready?*

Vocabulary Builder 1

▶ 1A Vocabulary Builder 1 (CD 1, Track 1)

Hello./Good afternoon.	こんにちは。	Konnichi wa.
Good morning.	おはようございます。	Ohayoo gozaimasu.
Good evening.	こんばんは。	Konban wa.
Good night.	おやすみなさい。	Oyasuminasai.
How do you do?	はじめまして。	Hajimemashite.
Nice to meet you.	どうぞよろしく。	Doozo yoroshiku.
What's your name?	おなまえは？	Onamae wa?
to be …	～です。	… desu.
I am …	わたしは～です。	Watashi wa… desu.

Note: In Japanese script, ～ indicates ellipses (…).

✎ Vocabulary Practice 1

Now let's practice what you've learned! Match the Japanese in the left column with the English equivalent in the right.

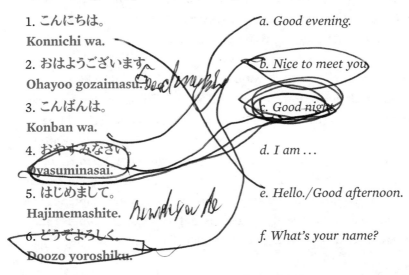

1. こんにちは。
Konnichi wa.

2. おはようございます。
Ohayoo gozaimasu.

3. こんばんは。
Konban wa.

4. おやすみなさい。
Oyasuminasai.

5. はじめまして。
Hajimemashite.

6. どうぞよろしく。
Doozo yoroshiku.

a. *Good evening.*

b. *Nice to meet you.*

c. *Good night.*

d. *I am …*

e. *Hello./Good afternoon.*

f. *What's your name?*

7. おなまえは？ *whats your name*   2   g. *Good morning.*
Onamae wa?

8. わたしは～です。 *I am*   h. *How do you do?* *hajimemashte*
Watashi wa ... desu.

ANSWER KEY
1. e; 2. g; 3. a; 4. c; 5. h; 6. b; 7. f; 8. d

Take It Further

Let's take a moment here to learn the basics of the Japanese writing system. Three different types of characters are used to write Japanese: ひらがな hiragana, カタカナ katakana, and かんじ kanji characters. Kanji is derived from the Chinese script, and is made up of ideographic symbols representing concepts or ideas rather than single sounds or syllables. In contrast, hiragana and katakana are syllabic: each character represents a single sound. Every Japanese word and expression can be written in hiragana, except for foreign loan words, which are written in katakana. Therefore, most students of Japanese first learn hiragana and katakana and add kanji later. As you learn kanji characters, you'll be able to write some words in kanji instead of hiragana. For more detailed overview of the Japanese writing system, please refer to Overview of the Japanese Writing System found in the *Guide to Reading and Writing Japanese*.

In *Essential Japanese*, all Japanese words and expressions will be written in hiragana (and katakana for foreign loan words). You'll also see the Japanese sounds transcribed into the Roman alphabet (also called romaji). Feel free to study only with the Roman alphabet transcriptions first. All of the written exercises in *Essential Japanese* are designed so that you can write in either Japanese characters or romaji. After each Vocabulary Practice section, you'll be introduced to new hiragana and katakana characters. After completing the course, you may want to review all the lessons and try reading examples and completing exercises in Japanese characters instead of romaji. And feel free to refer to the *Guide to Reading and Writing Japanese* at any time to study ahead of what is introduced in the lessons.

Grammar Builder 1

▶ 1B Grammar Builder 1 (CD 1, Track 2)

Let's review what you've learned in Vocabulary Builder 1. You learned how to greet a person:

in the morning	おはようございます。	Ohayoo gozaimasu.
in the afternoon	こんにちは。	Konnichi wa.
in the evening	こんばんは。	Konban wa.
parting at night or before going to sleep	おやすみなさい。	Oyasuminasai.

You also learned how to say *how do you do?* and *nice to meet you*:

How do you do?	はじめまして。	Hajimemashite.
Nice to meet you.	どうぞよろしく。	Doozo yoroshiku.

You also learned how to introduce yourself and ask someone for their name:

I am ...	わたしは〜です。	Watashi wa ... desu.
What's your name?	おなまえは？	Onamae wa?

The Japanese equivalent of *to be*, です **desu**, comes at the end of a sentence. わたし **Watashi** is the first person pronoun, the equivalent of *I* in English, and は **wa** is a particle that follows the topic of a sentence. Particles are used to indicate the different function of words in a sentence. In many cases, the topic particle は **wa** is used after the subject of a sentence. We'll learn more about other particles in future lessons.

When you are introducing yourself in Japanese, you should use your family name, as it is customary in Japan to call a person by his or her family name. However, most Japanese people know that first names are commonly used in English, and may offer to use first names in your conversation.

Now that you know how to greet people and introduce yourself, let's continue with some more words and expressions.

Vocabulary Builder 2

▶ 1C Vocabulary Builder 2 (CD 1, Track 3)

Long time no see.	ひさしぶりですね。	Hisashiburi desu ne.
How are you?	おげんきですか。	Ogenki desu ka.
I'm fine. (neutral)	げんきです。	Genki desu.
I'm fine. (polite)	おかげさまで。	Okagesama de.
Yes.	はい。	Hai.
Goodbye.	さようなら。	Sayoonara.
See you later.	それではまた。	Sorede wa mata.
Thank you.	ありがとうございます。	Arigatoo gozaimasu.
I'm sorry.	ごめんなさい。	Gomennasai.

✎ Vocabulary Practice 2

Now let's practice the new vocabulary. Fill in what is missing in each of the following expressions. You can use either romaji or Japanese characters.

1. _____ desu ne. (*Long time no see.*)

_____ ですね。

2. _____ desu ka. (*How are you? [lit. Are you well?]*)

_____ ですか。

3. **Hai,** _____ **desu.** (*Yes, I'm fine. [neutral]*)

はい、_____ です。

4. **Hai,** _____ **samade.** (*Yes, I'm fine. [polite]*)

はい、_____ さまで。

5. _____ **nara.** (*Goodbye.*)

_____ なら。

6. **Sorede wa** _____. (*See you later.*)

それでは _____。

7. _____ **gozaimasu.** (*Thank you.*)

_____ ございます。

8. _____ **nasai.** (*I'm sorry.*)

_____ なさい。

ANSWER KEY
1. **Hisashiburi** ひさしぶり; 2. **Ogenki** おげんき; 3. **genki** げんき; 4. **okage** おかげ; 5. **Sayoo** さよう; 6. **mata** また; 7. **Arigatoo** ありがとう; 8. **Gomen** ごめん

Take It Further

Okay, let's start learning some **hiragana**! All Japanese words, except for foreign loan words, can be written in **hiragana**. Modern Japanese uses 46 basic **hiragana** characters. The complete hiragana chart can be found in the *Guide to Reading and Writing Japanese*. Let's look at the first five characters, the vowels.

あぎょう AGYOO *THE A-LINE*		
あ	a	ありがとうございます。 **Arigatoo gozaimasu.** *Thank you.*
い	i	はい。 **Hai.** *Yes.*
う	u	うち **uchi** *home*
え	e	おなまえは？ **Onamae wa?** *What's your name?*
お	o	おなまえは？ **Onamae wa?** *What's your name?*

There is a slight difference between the typed style and the handwritten style, which is covered in the *Guide to Reading and Writing Japanese*.

You may want to note as well that the order of 46 characters will be introduced here in the same order as they would appear in the dictionary, though the glossary in these books will be alphabetized by the romaji.

Grammar Builder 2

▶ 1D Grammar Builder 2 (CD 1, Track 4)

Let's go back to the vocabulary that you learned in Vocabulary Builder 2. おげんきですか **Ogenki desu ka** (*How are you?*) literally means *Are you well?* So if you like, you can respond by first saying はい **Hai** (*Yes*), and then adding げんきです **Genki desu** (*I'm fine, neutral*) or おかげさまで **Okagesama de** (*I'm fine, polite*). げんきです **Genki desu** can be used with anyone, so you'll never sound rude by using this expression, but おかげさまで **Okagesama de** is an extra polite expression that will come in handy in more formal situations, such as a business meeting.

✎ Work Out 1

▶ 1E Work Out 1 (CD 1, Track 5)

Let's practice some of what you've learned in a listening comprehension exercise. Listen to the audio, and fill in the blanks with the words that you hear. If you want to do this exercise without the audio, use the English translation as a clue. Again, you may choose to use either romaji or Japanese characters.

1. *Good morning. How are you?*

   _____ gozaimasu. _____ desu ka.

   _____ ございます。 _____ ですか。

2. *Yes, I'm fine. Long time no see.*

   Hai, _____ desu. _____ desu ne.

   はい、_____ です。_____ ですね。

3. *Good evening.*

   _____ wa.

   _____ は。

4. *Hello. What's your name?*

   _____ wa. _____ wa?

   _____ は。_____ は?

5. *My name is Smith. Nice to meet you.*

_____ wa Sumisu _____. Doozo

_____.

_____ はスミス _____。どうぞ_____。

6. *How do you do?*

_____ mashite.

_____ まして。

7. *Good night. Goodbye.*

_____ nasai. _____ nara.

_____ なさい。_____ なら。

ANSWER KEY

1. **Oyahoo** おはよう, **Ogenki** おげんき; 2. **genki** げんき, **Hisashiburi** ひさしぶり; 3. **Konban** こんばん; 4. **Konnichi** こんにち, **Onamae** おなまえ; 5. **Watashi** わたし, **desu** です, **yoroshiku** よろしく; 6. **Hajime** はじめ; 7. **Oyasumi** おやすみ, **Sayoo** さよう

Bring It All Together

▶ 1F Bring It All Together (CD 1, Track 6)

Let's bring it all together in a couple of brief dialogues.

A. Hello!	こんにちは！	Konnichi wa!
B. Hello! How do you do?	こんにちは！はじめまして。	Konnichi wa! Hajimemashite.
A. What's your name?	おなまえは？	Onamae wa?
B. I'm Smith.	スミスです。	Sumisu desu.
A. I'm Yamada. Nice to meet you.	わたしはやまだです。どうぞよろしく。	Watashi wa Yamada desu. Doozo Yoroshiku.
B. Nice to meet you.	どうぞよろしく。	Doozo Yoroshiku.

Let's listen to another brief exchange.

A. Good evening.	こんばんは。	Konban wa.
B. Good evening. Long time no see!	こんばんは。ひさしぶりですね!	Konban wa. Hisashiburi desu ne!
A. How are you?	おげんきですか。	Ogenki desu ka.
B. I'm fine. How are you?	げんきです。おげんきですか。	Genki desu. Ogenki desu ka.
A. Yes, I'm fine.	はい、おかげさまで。	Hai, okagesama de.
B. See you later! Good night.	それではまた!おやすみなさい。	Sorede wa mata! Oyasuminasai.
A. Good night!	おやすみなさい!	Oyasuminasai!

Take It Further

Did you notice in the first dialogue that *I'm Smith* in Japanese was just スミス です **Sumisu desu** instead of わたしはスミスです **Watashi wa Sumisu desu?** In Japanese, the subject of a sentence, especially a pronoun, can be omitted when the subject is understood from the context. So when you introduce yourself, it is fine to simply say your name plus です **desu**.

Work Out 2

1G Work Out 2 (CD 1, Track 7)

Now let's practice some of what you've learned.

A. Translate the following phrases from Japanese to English.

1. おはようございます。

   Ohayoo gozaimasu.

   _____

2. こんばんは。

   Konban wa.

   _____

3. どうぞよろしく。

   Doozo yoroshiku.

   _____

4. げんきです。

   Genki desu.

   _____

5. ありがとうございます。

   Arigatoo gozaimasu.

   _____

6. ごめんなさい。

   Gomennasai.

   _____

B. Translate the following phrases and sentences from English to Japanese.

1. _Good afternoon._

   _____

2. *What's your name?*

_____

3. *How are you?*

_____

4. *Long time no see.*

_____

5. *See you later.*

_____

6. *Goodbye.*

_____

ANSWER KEY
A. 1. *Good morning.* 2. *Good evening.* 3. *Nice to meet you.* 4. *I'm fine. (neutral)* 5. *Thank you.* 6. *I'm sorry.*
B. 1. **Konnichi wa.** こんにちは。 2. **Onamae wa?** おなまえは？ 3. **Ogenki desu ka.** おげんきですか。 4. **Hisashiburi desu ne.** ひさしぶりですね。 5. **Sorede wa mata.** それではまた。 6. **Sayoonara.** さようなら。

✎ Drive It Home

Drive It Home exercises are designed to get you repeating material and committing it to memory. They may seem overly simple, but the repetition will help you better retain the words and phrases you learn in each lesson. Almost all of the Drive It Home exercises in Essential Japanese will focus on particles, but will review other vocabulary and structures as well. For your first Drive It Home exercises, use **desu** です and **wa** は to complete the following sentences.

1. **Genki** _____ . (*I'm fine.*)

   げんき_____。

2. **Ogenki** _____ ka. (*How are you?*)

   おげんき_____か。

3. **Sumisu** _____ . (*I'm Smith.*)

   スミス_____。

4. **Watashi wa Yamada** _____ . (*I'm Yamada.*)

   わたしはやまだ _____。

5. **Hisashiburi** _____ ne! (*Long time no see!*)

   ひさしぶり_____ね!

6. **Konnichi** _____ ! (*Hello!*)

   こんにち____ !

7. **Onamae** _____ ? (*What's your name?*)

   おなまえ____ ?

8. **Watashi** _____ **Yamada desu.** (*I'm Yamada.*)

   わたし____やまだです。

ANSWER KEY
1-5. all **desu** です; 6-8. all **wa** は

Parting Words

よくできました！**Yoku dekimashita!** *Well done!* You've just finished your first lesson, in which you learned some very useful basic vocabulary. You should now be able to:

☐ Use basic expressions to greet someone

☐ Introduce yourself and ask someone for their name

☐ Use the particle は **wa**

☐ Ask someone how they're doing

☐ Say *I'm fine* in both polite and neutral tones

☐ Use courtesy expressions such as *thank you* and *I'm sorry*

☐ Use what you've learned when meeting people for the first time

Take It Further

Japanese has different expressions which mean the same thing but differ in their degree of politeness. The language you'll hear in this audio course is neutral to polite, which is a great place to start. In the next lesson, you'll learn how to talk about your family and the families of others, but if you'd like to review Lesson 1 first, go right ahead! It is important that you learn at your own pace. だいにかでまたおあいしましょう！ **Dai nika de mata oai shimashoo!** *See you again in Lesson 2!*

Don't forget to practice and reinforce what you've learned by visiting **www.livinglanguage.com/ languagelab** for flashcards, games, and quizzes!

Word Recall

You will see a Word Recall section at the end of each lesson. It gives you the chance to review key vocabulary from all of the previous lessons up to that point, not only the lesson you've just completed. This will reinforce the vocabulary, as well as some of the structures, that you've learned so far in the course, to help you retain them in your long-term memory. Since this is your first Japanese lesson, in this Word Recall we'll just review the key vocabulary you learned in this lesson. Match the Japanese in the left column with the English equivalent in the right.

1. こんにちは。
Konnichi wa.

a. I'm fine. (polite)

2. おはようございます。
Ohayoo gozaimasu.

b. How are you?

3. こんばんは。
Konban wa.

c. See you later.

4. おやすみなさい。
Oyasuminasai.

d. Hello./Good afternoon.

5. どうぞよろしく。
Doozo yoroshiku.

e. Good evening.

6. ひさしぶりですね。
Hisashiburi desu ne.

f. I'm sorry.

7. おげんきですか。
Ogenki desu ka.

g. Thank you.

8. げんきです。
Genki desu.

h. Nice to meet you.

9. おかげさまで。
Okagesama de.

i. Long time no see.

10. それではまた。   *j. Good night.*
Sorede wa mata.

11. ありがとうございます。   *k. I'm fine. (neutral)*
Arigatoo gozaimasu.

12. ごめんなさい。   *l. Good morning.*
Gomennasai.

ANSWER KEY
1. d; 2. l; 3. e; 4. j; 5. h; 6. i; 7. b; 8. k; 9. a; 10. c; 11. g; 12. f

Lesson 2: People and Family

Dai nika: Hitobito to kazoku
だいにか : ひとびととかぞく

こんにちは。だいにかへようこそ。**Konnichi wa. Dai nika e yookoso.** *Hello. Welcome to Lesson 2.* By the end of this lesson, you'll be able to:

☐ Address and refer to people

☐ Express *to be* and *to not be*

☐ Use the particle の **no**

☐ Use basic vocabulary related to the family

☐ Express *I have, there is/are* (people and animals)

☐ Ask questions

☐ Use the particles が **ga** and か **ka**

☐ Begin to describe who people are and what they do
Let's get started with some vocabulary. じゅんびはいいですか。**Junbi wa ii desu ka.** *Are you ready?*

Vocabulary Builder 1

▶ 2A Vocabulary Builder 1 (CD 1, Track 8)

Mr./Ms. Yamada	やまださん	Yamada san
Prof./Dr. Tanaka	たなかせんせい	Tanaka sensee
person	ひと	hito
female	おんな	onna
male	おとこ	otoko
woman	おんなのひと	onna no hito
man	おとこのひと	otoko no hito
teacher	せんせい	sensee
student	がくせい	gakusee
to not be …	〜ではありません。	… de wa arimasen.

✎ Vocabulary Practice 1

Let's practice the vocabulary you've learned. Fill in what is missing in each of the following expressions and sentences.

1. **Yamada** _____ (*Mr./Ms. Yamada*)

   やまだ _____

2. **Tanaka** _____ (*Prof./Dr. Tanaka*)

   たなか _____

3. _____ **no** _____ (*man*)

   _____ の _____

4. _____ **no** _____ (*woman*)

   _____ の _____

5. Watashi wa _____ desu. (*I am a student.*)

   わたしは_____です。

6. Watashi wa _____ de wa arimasen. (*I am not a teacher.*)

   わたしは_____ではありません。

ANSWER KEY
1. san さん; 2. sensee せんせい; 3. otoko おとこ, hito ひと; 4. onna おんな, hito ひと; 5. gakusee がくせい;
6. sensee せんせい

Take It Further

In the last lesson, you learned the hiragana characters representing the vowels.
The rest of the characters represent consonant-vowel combinations. Let's take a
look at the characters that combine the k sound and the vowels (this combination
is called かぎょう kagyoo *the Ka-line*).

かぎょう KAGYOO *THE KA-LINE*		
か	ka	たなかさん Tana*ka* san *Mr./Ms. Tanaka*
き	ki	げんきです。 Gen*ki* desu. *I'm fine. (neutral)*
く	ku	がくせい ga*ku*see *student*
け	ke	とけい to*ke*e *watch/clock*

かぎょう KAGYOO *THE KA-LINE*		
こ	ko	おとこ oto*ko* *male*

Next, let's look at the characters that combine the s sound and the vowels (called さぎょう sagyoo *the Sa-line*):

さぎょう SAGYOO *THE SA-LINE*		
さ	sa	さようなら。 *Sa*yoonara. *Goodbye.*
し	shi	どうぞよろしく。 Doozo yoro*shi*ku. *Nice to meet you.*
す	su	〜です。 … de*su*. *to be…*
せ	se	せんせい *se*n*se*e *teacher*
そ	so	それではまた。 *So*rede wa mata. *See you later.*

Please note that the combination of the consonant s and the vowel i results in the sound shi in Japanese, not "si", a sound that doesn't exist in Japanese.

Good job! We'll continue with more hiragana in the next character section.

Grammar Builder 1

(▶) 2B Grammar Builder 1 (CD 1, Track 9)

Let's take a look at what you learned in Vocabulary Builder 1 in detail. When you address someone, you'll use さん **san** after the family name. You already learned in Lesson 1 that family names are commonly used when addressing people in Japanese.

さん **San** is similar to *Mr.* or *Ms.* in English. Be careful not to attach さん **san** to your own name. When referring to a doctor or a teacher — such as a physician, dentist, school teacher, and fitness instructor—use せんせい **sensee** instead of さん **san**. It would be rude to use さん **san** if he or she is a teacher or a doctor.

Now let's talk about some grammar. Do you remember the expression ～は～です … **wa** … **desu** from Lesson 1? です **Desu** is the Japanese equivalent of *to be*, and は **wa** is a particle that follows the topic of a sentence.

| *Mr./Ms.Yamada is a student.* | やまださんはがくせいです。 | **Yamada san wa gakusee desu.** |

If you want to turn it into a negative sentence, use ～ではありません … **de wa arimasen.**

| *Mr./Ms. Yamada is not a student.* | やまださんはがくせいではありません。 | **Yamada san wa gakusee de wa arimasen.** |

Another example of a particle is の **no**, which is used to connect two nouns. You just learned that おんな **onna** means *female*, and ひと **hito** means *person*. If you use の **no** to connect おんな **onna** and ひと **hito**, you'll have おんなのひと **onna no hito** (*female person*), or *woman*. Likewise, if you connect おとこ **otoko** (*male*) and ひと **hito** (*person*) with の **no**, you'll have おとこのひと **otoko no hito** (*male person*), or *man*.

Lastly, you may already have noticed that you don't need to use articles, such as *a*, *an*, or *the* before a noun in Japanese. Great news, isn't it?

Now let's learn how to talk about your family.

Vocabulary Builder 2

▶ 2C Vocabulary Builder 2 (CD 1, Track 10)

to have … /There is … (for a person or animal)	〜がいます。	… ga imasu.
question particle	か	ka
Do you have … ?/ Is there … ? (for a person or animal)	〜はいますか。	… wa imasu ka.
No.	いいえ。	Iie.
to not have … / There is not … (for a person or animal)	〜はいません。	… wa imasen.
siblings (one's own)	きょうだい	kyoodai
siblings (someone else's)	ごきょうだい	gokyoodai
older brother (one's own)	あに	ani
older brother (someone else's)	おにいさん	oniisan
younger brother (one's own)	おとうと	otooto
younger brother (someone else's)	おとうとさん	otootosan
older sister (one's own)	あね	ane

older sister (someone else's)	おねえさん	oneesan
younger sister (one's own)	いもうと	imooto
younger sister (someone else's)	いもうとさん	imootosan
son (one's own)	むすこ	musuko
son (someone else's)	むすこさん	musukosan
daughter (one's own)	むすめ	musume
daughter (someone else's)	むすめさん	musumesan
father (one's own)	ちち	chichi
father (someone else's)	おとうさん	otoosan
mother (one's own)	はは	haha
mother (someone else's)	おかあさん	okaasan

✎ Vocabulary Practice 2

Let's practice the vocabulary you've learned.

A. We'll first review the terms for referring to your own family members. Match the Japanese in the left column with the English equivalent in the right.

1. ちち chichi   a. *son*

2. はは haha   b. *older sister*

3. きょうだい kyoodai   c. *older brother*

4. あに ani   d. *mother*

5. あね ane   e. *younger brother*

6. おとうと otooto   f. *younger sister*

7. いもうと imooto   g. *siblings*

8. むすこ musuko   h. *daughter*

9. むすめ musume   i. *father*

B. Next, let's review the terms for referring to someone else's family members. Match the Japanese in the left column with the English equivalent in the right.

1. おとうさん otoosan
2. おかあさん okaasan
3. ごきょうだい gokyoodai
4. おにいさん oniisan
5. おねえさん oneesan
6. おとうとさん otootosan
7. いもうとさん imootosan
8. むすこさん musukosan
9. むすめさん musumesan

a. *siblings*
b. *younger sister*
c. *younger brother*
d. *older sister*
e. *father*
f. *mother*
g. *daughter*
h. *older brother*
i. *son*

ANSWER KEY
A. 1. i; 2. d; 3. g; 4. c; 5. b; 6. e; 7. f; 8. a; 9. h
B. 1. e; 2. f; 3. a; 4. h; 5. d; 6.c ; 7. b; 8. i; 9. g

Take It Further

Ready for some more hiragana? Let's take a look at the characters in たぎょう **tagyoo** *the Ta-line* and なぎょう **nagyoo** *the Na-line*.

たぎょう TAGYOO *THE TA-LINE*		
た	ta	たなかさん **Ta**naka san *Mr./Ms. Tanaka*
ち	chi	ちち *chichi* *father (one's own)*
つ	tsu	くつ ku**tsu** *shoes*

たぎょう TAGYOO *THE TA-LINE*		
て	te	はじめまし<u>て</u>。 **Hajimemashi<u>te</u>.** *(How do you do?)*
と	to	ひ<u>と</u> **hi<u>to</u>** *person*

なぎょう NAGYOO *THE NA-LINE*		
な	na	お<u>な</u>まえは? **O<u>na</u>mae wa?** *What's your name?*
に	ni	あ<u>に</u> **a<u>ni</u>** *older brother (one's own)*
ぬ	nu	い<u>ぬ</u> **i<u>nu</u>** *dog*
ね	ne	あ<u>ね</u> **a<u>ne</u>** *older sister (one's own)*
の	no	おんな<u>の</u>ひと **onna <u>no</u> hito** *woman*

Please note that the combination of the consonant **t** and the vowel **i** results in the sound **chi** not "ti." Likewise, the combination of the **t** and **u** results in the sound **tsu,** not "tu."

Excellent! That's it for now. Remember to use the *Guide to Reading and Writing Japanese* for more detailed guidance on Japanese characters and reading/writing exercises.

Grammar Builder 2

▶ 2D Grammar Builder 2 (CD 1, Track 11)

You've learned that there are two different sets of family terms. You have to use different words in Japanese depending on whether you are talking about members of your own family or someone else's family. It sounds like a lot to memorize, but notice that many of the words referring to someone else's family members are just the word used to refer to your own family members, plus さん **san**. So it won't be as difficult as it seems.

You also saw a new expression 〜がいます ... **ga imasu**, meaning *to have* or *there is*. います **Imasu** is a verb that literally means *to exist*. が **Ga** is another example of a particle in Japanese. There are several functions of the particle が **ga**, but one of its functions is to mark a subject. So if you say, おにいさんがいます **Oniisan ga imasu**, it literally means, *An older brother exists*, or *There is an older brother*. But you may wonder, "Whose older brother are you talking about?" Now, do you remember the topic particle は **wa**? If you add やまださんは **Yamada san wa** at the top of the sentence, you'll have やまださんはおにいさんがいます **Yamada san wa oniisan ga imasu**. This literally means, *As for Mr./Ms. Yamada, an older brother exists*, or *As for Mr./Ms. Yamada, there is an older brother*. It sounds very odd in English, but this is essentially what is going on in the Japanese sentence.

The natural English translation will be *Mr./Ms. Yamada has an older brother*. To summarize:

An older brother exists./ There is an older brother./ (You have/He has/She has) an older brother.	おにいさんがいます。	Oniisan ga imasu.
Mr./Ms. Yamada has an older brother.	やまださんはおにいさんがいます。	Yamada san wa oniisan ga imasu.

Please note that います **imasu** is used to talk about the existence of people or animals. You cannot use います **imasu** to talk about objects. You'll learn how to discuss objects in Lesson 4.

If you want to turn a sentence into a question, place the particle か **ka** at the end. Also note that in questions, the particle が **ga** is replaced by the particle は **wa**.

Mr./Ms. Yamada has an older brother.	やまださんはおにいさんがいます。	Yamada san wa oniisan ga imasu.
Does Mr./Ms. Yamada have an older brother?	やまださんはおにいさんはいますか。	Yamada san wa oniisan wa imasu ka.

The negative form of ～がいます … **ga imasu** is ～はいません … **wa imasen**. Just as in the question form we have just learned, the particle は **wa** replaces the particle が **ga** in a negative sentence.

Mr./Ms. Yamada has an older brother.	やまださんはおにいさんがいます。	Yamada san wa oniisan ga imasu.
Mr./Ms. Yamada doesn't have an older brother	やまださんはおにいさんはいません。	Yamada san wa oniisan wa imasen.

Take It Further

The particle か ka at the end of a sentence is enough to indicate a question in Japanese, so there is not normally a question mark (?) at the end of a question. However, if there is no か ka at the end of a question statement, you would need to use a question mark.

For example, do you remember the expression おなまえは？ Onamae wa? *What's your name?* The literal translation of this expression is *Your name?* It is an abbreviated form of おなまえはなんですか。Onamae wa nan desu ka. *What's your name?* Since the short form does not contain the question particle か ka, you need to use a question mark.

✎ Work Out 1

▶ 2E Work Out 1 (CD 1, Track 12)

Let's practice the verbs *to be* and *to have* in Japanese along with some of the words that you've learned in this lesson. Listen to the audio, and fill in the blanks with the words that you hear. Remember that personal pronouns such as *I, you, he, she* in Japanese are often omitted.

1. *Mr. Yamada is a student.*

   Yamada san _____ **gakusee** _____.

   やまださん_____ がくせい_____。

2. *(I am/You are/He is/She is) a student.*

   _____ **desu.**

   _____です。

3. *Mr. Yamada is not a teacher.*

   Yamada san _____ sensee _____.

   やまださん _____ せんせい _____。

4. *(I am/You are/He is/She is) not a teacher.*

   _____ de wa arimasen.

   _____ ではありません。

5. *Prof. Tanaka has an older brother.*

   Tanaka sensee _____ oniisan _____.

   たなかせんせい_____ おにいさん _____。

6. *(You have/He has/She has) an older brother.*

   _____ ga imasu.

   _____ がいます。

7. *I have an older brother.*

   _____ ga imasu.

   _____ がいます。

8. *Prof. Tanaka doesn't have a daughter.*

   Tanaka sensee _____ musumesan _____ imasen.

   たなかせんせい_____ むすめさん_____ いません。

9. *(You don't/He doesn't/She doesn't) have a daughter.*

   Musumesan wa _____.

   むすめさんは _____ 。

10. *I don't have a daughter.*

    Musume _____.

    むすめ _____ 。

11. *(Are you/Is he/Is she) a student?*

    Gakusee _____.

    がくせい _____ 。

12. *Is Mr. Yamada a student?*

    Yamada san _____ **gakusee** _____.

    やまださん_____ がくせい _____ 。

13. *(Do you/Does he/Does she) have an older sister?*

    Oneesan _____.

    おねえさん _____ 。

14. *Does Mr. Yamada have an older sister?*

    Yamada san _____ **oneesan** _____.

    やまださん_____ おねえさん _____ 。

ANSWER KEY

1. wa は, desu です; 2. Gakusee がくせい; 3. wa は, de wa arimasen ではありません; 4. Sensee せんせい; 5. wa は, ga imasu がいます; 6. Oniisan おにいさん; 7. Ani あに; 8. wa は, wa は; 9. imasen いません; 10. wa imasen はいません; 11. desu ka ですか; 12. wa は, desu ka ですか; 13. wa imasu ka はいますか; 14. wa は, wa imasu ka はいますか

◖ Bring It All Together

▶ 2F Bring It All Together (CD 1, Track 40)

Let's bring it all together in a brief dialogue.

A. Are you a student, Ms. Smith?	スミスさんはがくせいですか。	Sumisu san wa gakusee desu ka.
B. Yes, I am a student. And you, Mr. Yamada?	はい、がくせいです。やまださんは？	Hai, gakusee desu. Yamada san wa?
A. I am not a student.	わたしはがくせいではありません。	Watashi wa gakusee de wa arimasen.
B. Do you have siblings, Mr. Yamada?	やまださんはごきょうだいはいますか。	Yamada san wa gokyoodai wa imasu ka.
A. Yes, I have a younger sister. And you, Ms. Smith?	はい、いもうとがいます。スミスさんは？	Hai, imooto ga imasu. Sumisu san wa?
B. I don't have any siblings.	わたしはきょうだいはいません。	Watashi wa kyoodai wa imasen.
B. Is your sister a student?	いもうとさんはがくせいですか。	Imooto san wa gakusee desu ka.
A. Yes, she is a student.	はい、がくせいです。	Hai, gakusee desu.

Take It Further

As mentioned in Lesson 1, personal pronouns are often omitted in Japanese when it is understood from the context. In fact, the personal pronouns *you*, *he*, *she*, and *they* are almost never used in Japanese. If you want to avoid confusion, refer to a person by his or her name, rather than using a pronoun.

Possessive pronouns such as *your*, *his*, *her*, and *their* are also usually omitted. So, *Your/his/her younger sister is a student* is as simple as: いもうとさんはがくせい です。**Imootosan wa gakusee desu.**

If you want to ask *And you?* or *What about you?*, simply say 〜さんは？… *san wa?* Remember to always use the particle は *wa* after someone's name when you ask this question; otherwise, they would think that you're just calling their name!

✎ Work Out 2

▶ 2G Work Out 2 (CD 1, Track 14)

Now let's practice some of what you've learned.

A. Translate the following phrases from Japanese to English.

1. おかあさん

   okaasan

   _____

2. おんなのせんせい

   onna no sensee

   _____

3. ちちはせんせいです。

   Chichi wa sensee desu.

   _____

4. あねはいません。

   Ane wa imasen.

   _____

5. おねえさんはいますか。

Oneesan wa imasu ka.

B. Translate the following phrases from English to Japanese.

1. *Professor Tanaka*

---

2. *Professor Tanaka has a son.*

---

3. *I don't have a son.*

---

4. *Do you have siblings?*

---

5. *Is your younger brother a student?*

ANSWER KEY

A. 1. *mother (someone else's)*; 2. *female teacher*; 3. *My father is a teacher.* 4. *I don't have an older sister.* 5. *(Do you/Does he/Does she) have an older sister?*
B. 1. **Tanaka sensee たなかせんせい**; 2. **Tanaka sensee wa musukosan ga imasu. たなかせんせいはむ すこさんがいます。** 3. **Musuko wa imasen. むすこはいません。** 4. **Gokyoodai wa imasu ka. ごきょうだいは いますか。** 5. **Otootosan wa gakusee desu ka. おとうとさんはがくせいですか。**

✎ Drive It Home

Complete the following phrases and sentences by inserting the appropriate particles.

1. **Otootosan** _____ **gakusee desu.** *(Your younger brother is a student.)*

   おとうとさん _____ がくせいです。

2. **Haha** _____ **sensee de wa arimasen.** *(My mother is not a teacher.)*

   はは _____ せんせいではありません。

3. **Musumesan** _____ **imasen.** *(She does not have a younger sister.)*

   むすめさん _____ いません。

4. **Gokyoodai wa imasu** _____ . *(Do you have siblings?)*

   ごきょうだいはいます _____ 。

5. **Yamada san wa musumesan wa imasu** _____ . *(Does Mrs. Yamada have a daughter?)*

   やまださんはむすめさんはいます _____ 。

6. **Musuko** _____ **imasu.** *(I have a son.)*

   むすこ _____ います。

7. **Yamada san wa oniisan** _____ **imasu.** *(Mr./Ms. Yamada has an older brother.)*

   やまださんはおにいさん _____ います。

8. **onna** _____ **hito** (*woman*)

   おんな _____ ひと

9. **otoko** _____ **hito** (*man*)

   おとこ _____ ひと

ANSWER KEY

1-3. wa は; 4-5. ka か; 6-7. ga が; 8-9. no の

Parting Words

よくできました！**Yoku dekimashita!** *Well done!* You've learned so much in this lesson. You should now be able to:

☐ Address and refer to people

☐ Express *to be* and *to not be*

☐ Use the particle の no

☐ Use basic vocabulary related to the family

☐ Express *I have, there is/are* (people)

☐ Ask questions

☐ Use the particles が ga and か ka.

☐ Begin to describe who people are and what they do
  In the next lesson, we'll learn how to count in Japanese, but if you'd like to review Lesson 2 first, go right ahead! Remember to learn at a pace that is best for you.

Don't forget to practice and reinforce what you've learned by visiting **www.livinglanguage.com/languagelab** for flashcards, games, and quizzes!

Word Recall

1. ひと hito	a. younger brother (one's own)
2. せんせい sensee	b. person
3. いいえ。 Iie.	c. Yes.
4. はい。 Hai.	d. Goodbye.
5. ごきょうだい gokyoodai	e. What's your name?
6. おとうと otooto	f. mother (one's own)
7. むすこさん musukosan	g. siblings (someone else's)
8. むすめ musume	h. daughter (one's own)
9. さようなら。 Sayoonara.	i. father (someone else's)
10. おとうさん otoosan	j. teacher
11. おなまえは？ Onamae wa?	k. No.
12. はは haha	l. son (someone else's)

ANSWER KEY
1. b; 2. j; 3. k; 4. c; 5. g; 6. a; 7. l; 8. h; 9. d; 10. i; 11. e; 12. f

Lesson 3: Numbers

Dai sanka: Kazu
だいさんか：かず

こんにちは。だいさんかへようこそ。**Konnichi wa. Dai sanka e yookoso.** *Hello. Welcome to Lesson 3.* By the end of this lesson, you'll be able to:

☐ Count up to one hundred

☐ Express how many people there are with measure words

☐ Use what you've learned to talk about people and family

Vocabulary Builder 1

3A Vocabulary Builder 1 (CD 1, Track 15)

zero	ゼロ or れい	zero or ree
one	いち	ichi
two	に	ni
three	さん	san
four	よん or し	yon or shi
five	ご	go
six	ろく	roku
seven	なな or しち	nana or shichi
eight	はち	hachi
nine	きゅう or く	kyuu or ku
ten	じゅう	juu

You'll notice that there are two words in Japanese for the numbers zero, four, seven, and nine. Which number you use will depend on context. You'll learn about which number should be used for which situation in this lesson as well as in Lessons 4 and 8.

Now let's move on to numbers above ten. For numbers 11 to 19, just follow the word for *ten* —じゅう juu—with the appropriate word for 1 through 9. With this formula, *eleven* will be "ten one," *twelve* will be "ten two," and so on.

eleven	じゅういち	juuichi
twelve	じゅうに	juuni
thirteen	じゅうさん	juusan
fourteen	じゅうよん or じゅうし	juuyon or juushi
seventeen	じゅうなな or じゅうしち	juunana or juushichi
nineteen	じゅうきゅう or じゅうく	juukyuu or juuku

For 20, 30, 40, and so on, we'll use the opposite formula from what we used for 11 through 19. Say the Japanese number for 2 through 9, and then add the word for *ten*—じゅう juu—to it. *Twenty* will be "two ten," *thirty* will be "three ten," and so on.

20	にじゅう	nijuu
30	さんじゅう	sanjuu
40	よんじゅう	yonjuu
70	ななじゅう	nanajuu
90	きゅうじゅう	kyuujuu

✎ Vocabulary Practice 1

Let's practice the numbers you've learned. Match the Japanese in the left column with the English equivalent in the right.

1. さん san   a. *zero*

2. じゅう juu   b. *one*

3. ご go   c. *two*

4. に ni   d. *three*

5. なな nana or しち shichi   e. *four*

6. じゅういち juuichi   f. *five*

7. いち ichi   g. *six*

8. じゅうご juugo   h. *seven*

9. はち hachi   i. *eight*

10. はちじゅう hachijuu   j. *nine*

11. ろく roku   k. *ten*

12. きゅう kyuu or く ku   l. *eleven*

13. さんじゅう sanjuu   m. *fifteen*

14. よん yon or し shi   n. *thirty*

15. ゼロ zero or れい ree   o. *eighty*

Take It Further

Now it's hiragana time! Let's learn the characters in はぎょう hagyoo *the Ha-line* and まぎょう magyoo *the Ma-line*.

はぎょう HAGYOO *THE HA-LINE*		
は	ha	はち *hachi* *eight*
ひ	hi	ひらがな *hiragana* *hiragana*
ふ	fu	ふたり *futari* *two people*
へ	he	へや *heya* *room*
ほ	ho	ほん *hon* *book*

まぎょう MAGYOO *THE MA-LINE*		
ま	ma	います *imasu* *to have, there is, to exist*
み	mi	おやすみなさい。 **Oyasuminasai.** *Good night.*

まぎょう MAGYOO *THE MA-LINE*		
む	mu	む̲すこ **mu̲suko** *son (one's own)*
め	me	ごめ̲んなさい。 **Gome̲nnasai.** *I'm sorry.*
も	mo	いも̲うと **imo̲oto** *younger sister (one's own)*

Please note that the combination of **h** and **u** in Japanese results in **fu**, not "hu."

An important note on the character は **ha**: when this character is used as a particle, it's pronounced **wa**. This is the topic particle は **wa** that you already know from expressions you've seen in this course:

こんにち **konnichi** (*today*) + the particle は **wa** = こんにちは **konnichi wa** (*hello*)
こんばん **konban** (*this evening*) + the particle は **wa** = こんばんは **konban wa** (*good evening*)

You'll see this in other fixed expressions such as それではまた **sorede wa mata** (*see you later*) and ではありません **de wa arimasen** (*to not be*) whose **wa** sounds all originate from the particle は **wa**.

We'll cover the rest of the basic hiragana characters in the next character section. You're almost there!

Grammar Builder 1

▶ 3B Grammar Builder 1 (CD 1, Track 16)

Let's take a moment here to learn about how to deal with quantity in Japanese. When talking about the quantity of something, Japanese uses measure words, or words that come between the number and the item being counted. Measure words are similar to *pair of* in *one pair of shoes* or *glasses of* in *five glasses of wine*, but every noun in Japanese requires a measure word when talking about its quantity.

Let's first learn how to count people. The measure word for people is にん **nin**, but please note that *one person* and *two people* are irregular.

one person	ひとり	hitori
two people	ふたり	futari
three people	さんにん	sannin
four people	よにん	yonin
five people	ごにん	gonin
six people	ろくにん	rokunin
seven people	しちにん or ななにん	shichinin or nananin
eight people	はちにん	hachinin
nine people	きゅうにん or くにん	kyuunin or kunin
ten people	じゅうにん	juunin
eleven people	じゅういちにん	juuichinin
twelve people	じゅうににん	juuninin
thirteen people	じゅうさんにん	juusannin

よくできました！**Yoku dekimashita!** *Well done!*

Vocabulary Builder 2

▶ 3C Vocabulary Builder 2 (CD 1, Track 17)

Now let's learn some more numbers. From 21 to 99, just add 1 to 9 after the tens.

21	にじゅういち	nijuu ichi
22	にじゅうに	nijuu ni
23	にじゅうさん	nijuu san
34	さんじゅうよん or さんじゅうし	sanjuu yon or sanjuu shi
45	よんじゅうご	yonjuu go
56	ごじゅうろく	gojuu roku
67	ろくじゅうなな or ろくじゅうしち	rokujuu nana or rokujuu shichi
78	ななじゅうはち	nanajuu hachi
89	はちじゅうきゅう or はちじゅうく	hachijuu kyuu or hachijuu ku
91	きゅうじゅういち	kyuujuu ichi

After ninety-nine, we have *a hundred* (ひゃく hyaku).

100	ひゃく	hyaku

✎ Vocabulary Practice 2

Let's practice the numbers from 21 to 100. Match the Japanese in the left column with the English equivalent in the right.

1. ななじゅうに nanajuu ni   a. *twenty-four*

2. よんじゅういち yonjuu ichi   b. *thirty-seven*

3. ろくじゅうご rokujuu go   c. *forty-one*

4. ひゃく hyaku   d. *fifty-nine*

5. にじゅうよん **nijuu yon** or
にじゅうし **nijuu shi**

    e. *sixty-five*

6. はちじゅうろく **achijuu roku**

    f. *seventy-eight*

7. ななじゅうはち **nanajuu hachi**

    g. *seventy-two*

8. きゅうじゅうさん **kyuujuu san**

    h. *eighty-six*

9. さんじゅうなな **sanjuu nana** or
さんじゅうしち **sanjuu shichi**

    i. *ninety-three*

10. ごじゅうきゅう **gojuu kyuu** or
ごじゅうく **gojuu ku**

    j. *hundred*

ANSWER KEY
1. g; 2. c; 3. e; 4. j; 5. a; 6. h; 7. f; 8. i; 9. b; 10. d

Take It Further

Now let's learn the last set of the 46 hiragana characters, the ones in やぎょう
yagyoo *the Ya-line*, らぎょう **ragyoo** *the Ra-line*, and わぎょう **wagyoo** *the Wa-line*.

やぎょう YAGYOO *THE YA-LINE*		
や	ya	おやすみなさい。 **O***ya***suminasai.** *Good night.*
ゆ	ye	しょうゆ **shoo***yu* *soy sauce*
よ	yo	ようこそ。 ***Yo***okoso.** *Welcome.*

らぎょう RAGYOO *THE RA-LINE*		
ら	ra	ひらがな **hiragana** *hiragana*
り	ri	ありがとうございます。 **Arigatoo gozaimasu.** *Thank you.*
る	ru	くるま **kuruma** *car*
れ	re	れい **ree** *zero*
ろ	ro	ろく **roku** *six*

わぎょう WAGYOO *THE WA-LINE*		
わ	wa	わたし **watashi** *I*
を	o	を **o** *the particle* o

Did you notice that there are only three characters in the **Ya**-line and only two characters in the **Wa**-line? Historically, there used to be five characters in those two lines, but modern Japanese only uses three in the **Ya**-line and two in the **Wa**-line. Please note that the character を is pronounced **o**, not "**wo**." In modern

Japanese, this character is used only as the particle を o, whose main function is to mark an object in a sentence. You'll learn the particle を o in Lesson 7.

Have you counted how many characters you learned so far? You've learned 45 characters. But wait, there should be 46 characters, shouldn't they? Here's the very last character for you:

ん	n	こんばんは。 **Ko**n**ban** wa. *Good evening.*

The character ん does not belong to any line. This character is special also because it represents a single consonant sound, as opposed to a combination of consonant + vowel.

おめでとうございます！**Omedetoo gozaimasu!** *Congratulations!* Now you know all the basic hiragana characters! In the next character sections, we'll guide you through diacritics and special character combinations.

Grammar Builder 2

▶ 3D Grammar Builder 2 (CD 1, Track 18)

In Japanese, there is no plural form for nouns. That means when the quantity changes, the noun stays the same. Here are some examples:

I have one older sister.	あねがひとりいます。	**Ane ga hitori imasu.**
I have two older sisters.	あねがふたりいます。	**Ane ga futari imasu.**
I have three older sisters.	あねがさんにんいます。	**Ane ga sannin imasu.**

Note that あね **ane** *older sister* followed by the particle が **ga** comes before the measure word. This is one of the several possible word order, but we'll stick to this neutral word order in *Essential Japanese*.

✎ Work Out 1

▶ 3E Work Out 1 (CD 1, Track 19)

Let's put the numbers together with the measure word にん nin in some
sentences using some grammar you already know: the verb *to have*. Listen to the
audio, and fill in the blanks with the words that you hear.

1. *I have one younger sister.*

   Imooto ga _____ imasu.

   いもうとが _____ います。

2. *I have two younger brothers.*

   Otooto ga _____ imasu.

   おとうとが _____ います。

3. *I have three older brothers.*

   Ani ga _____ imasu.

   あにが _____ います。

4. *I have four daughters.*

   Musume ga _____ imasu.

   むすめが _____ います。

5. *I have five siblings.*

   Kyoodai ga _____ imasu.

   きょうだいが _____ います。

   ANSWER KEY
   1. hitori ひとり; 2. futari ふたり; 3. sannin さんにん; 4. yonin よにん; 5. gonin ごにん

🎧 Bring It All Together
▶ 3F Bring It All Together (CD 1, Track 20)

Now we'll bring it all together in a short monologue.

I have one older brother.	あにがひとりいます。	**Ani ga hitori imasu.**
You have two younger sisters.	いもうとさんがふたりいます。	**Imootosan ga futari imasu.**
Mr. Yamada has three older brothers.	やまださんはおにいさんがさんにんいます。	**Yamada san wa oniisan ga sannin imasu.**
Professor Tanaka has four daughters.	たなかせんせいはむすめさんがよにんいます。	**Tanaka sensee wa musumesan ga yonin imasu.**
There are six people.	ひとがろくにんいます。	**Hito ga rokunin imasu.**
There are seven men.	おとこのひとがしちにんいます。	**Otoko no hito ga shichinin imasu.**
There are nine female teachers.	おんなのせんせいがきゅうにんいます。	**Onna no sensee ga kyuunin imasu.**
There are eleven students.	がくせいがじゅういちにんいます。	**Gakusee ga juuichinin imasu.**

✏️ Work Out 2
▶ 3G Work Out 2 (CD 1, Track 21)

A. We'll give you a simple addition or subtraction problem below. Write down the answers in Japanese.

1. *1 + 1 =* _____

2. *3 + 3 =* _____

3. *10 + 10 =* _____

4. *100 – 50 =* _____

5. *6 + 6 =* _____

6. *40 – 4 =* _____

7. *44 + 56 =* _____

B. Now try using the measure word for people. Fill in what is missing in each of the following sentences.

1. **Musuko ga** _____ **imasu.** (*I have one son.*)

   むすこが _____ います。

2. **Musuko ga** _____ **imasu.** (*I have two sons.*)

   むすこが _____ います。

3. **Musuko ga** _____ **imasu.** (*You have three sons.*)

   むすこが _____ います。

4. **Musuko ga** _____ **imasu.** (*He has four sons.*)

   むすこが _____ います。

5. **Sensee ga** _____ **imasu.** (*There are five teachers.*)

   せんせいが _____ います。

6. **Gakusee ga** _____ **imasu.** (*There are six students.*)

   がくせいが _____ います。

7. **Onna no hito ga** _____ **imasu.** (*There are seven women.*)

   おんなのひとが _____ います。

8. **Otoko no sensee ga** _____ **imasu.**

(There are eight male teachers.)

おとこのせんせいが _____ います。

ANSWER KEY
A. 1. ni に; 2. roku ろく; 3. nijuu にじゅう; 4. gojuu ごじゅう; 5. juuni じゅうに;
6. sanjuu roku さんじゅうろく; 7. hyaku ひゃく
B. 1. hitori ひとり; 2. futari ふたり; 3. sannin さんにん; 4. yonin よにん; 5. gonin ごにん;
6. rokunin ろくにん; 7. shichinin しちにん *or* nananin ななにん; 8. hachinin はちにん

✎ Drive It Home

How do you count from one to ten in Japanese?

1. *one* _____

2. *two* _____

3. *three* _____

4. *four* _____

5. *five* _____

6. *six* _____

7. *seven* _____

8. *eight* _____

9. *nine* _____

10. *ten* _____

ANSWER KEY
1. ichi いち; 2. ni に; 3. san さん; 4. yon よん or shi し; 5. go ご; 6. roku ろく; 7. nana なな or shichi しち;
8. hachi はち; 9. kyuu きゅう or ku く; 10. juu じゅう

Parting Words

よくできました！**Yoku dekimashita!** *Well done!* You've finished the lesson. You've learned how to count, how to use a measure word, and how to put them together in sentences. You'll learn more measure words in the next lesson to help you express yourself even more with numbers. You should now be able to:

☐ Count up to one hundred

☐ Express how many people there are with measure words

☐ Use what you've learned to talk about people and family

Don't forget to practice and reinforce what you've learned by visiting **www.livinglanguage.com/languagelab** for flashcards, games, and quizzes!

Word Recall

1. よんじゅうご yonjuu go a. *female*

2. おんな onna b. *daughter (someone else's)*

3. ひとり hitori c. *How do you do?*

4. はじめまして。Hajimemashite. d. *one person*

5. はちにん hachinin e. *45*

6. がくせい gakusee f. *eight people*

7. じゅうにん juunin g. *two people*

8. ちち chichi h. *student*

9. ふたり futari i. *ten people*

10. むすめさん musumesan j. *78*

11. ななじゅうはち nanajuu hachi k. *father (one's own)*

12. おとこのひと otoko no hito l. *man*

ANSWER KEY
1. e; 2. a; 3. d; 4. c; 5. f; 6. h; 7. i; 8. k; 9. g; 10. b; 11. j; 12. l

Lesson 4: At Home
Dai yonka: Uchi de
だいよんか：うちで

こんにちは。だいよんかへようこそ。**Konnichi wa. Dai yonka e yookoso.** *Hello. Welcome to Lesson 4.* By the end of this lesson, you'll be able to:

☐ Express the names of different objects around the home

☐ Express *I have, there is/are* (objects)

☐ Ask a question *What is there?*

☐ Use the particle と **to**

☐ Use measure words for counting books and machines

☐ Use native Japanese numbers

☐ Use what you've learned to describe objects around the home
    As usual, let's get started with some words and phrases.

Vocabulary Builder 1

4A Vocabulary Builder 1 (CD 1, Track 22)

There is … / to have … (for an object)	〜があります。	… ga arimasu.
Is there … / Do you have … (for an object)	〜はありますか。	… wa arimasu ka.
There is not … /to not have … (for an object)	〜はありません。	… wa arimasen.
what	なに or なん	nani or nan
What is there?	なにがありますか。	Nani ga arimasu ka.
and	と	to
book	ほん	hon
table	テーブル	teeburu
chair	いす	isu
television	テレビ	terebi
computer	コンピューター	konpyuutaa
telephone	でんわ	denwa
refrigerator	れいぞうこ	reezooko
car	くるま	kuruma

Vocabulary Practice 1

Let's practice what you've learned! Match the Japanese in the left column with the English equivalent in the right.

1. ほん hon
2. テーブル teeburu
3. いす isu
4. テレビ terebi

a. television
b. refrigerator
c. table
d. telephone

5. コンピューター konpyuutaa   e. *car*

6. でんわ denwa   f. *book*

7. れいぞうこ reezooko   g. *chair*

8. くるま kuruma   h. *computer*

ANSWER KEY
1. f; 2. c; 3. g; 4. a; 5. h; 6. d; 7. b; 8. e

Take It Further

Now that you've learned the 46 basic hiragana characters, let's look at the two types of diacritics used with some of the characters to create additional sounds.

There is a two-dot symbol called だくてん dakuten, which can be placed to the upper right of the characters in かぎょう kagyoo *the Ka-line*, さぎょう sagyoo *the Sa-line*, たぎょう tagyoo *the Ta-line*, and はぎょう hagyoo *the Ha-line*. Let's see what they look like and how those characters sound.

かぎょう KAGYOO *THE KA-LINE*		かぎょう KAGYOO *THE KA-LINE* WITH だくてん DAKUTEN	
か	ka	が	ga
き	ki	ぎ	gi
く	ku	ぐ	gu
け	ke	げ	ge
こ	ko	ご	go

さぎょう SAGYOO *THE SA-LINE*		さぎょう SAGYOO *THE SA-LINE* WITH だくてん DAKUTEN	
さ	sa	ざ	za
し	shi	じ	ji
す	su	ず	zu
せ	se	ぜ	ze
そ	so	ぞ	zo

たぎょう TAGYOO *THE TA-LINE*		たぎょう TAGYOO *THE TA-LINE* **WITH** だくてん DAKUTEN	
た	ta	だ	da
ち	chi	ぢ	ji
つ	tsu	づ	zu
て	te	で	de
と	to	ど	do

はぎょう HAGYOO *THE HA-LINE*		はぎょう HAGYOO *THE HA-LINE* **WITH** だくてん DAKUTEN	
は	ha	ば	ba
ひ	hi	び	bi
ふ	fu	ぶ	bu
へ	he	べ	be
ほ	ho	ぼ	bo

There is another kind of diacritic called はんだくてん handakuten, which is a little circle and it is only used over the characters in はぎょう hagyoo *the Ha-line*:

はぎょう HAGYOO *THE HA-LINE*		はぎょう HAGYOO *THE HA-LINE* **WITH** はんだくてん HANDAKUTEN	
は	ha	ぱ	pa
ひ	hi	ぴ	pi
ふ	fu	ぷ	pu
へ	he	ぺ	pe
ほ	ho	ぽ	po

Note that じ ji and ぢ ji have the same pronunciation. They are, however, not interchangeable. For example, the word that means *time* must always be written with じ as in じかん jikan, but not ぢかん. In fact, the character ぢ is rarely used.

The following pairs of examples illustrate the contrast between words with and without a だくてん dakuten:

WORD WITHOUT だくてん DAKUTEN			WORD WITH だくてん DAKUTEN		
とく	toku	*virtue*	どく	doku	*poison*
せん	sen	*thousand*	ぜん	zen	*Zen Buddhism*
か	ka	*mosquito*	が	ga	*moth*
ふた	futa	*lid*	ぶた	buta	*pig*

Great! Now you know the two types of diacritics, だくてん dakuten and はんだくてん handakuten, and how they change the sounds of some of the characters. In the next character section, we'll go over special character combinations.

Grammar Builder 1
▶ 4B Grammar Builder 1 (CD 1, Track 23)

Do you remember the expression います imasu from Lesson 2? This expression is used when you talk about people or animals. Now let's learn a similar expression あります arimasu, which is used for objects.

There is a car.	くるまがあります。	Kuruma ga arimasu.
Is there a car?	くるまはありますか。	Kuruma wa arimasu ka.
There isn't a car.	くるまはありません。	Kuruma wa arimasen.

You use あります arimasu in a sentence exactly the same way you use います imasu. The only difference is that あります arimasu is used for objects, while います imasu is used for people and animals.

If you want to ask, *What is there?*, use the question word なに **nani** and the question particle か **ka**.

What is there?	なにがありますか。	Nani ga arimasu ka.

The question word なに **nani** should be followed by the particle が **ga**. Compare it with a *yes/no* question such as くるまはありますか **Kuruma wa arimasu ka** (*Is there a car?*), where you use the particle は **wa**. The particle は **wa** is commonly used in *yes/no* questions. In contrast, question words such as *what*, *who*, *where* in Japanese should not be followed by the particle は **wa**. We'll learn more about the question words later.

If you want to say *and* in Japanese, use the noun connecting particle と **to**.

There is a table and a chair.	テーブルといすがあります。	Teeburu to isu ga arimasu.

Be careful to note that と **to** is used only to connect nouns, such as *a table and a chair*. You cannot use と **to** to connect adjectives, verbs, and sentences.

The expression あります **arimasu** can also be used to express possession. Just add the particle は **wa** after someone's name, and follow it by the object of possession and the particle が **ga**, and follow it with あります **arimasu**. To say that Mr. Yamada has a car, for example, you would say:

Mr. Yamada has a car.	やまださんはくるまがあります。	Yamada san wa kuruma ga arimasu.

As you already know, personal pronouns are often omitted in Japanese. So, depending on the context, くるまがあります **Kuruma ga arimasu** could mean *I have a car*, *You have a car*, *He has a car*, *She has a car*, and of course, *There is a car*.

Vocabulary Builder 2

▶ 4C Vocabulary Builder 2 (CD 1, Track 24)

Let's learn more measure words and see how they work with a few numbers.

Measure word for books, photo albums, magazines	さつ	satsu
1, 2, 3	いっさつ、にさつ、さんさつ	issatsu, nisatsu, sansatsu
4, 5, 6	よんさつ、ごさつ、ろくさつ	yonsatsu, gosatsu, rokusatsu
7, 8, 9, 10	ななさつ、はっさつ、きゅうさつ、じゅっさつ	nanasatsu, hassatsu, kyuusatsu, jussatsu

Measure word for cars, machines	だい	dai
1, 2, 3	いちだい、にだい、さんだい	ichidai, nidai, sandai
4, 5, 6,	よんだい、ごだい、ろくだい	yondai, godai, rokudai
7, 8, 9, 10	ななだい、はちだい、きゅうだい、じゅうだい	nanadai, hachidai, kyuudai, juudai

The numbers you have learned so far are mostly of Chinese origin, but there is also a set of native Japanese numbers, which are used to count small and round objects, furniture, rooms among other things. Let's listen to these numbers now.

1	ひとつ	hitotsu
2	ふたつ	futatsu
3	みっつ	mittsu
4	よっつ	yottsu
5	いつつ	itsutsu

6	むっつ	muttsu
7	ななつ	nanatsu
8	やっつ	yattsu
9	ここのつ	kokonotsu
10	とお	too

✏ Vocabulary Practice 2

Complete each of the following sentences by inserting the appropriate number and measure word combination or native Japanese number.

1. **Hon ga** _____ **arimasu.** (*There is one book.*)

   ほんが _____ あります。

2. **Hon ga** _____ **arimasu.** (*There are two books.*)

   ほんが _____ あります。

3. **Hon ga** _____ **arimasu.** (*There are three books.*)

   ほんが _____ あります。

4. **Kuruma ga** _____ **arimasu.** (*There are four cars.*)

   くるまが _____ あります。

5. **Kuruma ga** _____ **arimasu.** (*There are five cars.*)

   くるまが _____ あります。

6. **Kuruma ga** _____ **arimasu.** (*There are six cars.*)

   くるまが _____ あります。

7. **Isu ga** _____ **arimasu.** (*There are seven chairs.*)

   いすが _____ あります。

8. **Isu ga** _____ **arimasu.** (*There are eight chairs.*)

いすが _____ あります。

9. **Isu ga** _____ **arimasu.** (*There are nine chairs.*)

いすが _____ あります。

ANSWER KEY

1. issatsu いっさつ; 2. nisatsu にさつ; 3. sansatsu さんさつ; 4. yondai よんだい; 5. godai ごだい; 6. rokudai ろくだい; 7. nanatsu ななつ; 8. yattsu やっつ; 9. kokonotsu ここのつ

Take It Further

In the next several character sections, you'll learn special character combinations and how they sound. We'll start with character combinations that create a type of sound called *glide*. A glide is a sound that contains a consonant and y, such as **kya**. Glides are written with the combination of the hiragana containing the vowel i and small や **ya**, ゆ **yu**, or よ **yo**. There are 36 glides, but let's look at the first nine glides here along with word examples:

	K	S	T
ya	きゃ kya	しゃ sha	ちゃ cha
	きゃく *kya*ku customer	いしゃ i*sha* medical doctor	おちゃ o*cha* Japanese tea
yu	きゅ kyu	しゅ shu	ちゅ chu
	きゅう *kyu*u nine	こんしゅう kon*shuu* this week	ちゅうしょく *chuu*shoku lunch (*fml.*)
yo	きょ kyo	しょ sho	ちょ cho
	きょうだい *kyo*odai siblings (*one's own*)	しょうゆ *sho*oyu soy sauce	ちょうしょく *choo*shoku breakfast (*fml.*)

Note that the romaji for glides does not necessarily contain the alphabet character y, such as ちゃ **cha** and しゅ **shu**. However, if you pronounce them, you'll hear the sound "y". It is very important that the characters や **ya**, ゆ **yu**, and よ **yo** are written small in glides. Written big, it may result in a completely different word. Here are some examples:

WORD WITH A GLIDE			WORD WITHOUT A GLIDE		
きゃく	kyaku	*customer*	きやく	kiyaku	*agreement, rules*
きょう	kyoo	*today*	きよう	kiyoo	*promotion, appointment*

You'll learn 24 more glides in the next two character sections.

Grammar Builder 2

▶ 4D Grammar Builder 2 (CD 1, Track 25)

You've just learned two new measure words. The first is さつ **satsu**, which is used for counting things like books, photo albums, and magazines. Did you notice the special pronunciation for 1, 8, and 10? Let's hear them again.

1, 8, 10	いっさつ、はっさつ、じゅっさつ	issatsu, hassatsu, jussatsu
There are eight books.	ほんがはっさつあります。	**Hon ga hassatsu arimasu.**

The second measure word you learned was だい **dai**. This is used for counting cars and machines such as computers, televisions, telephones, and refrigerators.

There are three computers.	コンピューターがさんだいあります。	**Konpyuutaa ga sandai arimasu.**

You also learned the native Japanese numbers. They are convenient to remember because you can use them to count many different objects, such as small and round objects, pieces of furniture, rooms, and abstract things. Native Japanese numbers can also be used instead of a particular measure word if you don't happen to know the appropriate one to use. Please note that native Japanese numbers only exist to count from one to ten.

| *There are three chairs.* | いすがみっつあります。 | **Isu ga mittsu arimasu.** |

✎ Work Out 1

 4E Work Out 1 (CD 1, Track 26)

Okay, let's put everything you've learned so far together in a short comprehension exercise. Listen to the audio, and fill in the blanks with the words that you hear.

1. *What is there?*

   _____ ga arimasu ka.

   _____ がありますか。

2. *There is a table and a chair.*

   Teeburu _____ **isu ga arimasu.**

   テーブル _____ いすがあります。

3. *Is there a telephone?*

   Denwa wa _____.

   でんわは _____。

4. *There isn't a refrigerator.*

   Reezooko wa _____.

   れいぞうこは _____。

5. *Mr. Yamada has a car.*

   Yamada san wa kuruma ga _____.

   やまださんはくるまが_____ 。

6. *There are two books.*

   Hon ga _____ **arimasu.**

   ほんが_____ あります。

7. *There are two chairs.*

   Isu ga _____ **arimasu.**

   いすが_____ あります。

8. *There are two televisions.*

   Terebi ga _____ **arimasu.**

   テレビが_____ あります。

ANSWER KEY
1. **Nani** なに; 2. **to** と; 3. **arimasu ka** ありますか; 4. **arimasen** ありません; 5. **arimasu** あります; 6. **nisatsu** にさつ; 7. **futatsu** ふたつ; 8. **nidai** にだい

🎧 Bring It All Together

▶ 4F Bring It All Together (CD 1, Track 27)

Let's bring it all together, and add a little more structure.

A. *What is there?*	なにがありますか。	**Nani ga arimasu ka.**
B. *There are five books.*	ほんがごさつあります。	**Hon ga gosatsu arimasu.**
A. *Is there a chair?*	いすはありますか。	**Isu wa arimasu ka.**
B. *Yes, there are two chairs.*	はい、いすがふたつあります。	**Hai, isu ga futatsu arimasu.**

A. Is there a television and a telephone?	テレビとでんわはありますか。	Terebi to denwa wa arimasu ka.
B. There is a television. There isn't a telephone.	テレビがあります。でんわはありません。	Terebi ga arimasu. Denwa wa arimasen.
A. Is there a car?	くるまはありますか。	Kuruma wa arimasu ka.
B. Yes, there are two cars.	はい、くるまがにだいあります。	Hai, kuruma ga nidai arimasu.

✎ Work Out 2

▶ 4G Work Out 2 (CD 1, Track 28)

A. Translate the following sentences from English to Japanese.

1. *There is one book.*

   _____

2. *There are two books.*

   _____

3. *There are three books.*

   _____

4. *There is one table.*

   _____

5. *There are two tables.*

   _____

6. *There are three tables.*

   _____

7. *There is one computer.*

_____

8. *There are two computers.*

_____

9. *There are three computers.*

_____

B. Give the native Japanese numbers from one to ten.

1. *one*

_____

2. *two*

_____

3. *three*

_____

4. *four*

_____

5. *five*

_____

6. *six*

_____

7. *seven*

_____

8. *eight*

_____

9. *nine*

_____

10. *ten*

_____

ANSWER KEY

A. 1. Hon ga issatsu arimasu. ほんがいっさつあります。 2. Hon ga nisatsu arimasu. ほんがにさつあり
ます。 3. Hon ga sansatsu arimasu. ほんがさんさつあります。 4. Teeburu ga hitotsu arimasu. テーブル
がひとつあります。 5. Teeburu ga futatsu arimasu. テーブルがふたつあります。 6. Teeburu ga mittsu
arimasu. テーブルがみっつあります。 7. Konpyuutaa ga ichidai arimasu. コンピューターがいちだいあ
ります。 8. Konpyuutaa ga nidai arimasu. コンピューターがにだいあります。 9. Konpyuutaa ga sandai
arimasu. コンピューターがさんだいあります。

B. 1. hitotsu ひとつ; 2. futatsu ふたつ; 3. mittsu みっつ; 4. yottsu よっつ; 5. itsutsu いつつ; 6. muttsu む
っつ; 7. nanatsu ななつ; 8. hattsu やっつ; 9. kokonotsu ここのつ; 10. too とお

✎ Drive It Home

Complete the following sentences by inserting appropriate particles.

1. **Kuruma** _____ **arimasu.** (*There is a car.*)

   くるま _____ あります。

2. **Kuruma** _____ **arimasu** _____. (*Is there a car?*)

   くるま _____ あります _____。

3. **Kuruma** _____ **arimasen.** (*There isn't a car.*)

   くるま _____ ありません。

4. **Nani** _____ **arimasu ka.** (*What is there?*)

   なに _____ ありますか。

5. **Yamada san** _____ **kuruma** _____ **arimasu.** *(Mr./Ms. Yamada has a car.)*

やまださん _____ くるま _____ あります。

ANSWER KEY
1. ga が; 2. wa は, ka か; 3. wa は; 4. ga が; 5. wa は, ga が

Parting Words

Congratulations. おめでとうございます。**Omedetoo gozaimasu.** You did a great job! You learned new measure words and more about how to talk about objects around you. You should now be able to:

☐ Express the names of different objects around the home

☐ Express *I have, there is/are* (objects)

☐ Ask a question *What is there?*

☐ Use the particle と **to**

☐ Use measure words for counting books and machines

☐ Use native Japanese numbers

☐ Use what you've learned to describe objects around the home

Take It Further
▶ 4H Take It Further (CD 1, Track 29)

Throughout your studies, you'll come across several words in Japanese that may seem familiar because they are very similar to English words. These words are called loan words, and Japanese uses many of them. When talking about computers, for instance, many English loan words are used. You will hear words such as:

| *mouse* | マウス | mausu |
| *keyboard* | キーボード | kiiboodo |

display	ディスプレイ	disupurei
monitor	モニター	monitaa
software	ソフトウェア	sofutowea
hardware	ハードウェア	haadowea
e-mail	イーメール	iimeeru
internet	インターネット	intaanetto

Be sure to practice the Japanese pronunciation of these words!

And one more note: the above are all written in katakana as is typical for loan words. You'll start learning katakana in Lesson 7, but feel free to skip ahead and start studying it in the *Guide to Reading and Writing Japanese*.

Don't forget to practice and reinforce what you've learned by visiting **www.livinglanguage.com/languagelab** for flashcards, games, and quizzes!

Word Recall

1. ろくにん rokunin

2. きょうだい kyoodai

3. いす isu

4. に ni

5. いもうとさん imootosan

6. テレビ terebi

7. でんわ denwa

8. くるま kuruma

9. わたしは〜です。
Watashi wa ... desu.

10. コンピューター konpyuutaa

11. きゅうじゅういち kyuujuu ichi

12. れいぞうこ reezooko

a. *computer*

b. *two*

c. *car*

d. *siblings (one's own)*

e. *refrigerator*

f. *younger sister (someone else's)*

g. *chair*

h. *television*

i. *six people*

j. *telephone*

k. *91*

l. *I am ...*

ANSWER KEY
1. i; 2. d; 3. g; 4. b; 5. f; 6. h; 7. j; 8. c; 9. l; 10. a; 11. k; 12. e

Lesson 5: Describing Things

Dai goka: Mono no setsumee
だいごか：もののせつめい

こんにちは。**Konnichi wa.** *Hello.* By the end of this lesson, you'll be able to:

☐ Express possession

☐ Express *this* and *that*

☐ Use *i*-adjectives

☐ Describe things with adjectives
Let's get started with vocabulary related to some everyday objects you might encounter and need to describe.

Vocabulary Builder 1

▶ 5A Vocabulary Builder 1 (CD 2, Track 1)

pen	ペン	pen
watch/clock	とけい	tokee
shirt	シャツ	shatsu
shoes	くつ	kutsu
bag	バッグ	baggu
house	いえ	ie
apartment	アパート	apaato
dog	いぬ	inu
cat	ねこ	neko
my pen	わたしのペン	watashi no pen
this	これ	kore
that (far from the speaker but close to the listener)	それ	sore
that (far from both the speaker and the listener)	あれ	are
this pen (close to the speaker)	このペン	kono pen
that pen (far from the speaker but close to the listener)	そのペン	sono pen
that pen (far from both the speaker and the listener)	あのペン	ano pen
What is ... ?	～はなんですか。	... wa nan desu ka.

✎ Vocabulary Practice 1

Now let's practice the new vocabulary. Fill in what is missing in each of the following phrases and sentences.

1. Kore wa _____desu. (*This is a watch/clock.*)

   これは _____ です。

2. _____ wa pen desu. (*That is a pen. [far from the speaker but close to the listener]*)

   _____はペンです。

3. _____ wa _____ desu. (*That is an apartment. [far from both the speaker and the listener]*)

   _____ は _____ です。

4. _____ to _____ (*a dog and a cat*)

   _____ と _____

5. kono _____ (*these shoes*)

   この _____

6. _____ shatsu (*this shirt*)

   _____シャツ

7. sono _____ (*that bag [far from the speaker but close to the listener]*)

   その _____

8. Are wa _____ desu ka. (*What is that? [far from both the speaker and the listener]*)

   あれは _____ ですか。

Take It Further

Ready for another set of hiragana glides? Here are twelve more:

	N	H	M	R
ya	にゃ nya	ひゃ hya	みゃ mya	りゃ rya
	こんにゃく kon*nya*ku *potato*	ひゃく *hya*ku *hundred*	みゃく *mya*ku *pulse*	りゃくご *rya*kugo *abbreviation*
yu	にゅ nyu	ひゅ hyu	みゅ myu	りゅ ryu
	とうにゅう too*nyu*u *soy milk*	ひゅう *hyu*u *onomatopoeia representing the sound of blowing wind*	n/a	りゅう *ryu*u *dragon*
yo	にょ nyo	ひょ hyo	みょ myo	りょ ryo
	にょう *nyo*o *urine*	ひょうげん *hyo*ogen *expression*	みょう *myo*o *strange*	りょうり *ryo*ori *cooking*

As noted in the previous character section, the characters や ya, ゆ yu, and よ yo must be written small in glides; otherwise, the word may mean something completely different. Here are some examples:

WORD WITH A GLIDE			WORD WITHOUT A GLIDE		
ひゃく	**hyaku**	*hundred*	ひやく	**hiyaku**	*leap*
りゅう	**ryuu**	*dragon*	りゆう	**riyuu**	*reason*

You'll learn the rest of the glides in the next Take It Further character section.

Grammar Builder 1

▶ 5B Grammar Builder 1 (CD 2, Track 2)

Do you remember the particle の no from Lesson 2? The particle の no connects two nouns. For example, you can connect おんな onna (*female*) and せんせい sensee (*teacher*) with の no, and you get おんなの せんせい onna no sensee (*female teacher*). You can also use the particle の no, to express possession. For example, わたしのペン watashi no pen means *my pen*, and やまださんのペン Yamada san no pen means *Mr./Ms. Yamada's pen*.

Did you notice that there are two different words meaning *that* in Japanese? One is それ sore, and the other is あれ are. You use それ sore when the object you're referring to is close to the listener but far from you. In contrast, あれ are is used when the object you're referring to is far from both you and the listener. While これ kore, それ sore, and あれ are stand alone in a sentence, この kono, その sono, and あの ano are all followed by nouns.

This is Mr./Ms. Yamada's pen.	これはやまださんのペンです。	Kore wa Yamada san no pen desu.
This pen is Mr./Ms. Yamada's pen.	このペンはやまださんのペンです。	Kono pen wa Yamada san no pen desu.
That is Mr./Ms. Yamada's pen. (far from the speaker but close to the listener)	それはやまださんのペンです。	Sore wa Yamada san no pen desu.
That pen is Mr./Ms. Yamada's pen. (far from the speaker but close to the listener)	そのペンはやまださんのペンです。	Sono pen wa Yamada san no pen desu.
That is Mr./Ms. Yamada's pen. (far from both the speaker and the listener)	あれはやまださんのペンです。	Are wa Yamada san no pen desu.

| That pen is Mr./Ms. Yamada's pen. (far from both the speaker and the listener) | あのペンはやまださんの ペンです。 | Ano pen wa Yamada san no pen desu. |

Now let's learn some adjectives to describe the nouns you've just learned.

Vocabulary Builder 2

▶ 5C Vocabulary Builder 2 (CD 2, Track 3)

big	おおきい	ookii
big house	おおきいいえ	ookii ie
small	ちいさい	chiisai
small apartment	ちいさいアパート	chiisai apaato
expensive	たかい	takai
expensive car	たかいくるま	takai kuruma
cheap	やすい	yasui
cheap bag	やすいバッグ	yasui baggu
new	あたらしい	atarashii
new book	あたらしいほん	atarashii hon
old	ふるい	furui
old clock	ふるいとけい	furui tokee
black	くろい	kuroi
black pen	くろいペン	kuroi pen
white	しろい	shiroi
white cat	しろいねこ	shiroi neko
very	とても	totemo
very big	とてもおおきい	totemo ookii

| It's big. | おおきいです。 | Ookii desu. |
| It's very big. | とてもおおきいです。 | Totemo ookii desu. |

✎ Vocabulary Practice 2

Let's practice the new vocabulary. Fill in what is missing in each of the following phrases and sentences.

1. _____ inu (*black dog*)

   _____ いぬ

2. _____kutsu (*new shoes*)

   _____ くつ

3. _____ kuruma (*big car*)

   _____ くるま

4. _____ tokee (*expensive watch/clock*)

   _____ とけい

5. _____desu. (*It's cheap.*)

   _____ です。

6. _____ desu. (*It's old.*)

   _____ です。

7. Totemo _____ desu. (*It's very small.*)

   とても _____ です。

8. _____ takai desu. (*It's very expensive.*)

   _____ たかいです。

9. _____ ie desu. *(It's a white house.)*

_____いえです。

ANSWER KEY

1. kuroi くろい ; 2. atarashii あたらしい; 3. ookii おおきい; 4. takai たかい; 5. Yasui やすい; 6. Furui ふるい; 7. chiisai ちいさい; 8. Totemo とても; 9. Shiroi しろい

Take It Further

Now let's look at the rest of the glides. These glides contain characters with the diacritics, だくてん dakuten and はんだくてん handakuten.

	G	Z	D	B	P
ya	ぎゃ gya	じゃ ja	ぢゃ ja	びゃ bya	ぴゃ pya
	ぎゃく *gyaku* opposite	じゃま *jama* intrusion	めおとぢゃわん **meotojawan** "his and hers" rice bowl set	びゃくや *byakuya* white night	はっぴゃく *happyaku* eight hundred
yu	ぎゅ gyu	じゅ ju	ぢゅ ju	びゅ byu	ぴゅ pyu
	ぎゅうにく **gyuuniku** beef	じゅう *juu* ten	n/a	ごびゅう **gobyuu** error (fml.)	ぴゅう *pyuu* onomatopoeia representing the sound of blowing wind
yo	ぎょ gyo	じょ jo	ぢょ jo	びょ byo	ぴょ pyo
	しょくぎょう **shokugyoo** occupation	てんじょう **tenjoo** ceiling	いっぽんぢょうし **ipponjooshi** monotonous	びょういん **byooin** hospital	はっぴょう *happyoo* presentation

Some glides are rarely used in everyday Japanese, however it is still good to know that these character combinations exist and what they sound like. Several of the example words above (such as めおとぢゃわん **meotojawan**, ごびゆう **gobyuu**, and びゃくや **byakuya**) are not everyday words, so don't worry too much about memorizing them all for now.

Note that じゃ **ja** and ぢゃ **ja** have the same pronunciation. The same goes for じゅ **ju** and ぢゅ **ju**, じょ **jo**, and ぢょ **jo**. However, they are not interchangeable. For example, the word that means *ten* must always be written with じゅ as in じゅう, but not ぢゅう.

In the next Take It Further character section, you'll learn another character combination: double consonants.

Grammar Builder 2

▶ 5D Grammar Builder 2 (CD 2, Track 4)

There are two types of adjectives in Japanese: *i*-adjectives and *na*-adjectives. The adjectives that you just learned are called *i*-adjectives because they end with the sound い **i**. Let's hear how the *i*-adjective たかい **takai** (*expensive*) is used in sentences.

This watch is expensive.	このとけいはたかいです。	Kono tokee wa takai desu.
My watch is very expensive	わたしのとけいはとてもたかいです。	Watashi no tokee wa totemo takai desu.
There is an expensive watch.	たかいとけいがあります。	Takai tokee ga arimasu.
This is an expensive watch.	これはたかいとけいです。	Kore wa takai tokee desu.

| *This is not an expensive watch.* | これはたかいとけいではありません。 | **Kore wa takai tokee de wa arimasen.** |

In Lesson 7, you'll learn how to negate *i*-adjectives to say sentences such as *This watch is not expensive* and *My watch is not expensive*. For now, however, you can still use an *i*-adjective in a negative sentence using the copula ではありません **de wa arimasen**, as in これはたかいとけいではありません **Kore wa takai tokee de wa arimasen** (*This is not an expensive watch*).

✎ Work Out 1

▶ 5E Work Out 1 (CD 2, Track 5)

Okay, let's review everything you've learned so far. Listen to the audio, and fill in the blanks with the words that you hear.

1. *What is that?*

   Sore wa _____.

   それは _____ 。

2. *This is a bag.*

   _____ **baggu desu.**

   _____ バッグです。

3. *Is that Mr. Yamada's house over there?*

   Are wa _____ **desu ka.**

   あれは _____ ですか。

4. *My dog is white.*

   Watashi no inu wa _____.

   わたしのいぬは _____ 。

5. *That shirt is very cheap.*

   Kono shatsu wa _____ **desu.**

   このシャツは _____ です。

6. *That is a big cat.*

   Are wa _____ **desu.**

   あれは _____ です。

7. *This is not a new apartment.*

   Kore wa _____ **de wa arimasen.**

   これは _____ ではありません。

ANSWER KEY

1. nan desu ka なんですか; 2. Kore wa これは; 3. Yamada san no ie やまださんのいえ; 4. shiroi desu しろいです; 5. totemo yasui とてもやすい; 6. ookii neko おおきいねこ; 7. atarashii apaato あたらしいアパート

Bring It All Together

▶ 5F Bring It All Together (CD 2, Track 6)

Now let's bring it all together, and add a little bit more vocabulary and structure.

| A: What is that? | それはなんですか。 | Sore wa nan desu ka. |
| B: This is my new bag. | これはわたしのあたらしいバッグです。 | Kore wa watashi no atarashii baggu desu. |

A: Is it expensive?	たかいですか。	Takai desu ka.
B: Yes, it is expensive.	はい、たかいです。	Hai, takai desu.
A: What are these?	これはなんですか。	Kore wa nan desu ka.
B: Those are my younger sister's shoes.	それはいもうとのくつですよ。	Sore wa imooto no kutsu desu yo.
A: Are they new?	あたらしいですか。	Atarashii desu ka.
B: No, they're old.	いいえ、ふるいです。	Iie, furui desu.
A: Do you have a dog?	いぬはいますか。	Inu wa imasu ka.
B: Yes. I have a small dog.	はい、ちいさいいぬがいます。	Hai, chiisai inu ga imasu.
A: Is the dog white?	いぬはしろいですか。	Inu wa shiroi desu ka.
B: No, it's black.	いいえ、くろいですよ。	Iie, kuroi desu yo.

Take It Further

You may have noticed in the dialogue that a couple of sentences ended with
よ yo: それはいもうとのくつですよ Sore wa imooto no kutsu desu yo (*Those
are my younger sister's shoes*) and いいえ、くろいですよ Iie, kuroi desu yo (*No,
it's black*). This is a particle that comes at the end of a sentence just as the
particle か ka. Using the particle よ yo, you imply that you are trying to give new
information, attract the listener's attention, or emphasize the statement. The
English equivalent would be *you know*, but it is more subtle, and therefore it is
not necessarily translated into English. The particle よ yo is used very often in
colloquial Japanese, and it adds a natural flow to a conversation.

✎ Work Out 2

▶ 5G Work Out 2 (CD 2, Track 7)

Let's practice some of what you've learned.

A. Translate the following phrases from Japanese to English.

1. このシャツはあたらしいです。

   Kono shatsu wa atarashii desu.

   _____

2. あれはやまださんのねこですか。

   Are wa Yamada san no neko desu ka.

   _____

3. それはちいさいくつです。

   Sore wa chiisai kutsu desu.

   _____

4. わたしのいえはとてもふるいです。

   Watashi no ie wa totemo furui desu.

   _____

5. これはやすいとけいではありません。

   Kore wa yasui tokee de wa arimasen.

   _____

B. Translate the following phrases and sentences from English to Japanese.

1. *This is a white bag.*

   _____

2. *This bag is black.*

   _____

3. *That is not my bag. (far from both the speaker and the listener)*

   _____

4. *That big bag is expensive.*

   _____

5. *My bag is small.*

   _____

ANSWER KEY
A. 1. *This shirt is new.* 2. *Is that Mr./Ms. Yamada's cat?* 3. *Those are small shoes.* 4. *My house is very old.*
5. *This is not a cheap watch.*
B. 1. **Kore wa shiroi baggu desu.** これはしろいバッグです。 2. **Kono baggu wa kuroi desu.** このバッグは
くろいです。 3. **Are wa watashi no baggu de wa arimasen.** あれはわたしのバッグではありません。
4. **Ano ookii baggu wa takai desu.** あのおおきいバッグはたかいです。 5. **Watashi no baggu wa chiisai
desu.** わたしのバッグはちいさいです。

✎ Drive It Home

Complete the following phrases and sentences based on the English translations.

1. _____ ie *(this house)*

   _____ いえ

2. _____ ie *(that house [far from the speaker but close to the listener])*

   _____ いえ

3. _____ ie *(that house [far from both the speaker and the listener])*

    _____ いえ

4. _____ wa ie desu. *(This is a house.)*

    _____ はいえです。

5. _____ wa ie desu. *(That is a house. [far from the speaker but close to*

the listener])

    _____ はいえです。

6. _____ wa ie desu. *(That is a house. [far from both the speaker and*

the listener])

    _____ はいえです。

ANSWER KEY
1. kono この; 2. sono その; 3. ano あの; 4. Kore これ; 5. Sore それ; 6. Are あれ

Parting Words

Well done! よくできました！ **Yoku dekimashita!** *You're halfway there!* You've learned the basic vocabulary and grammar you need to describe things. You should now be able to:

☐ Express possession

☐ Express *this* and *that*

☐ Use *i*-adjectives

☐ Describe things with adjectives

Take It Further

▶ 5H Take It Futher (CD 2, Track 8)

Before we move on, you may want to know some more *i*-adjectives:

good	いい	ii
cute	かわいい	kawaii
easy, kind	やさしい	yasashii
difficult	むずかしい	muzukashii
interesting	おもしろい	omoshiroi
busy	いそがしい	isogashii
long	ながい	nagai
short	みじかい	mijikai
heavy	おもい	omoi
light	かるい	karui
early	はやい	hayai
late	おそい	osoi
far	とおい	tooi
close	ちかい	chikai

Don't forget to practice and reinforce what you've learned by visiting **www.livinglanguage.com/languagelab** for flashcards, games, and quizzes!

Word Recall

1. おおきいいえ ookii ie
2. たかいくるま takai kuruma
3. あに ani
4. やすいバッグ yasui baggu
5. あたらしいほん atarashii hon
6. ふるいとけい furui tokee
7. くろいペン kuroi pen
8. ごにん gonin
9. と to
10. テーブル teeburu
11. しろいねこ shiroi neko
12. はち hachi

a. *new book*
b. *five people*
c. *black pen*
d. *and*
e. *cheap bag*
f. *big house*
g. *expensive car*
h. *old clock*
i. *eight*
j. *white cat*
k. *table*
l. *older brother (one's own)*

ANSWER KEY
1. f; 2. g; 3. l; 4. e; 5. a; 6. h; 7. c; 8. b; 9. d; 10. k; 11. j; 12. i

Essential Japanese

Quiz 1
テスト 1

Now let's see how you've done so far. In this section you'll find a short quiz testing what you learned in Lessons 1-5. After you've answered all of the questions, score your quiz and see how you did! If you find that you need to go back and review, please do so before continuing on to Lesson 6.

You'll get a second quiz after Lesson 10, followed by a final review with five dialogues and comprehension questions.

Let's get started!

A. Match the following English words to the correct Japanese translations.

1. がくせい gakusee
2. いいえ iie
3. はちにん hachinin
4. でんわ denwa
5. あたらしい atarashii

    a. *telephone*
    b. *student*
    c. *new*
    d. *eight people*
    e. *no*

B. Translate the following English expressions into Japanese.

1. *Good morning.* _____

2. *What's your name?* _____

3. *How are you?* _____

4. *Thank you.* _____

5. *I'm sorry.* _____

C. Complete the following phrases and sentences by inserting appropriate particles.

1. **Kuruma** _____ **arimasen.** (*There isn't a car.*)

   くるま_____ありません。

2. **Watashi** _____ **inu wa chiisai desu.** (*My dog is small.*)

   わたし_____いぬはちいさいです。

3. **Yamada san wa gakusee desu** _____. (*Is Mr. Yamada a student?*)

   やまださんはがくせいです_____。

4. **Nani** _____ **arimasu ka.** (*What is there?*)

   なに_____ありますか。

5. **Yamada san** _____ **otootosan ga imasu.** (*Mr. Yamada has a younger brother.*)

   やまださん_____おとうとさんがいます。

D. Fill in the table with the appropriate words.

	ONE'S OWN	SOMEONE ELSE'S
mother	1.	おかあさん okaasan
siblings	きょうだい kyoodai	2.
son	むすこ musuko	3.
younger sister	4.	いもうとさん imootosan
older brother	あに ani	5.

ANSWER KEY

A. 1. b; 2. e; 3. d; 4. a; 5. c

B. 1. **Ohayoo gozaimasu.** おはようございます。 2. **Onamae wa?** おなまえは？
3. **Ogenki desu ka.** おげんきですか。 4. **Arigatoo gozaimasu.** ありがとうございます。
5. **Gomennasai.** ごめんなさい。

C. 1. wa は; 2. no の; 3. ka か; 4. ga が; 5. wa は

D. 1. haha はは; 2. gokyoodai ごきょうだい; 3. musukosan むすこさん; 4. imooto いもうと;
5. oniisan おにいさん

How Did You Do?

Give yourself a point for every correct answer, then use the following key to
determine whether or not you're ready to move on:

0-7 points: It's probably best to go back and study the lessons again to make sure
you understood everything completely. Take your time; it's not a race! Make sure
you spend time reviewing the vocabulary and reading through each Grammar
Builder section carefully.

8-16 points: If the questions you missed were in sections A, B, or D, you may
want to review the vocabulary from previous lessons again; if you missed answers
mostly in section C, check the Grammar Builder sections to make sure you have
your grammar basics down.

17-20 points: Feel free to move on to Lesson 6! You're doing a great job.

☐☐ **points**

Lesson 6: Around Town

Dai rokka: Machi de
だいろっか：まちで

ようこそ！**Yookoso!** *Welcome!* By the end of this lesson, you'll be able to:

☐ Express *here* and *there*

☐ Ask for directions using the question word *where*

☐ Use expressions referring to locations of things

☐ Use the action verb *to go*

☐ Use the particle にni

☐ Ask for directions to get around town and express where things are
   As usual, let's get started with some vocabulary. じゅんびはいいですか。**Junbi wa ii desu ka.** *Are you ready?*

Vocabulary Builder 1

▶ 6A Vocabulary Builder 1 (CD 2, Track 9)

here	ここ	koko
there (far from the speaker but close to the listener)	そこ	soko
there (far from both the speaker and the listener)	あそこ	asoko
where	どこ	doko
Where is … ?	〜はどこですか。	… wa doko desu ka.
hotel	ホテル	hoteru
restaurant	レストラン	resutoran
department store	デパート	depaato
restroom	おてあらい	otearai
next to …	〜のとなり	… no tonari
across from …	〜のむかいがわ	… no mukai gawa
right	みぎ	migi
left	ひだり	hidari

Vocabulary Practice 1

Let's practice the new vocabulary. Fill in what is missing in each of the following phrases and sentences.

1. _____ to _____ *(right and left)*

    _____ と _____

2. _____ wa doko desu ka. *(Where is the restroom?)*

    _____ はどこですか。

3. _____ wa doko desu ka. *(Where is the department store?)*

   _____ はどこですか。

4. hoteru no _____ *(next to the hotel)*

   ホテルの _____

5. hoteru no _____ *(across from the hotel)*

   ホテルの _____

6. Resutoran wa _____ desu ka. *(Where is the restaurant?)*

   レストランは _____ですか。

7. _____ desu. *(It's here.)*

   _____です。

8. _____ desu. *(It's there. [far from the speaker but close to the listener])*

   _____です。

9. Depaato wa _____ desu. *(The department store is over there. [far from both the speaker and the listener])*

   デパートは _____です。

ANSWER KEY
1. migi みぎ, hidari ひだり; 2. Otearai おてあらい; 3. Depaato デパート; 4. tonari となり; 5. mukai gawa むかいがわ; 6. doko どこ; 7. Koko ここ; 8. Soko そこ; 9. asoko あそこ

Take It Further

Welcome to another hiragana lesson! Let's learn about double consonants. A double consonant can be recognized by a brief pause between sounds within a word, such as がっこう gakkoo *school*. Double consonants are written with a small

つ**tsu** placed immediately before the consonant to be doubled. Below are some examples:

がっこう	**ga**k**koo**	*school*
いっさつ	**i**ss**atsu**	*one (book, magazine)*
はっさつ	**ha**ss**atsu**	*eight (books, magazines)*
いっしょに	**i**ss**ho ni**	*together*
みっつ	**mi**tt**su**	*three (native Japanese number)*
よっつ	**yo**tt**su**	*four (native Japanese number)*
いっぱい	**i**pp**ai**	*a glass/cup/bowl of*
すっぱい	**su**pp**ai**	*sour*
いっぷん	**i**pp**un**	*one minute*
ろっぷん	**ro**pp**un**	*six minutes*

Keep in mind that double **n** are not considered as double consonants. This is because the first **n** is represented by the character ん**n**, as illustrated in the following examples:

さんにん	**sa**nn**in**	*three people*
どんな	**do**nn**a**	*what kind of*

Good job! In the next two character sections, you'll learn how long vowels are represented in hiragana.

Grammar Builder 1

▶ 6B Grammar Builder 1 (CD 2, Track 10)

Okay, you've just learned demonstrative expressions and a question word for places:

ここ koko (*here*), そこ soko (*there*), あそこ asoko (*there*), どこ doko (*where*). They all end with the sound こ ko, and you have probably noticed that ここ koko, そこ soko, あそこ asoko, are related to これ kore, それ sore, あれ are, and この kono, その sono, あの ano.

To ask where things are, use どこですか doko desu ka. If you want to ask where a hotel is, you can say, ホテルはどこですか Hoteru wa doko desu ka.

You've also learned some expressions to talk about where things are: みぎ migi (*right*), ひだり hidari (*left*), 〜のとなり ... no tonari (*next to* ...), and 〜のむかいがわ ... no mukai gawa (*across from* ...). Let's hear how to use these expressions in sentences.

Where is the restaurant?	レストランはどこですか。	Resutoran wa doko desu ka.
The restaurant is on the right.	レストランはみぎです。	Resutoran wa migi desu.
Where is the hotel?	ホテルはどこですか。	Hoteru wa doko desu ka.
The hotel is on the left.	ホテルはひだりです。	Hoteru wa hidari desu.
Where is the department store?	デパートはどこですか。	Depaato wa doko desu ka.
The department store is next to the hotel.	デパートはホテルのとなりです。	Depaato wa hoteru no tonari desu.
Where is the restaurant?	レストランはどこですか。	Resutoran wa doko desu ka.
The restaurant is across from the department store.	レストランはデパートのむかいがわです。	Resutoran wa depaato no mukai gawa desu.

Note the word order of each sentence: the location simply replaces the どこ doko in the question.

Vocabulary Builder 2

▶ 6C Vocabulary Builder 2 (CD 2, Track 11)

Let's learn some more words that will help you get around town.

east side	ひがしがわ	higashi gawa
west side	にしがわ	nishi gawa
south side	みなみがわ	minami gawa
north side	きたがわ	kita gawa
to go to . . .	～にいきます。	. . . ni ikimasu.
to not go to . . .	～にはいきません。	. . . ni wa ikimasen.
Do you go to . . . ?	～にはいきますか。	. . . ni wa ikimasu ka.
Where do you go?	どこにいきますか。	Doko ni ikimasu ka.
hospital	びょういん	byooin
station	えき	eki
park	こうえん	kooen
store	みせ	mise
convenience store	コンビニ	konbini
police booth	こうばん	kooban

Vocabulary Practice 2

Let's practice this new vocabulary. Fill in the word or phrase missing in each of the following phrases and sentences.

1. _____ ni ikimasu. (*I'm going to the police booth.*)

   _____ にいきます。

2. _____ ni wa ikimasen. (*I'm not going to the store.*)

   _____ にはいきません。

3. _____ ni wa ikimasu ka? (*Are you going to the*

   convenience store?)

   _____ にはいきますか。

4. _____ ni ikimasu ka? (*Where are you going?*)

   _____にいきますか。

5. _____ no minami gawa (*the south side of the park*)

   _____のみなみがわ

6. _____ no higashi gawa (*the east side of the station*)

   _____のひがしがわ

7. _____ no nishi gawa (*the west side of the hospital*)

   _____のにしがわ

8. Hoteru no _____ (*the north side of the hotel*)

   ホテルの _____

ANSWER KEY
1. Kooban こうばん; 2. Mise みせ; 3. Konbini コンビニ; 4. Doko どこ; 5. kooen こうえん; 6. eki えき;
7. byooin びょういん; 8. kita gawa きたがわ

Take It Further

There's just one more type of combination characters to master: long vowels.
Long vowels are created by the consecutive appearance of two identical vowel
sounds in a single word. Keep in mind that the two vowels are pronounced as a
continuous sound (thus creating a long vowel), not as two separate vowels. Here,
we'll take a look at some of the possible character combinations that create long
vowel sounds.

	A	K	S	T	N
aa	ああ aa	かあ kaa	さあ saa	たあ taa	なあ naa
ii	いい ii	きい kii	しい sii	ちい chii	にい nii
uu	うう uu	くう kuu	すう suu	つう tsuu	ぬう nuu
ee	えい ee ええ ee	けい kee	せい see	てい tee	ねい nee ねえ nee
oo	おう oo おお oo	こう koo こお koo	そう soo	とう too とお too	のう noo

As you can see in the chart above, different character combinations sometimes share the identical sound. For example, おう oo and おお oo, こう koo and こお koo. Notice that the second vowel in the sequence ee is often written with the character い i instead of え e. Likewise, the second vowel in the sequence oo is often written with the character う u instead of お o. When you see these combinations, be sure to pronounce them correctly.

Below are some example words that appear in *Essential Japanese* containing long vowels:

いいえ	*iie*	*no*
えいが	*eega*	*movie*
おおきい	*ookii*	*big*
おかあさん	o*kaa*san	*mother (someone else's)*
とけい	to*kee*	*watch, clock*
こうこうせい	*kookoosee*	*high school student*
せんせい	sen*see*	*teacher*
バスてい	basu*tee*	*bus stop*
おとうさん	o*too*san	*father (someone else's)*
おにいさん	o*nii*san	*older brother (someone else's)*
おねえさん	o*nee*san	*older sister (someone else's)*

Fantastic! You only have one more hiragana section to go, where we'll go through the rest of the long vowel combinations.

Grammar Builder 2

▶ 6D Grammar Builder 2 (CD 2, Track 12)

You've just learned more expressions useful for getting around town, including your first action verb, いきます ikimasu (*to go*). When you use いきます ikimasu, you also want to use the particle に ni with it. One of the functions of に ni is to express the direction of an action, something like *to* in English. To say *I go to a restaurant* in Japanese, say レストランにいきます Resutoran ni ikimasu. As you already know, Japanese pronouns are often omitted, so レストランにいきます Resutoran ni ikimasu can in fact mean *I go to a restaurant, You go to a restaurant, She goes to a restaurant, We go to a restaurant*, etc, depending on its context. If you want to say *Mr. Yamada goes to a restaurant*, it will be やまださんはレストランにいきます。 Yamada san wa resutoran ni ikimasu. The negative form of いきます ikimasu is いきません ikimasen, and requires the particle は wa following the particle に ni. So, *I don't go to a restaurant* in Japanese will be レストランにはいきません Resutoran ni wa ikimasen. Similarly, to ask a *yes/no* question, use the particle は wa following the particle に ni. So, *Do you go to a restaurant?* in Japanese will be レストランにはいきますか Resutoran ni wa ikimasu ka. However, when you ask a question using the question word どこ doko, do not use the particle は wa. So, *Where do you go?* in Japanese will be どこにいきますか Doko ni ikimasu ka.

All Japanese action verbs end with ます masu and their negative forms end with ません masen. So all you have to do is to memorize the part that comes before ます masu and ません masen when you learn more action verbs later.

There's more good news: Japanese present tense action verbs are also used to talk about the future. You don't have to learn future tense verb forms. So レストランにいきます **Resutoran ni ikimasu** can mean any one of the following: *I go to a restaurant, I'm going to a restaurant*, and *I will go to a restaurant*. The appropriate interpretation depends on its context.

✎ Work Out 1
▶ 6E Work Out 1 (CD 2, Track 13)

Let's put everything you've learned so far together in a short comprehension exercise. Listen to the audio, and fill in the blanks with the words that you hear.

1. *Where is a convenience store?*

   Konbini wa _____.

   コンビニは _____。

2. *Where is the restroom?*

   _____**doko desu ka.**

   _____ どこですか。

3. *Is the station over there?*

   Eki wa _____.

   えきは_____ 。

4. *The department store is across from the station.*

   Depaato wa eki no _____.

   デパートはえきの _____ 。

5. *The hospital is on the south side of the park.*

   Byooin wa kooen no _____.

   びょういんはこうえんの _____ 。

6. *The convenience store is next to the hotel.*

   Konbini wa hoteru no _____.

   コンビニはホテルの _____ 。

7. *I'm going to a store.*

   Mise ni _____.

   みせに_____ 。

8. *Are you going to the station?*

   Eki ni wa _____.

   えきには_____ 。

9. *I'm not going to a police booth.*

   Kooban ni wa _____.

   こうばんには_____ 。

10. *Where are you going?*

    _____ **ikimasu ka.**

    _____ いきますか。

ANSWER KEY
1. doko desu ka どこですか; 2. Otearai wa おてあらいは; 3. asoko desu ka あそこですか; 4. mukai gawa desu むかいがわです; 5. minami gawa desu みなみがわです; 6. tonari desu となりです; 7. Ikimasu いきます; 8. ikimasu ka いきますか; 9. ikimasen いきません; 10. Doko ni どこに

🔊 Bring It All Together

▶ 6F Bring It All Together (CD 2, Track 14)

Let's bring it all together, and add a little bit more vocabulary and structure.

A. Ms. Smith, where are you going?	スミスさんはどこにいきますか。	Sumisu san wa doko ni ikimasu ka.
B. I'm going to a department store.	デパートにいきます。	Depaato ni ikimasu.
A. Where is the department store?	デパートはどこですか。	Depaato wa doko desu ka.
B. It's next to the station. It's a big department store. Where are you going, Mr. Yamada?	えきのとなりです。おおきいデパートです。やまださんはどこにいきますか。	Eki no tonari desu. Ookii depaato desu. Yamada san wa doko ni ikimasu ka.
A. I'm going to a restaurant.	わたしはレストランにいきます。	Watashi wa resutoran ni ikimasu.
B. Where is the restaurant?	レストランはどこですか。	Resutoran wa doko desu ka.
A. It's across from the park. It's a new restaurant.	こうえんのむかいがわです。あたらしいレストランです。	Kooen no mukai gawa desu. Atarashii resutoran desu.

✎ **Work Out 2**

▶ 6G Work Out 2 (CD 2, Track 15)

Now let's practice some of what you've learned.

A. Translate the following sentences from Japanese to English.

1. おてあらいはあそこです。

   Otearai wa asoko desu.

   _____

2. えきはどこですか。

   Eki wa doko desu ka.

   _____

3. デパートにいきます。

   Depaato ni ikimasu.

   _____

4. レストランはえきのみなみがわです。

   Resutoran wa eki no minami gawa desu.

   _____

5. ホテルはひだりです。

   Hoteru wa hidari desu.

   _____

B. Translate the following sentences from English to Japanese.

1. *I'm going to a police booth.*

   _____

2. *The convenience store is on the east side of the hospital.*

   _____

3. *I'm not going to the station.*

   _____

4. *Where is the park?*

   _____

5. *The store is over there.*

   _____

ANSWER KEY

A. 1. *The restroom is over there.* 2. *Where is the station?* 3. *I'm going to a department store.* 4. *The restaurant is on the south side of the station.* 5. *The hotel is on the left.*

B. 1. **Kooban ni ikimasu. こうばんにいきます。** 2. **Konbini wa byooin no higashi gawa desu. コンビニは びょういんのひがしがわです。** 3. **Eki ni wa ikimasen. えきにはいきません。** 4. **Kooen wa doko desu ka. こうえんはどこですか。** 5. **Mise wa asoko desu. みせはあそこです。**

✎ Drive It Home

Complete the following phrases and sentences by inserting appropriate particles.

1. **Doko** _____ **ikimasu** _____ . *(Where are you going?)*

   どこ _____ いきます _____ 。

2. **Depaato** _____ **ikimasen.** *(I'm not going to the department store.)*

   デパート _____ いきません。

3. Eki _____ ikimasu. (*I'm going to the station.*)

   えき _____ いきます。

4. Resutoran _____ doko desu _____. (*Where is the restaurant?*)

   レストラン _____ どこです_____。

5. Hoteru_____ kooen _____ higashi gawa desu. (*The hotel is on the east side of the park*)

   ホテル _____こうえん _____ひがしがわです。

6. kooen _____ mukai gawa (*across from the park*)

   こうえん_____むかいがわ

ANSWER KEY
1. ni に, ka か; 2. ni wa には; 3. ni に; 4. wa は, ka か; 5. wa は, no の; 6. no の

Parting Words

おめでとうございます！Omedetoo gozaimasu! *Congratulations!* You've finished the lesson. You've learned the basic vocabulary to get around town. You should now be able to:

☐ Express *here* and *there*

☐ Ask for directions using the question word *where*

☐ Use expressions referring to locations of things

☐ Use the action verb *to go*

☐ Use the particle に ni

☐ Ask for directions to get around town and express where things are

Take It Further

 6H Take It Further (CD 2, Track 16)

You may of course want to extend your vocabulary a bit. Some other useful vocabulary to know is:

school	がっこう	gakkoo
subway	ちかてつ	chikatetsu
bus stop	バスてい	basutee
supermarket	スーパー	suupaa
book store	ほんや	hon-ya

Don't forget to practice and reinforce what you've learned by visiting **www.livinglanguage.com/languagelab** for flashcards, games, and quizzes!

Word Recall

1. にしがわ nishi gawa
2. じゅういちにん juuichinin
3. いぬ inu
4. えき eki
5. むっつ muttsu
6. コンビニ konbini
7. シャツ shatsu
8. みなみがわ minami gawa
9. おてあらい otearai
10. くつ kutsu
11. おかあさん okaasan
12. ここ koko

a. *convenience store*
b. *restroom*
c. *shirt*
d. *west side*
e. *6 (native Japanese number)*
f. *station*
g. *south side*
h. *shoes*
i. *mother (someone else's)*
j. *eleven people*
k. *here*
l. *dog*

ANSWER KEY
1. d; 2. j; 3. l; 4. f; 5. e; 6. a; 7. c; 8. g; 9. b; 10. h; 11. i; 12. k

Lesson 7: At a Restaurant

Dai nanaka: Resutoran de
だいななか：レストランで

It's about time to grab something to eat. In this lesson you'll learn how to order your favorite foods and drinks at a restaurant. By the end of this lesson, you'll be able to:

☐ Make polite requests

☐ Use the particle を o

☐ Use a measure word that corresponds to *a glass/cup/bowl of*

☐ Use the negative forms of *i*-adjectives

☐ Recognize very polite language with some honorific forms

☐ Use what you've learned to order food and drinks at a restaurant
Ready for some vocabulary?

Vocabulary Builder 1

7A Vocabulary Builder 1 (CD 2, Track 17)

Excuse me.	すみません。	Sumimasen.
Please give me ...	〜をください。	... o kudasai.
I'd like to have ...	〜をおねがいします。	... o onegaishimasu.
order	ちゅうもん	chuumon
menu	メニュー	menyuu
drink	のみもの	nomimono
meal	しょくじ	shokuji
a glass/cup/bowl of	いっぱい	ippai
two glasses/cups/bowls of	にはい	nihai
three glasses/cups/bowls of	さんばい	sanbai
water	おみず or みず	omizu or mizu
alcoholic beverage	おさけ or さけ	osake or sake
beer	ビール	biiru
wine	ワイン	wain
sake	にほんしゅ	nihonshu
bread	パン	pan
rice (cooked)	ごはん	gohan
vegetable	やさい	yasai
salad	サラダ	sarada
fish	さかな	sakana
meat	にく	niku

chicken	とりにく	toriniku
beef	ぎゅうにく	gyuuniku
pork	ぶたにく	butaniku
set meal	ていしょく	teeshoku

Note that ていしょく teeshoku (*set meal*) is a bit like a fixed price meal, including a main course and one or two side dishes, often miso soup and a vegetable.

Vocabulary Practice 1

Let's practice what you've learned! Match the Japanese in the left column with the English equivalent in the right.

1. ごはん gohan
2. のみもの nomimono
3. すみません。 Sumimasen.
4. にほんしゅ nihonshu
5. やさい yasai
6. とりにく toriniku
7. パン pan
8. ぶたにく butaniku
9. しょくじ shokuji
10. ちゅうもん chuumon
11. ぎゅうにく gyuuniku
12. みず mizu

a. *bread*
b. *order*
c. *pork*
d. *meal*
e. *vegetable*
f. *beef*
g. *sake*
h. *rice (cooked)*
i. *drink*
j. *Excuse me.*
k. *water*
l. *chicken*

ANSWER KEY
1. h; 2. i; 3. j; 4. g; 5. e; 6. l; 7. a; 8. c; 9. d; 10. b; 11. f; 12. k

Take It Further

Now let's take a look at the rest of the long vowels.

	H	M	Y	R	W
aa	はあ haa	まあ maa	やあ yaa	らあ raa	わあ waa
ii	ひい hii	みい mii		りい rii	
uu	ふう fuu	むう muu	ゆう yuu	るう ruu	
ee	へい hee	めい mee		れい ree	
oo	ほう hoo おお hoo	もう moo	よう yoo	ろう roo	

Below are some example words containing long vowels you've just learned:

ほうこう	*hoo*koo	*direction*
せつめい	setsu*mee*	*description*
いもうと	i*moo*to	*younger sister (one's own)*
れい	*ree*	*zero*
ろうか	*roo*ka	*hallway*

In addition to the character combinations you've learned, long vowels can be created in hiragana with diacritics and glides. Below are some examples:

ぐうぜん	*guu*zen	*coincidence*
れいぞうこ	*ree*zooko	*refrigerator*
じゅう	*juu*	*ten*
こんしゅう	kon*shuu*	*this week*
きょう	*kyoo*	*today*

おめでとうございます！Omedetoogozaimasu! *Congratulations!* You finished all the hiragana lessons! In the following characters sections, you'll learn katakana.

It won't be too hard because you've already mastered the basics of hiragana and a lot of the same principles apply to katakana. If you like to spend more time with hiragana, feel free to go back and review any of the sections in the lessons or the reading and writing exercises in the *Guide to Reading and Writing Japanese*. Remember: it's very important to learn at the pace you feel comfortable with.

Grammar Builder 1

▶ 7B Grammar Builder 1 (CD 2, Track 18)

You've learned a lot of useful vocabulary for food and other items associated with eating at home or in a restaurant. When you order something or ask for something in a restaurant, you'll use either ください **kudasai** or おねがいします **onegaishimasu**. Be sure to use the particle を **o** with these expressions. In many cases, the particle を **o** marks the direct object of a verb. For example, to say *Please give me a menu* in Japanese, you'd say メニューをください **Menyuu o kudasai**. Notice that the particle を **o** follows メニュー **menyuu**, which is the direct object in the sentence.

At a restaurant, you may need to specify quantities of various things. The measure word that corresponds to *a glass of*, *a cup of*, or *a bowl of* is はい **hai**, but the pronunciation sometimes changes to ぱい **pai** or ばい **bai** depending on the number. *Please give me a glass of water* will be おみずをいっぱいください **Omizu o ippai kudasai**. To specify quantities of other items you may see on the menu, you may use the convenient Japanese native numbers. For example, if you want to say *We'd like to have two orders of tempura meals*, you'd say てんぷらていしょくをふたつおねがいします **Tempura teeshoku o futatsu onegaishimasu**.

Let's continue with more vocabulary related to eating and drinking.

Vocabulary Builder 2

▶ 7C Vocabulary Builder 2 (CD 2, Track 19)

salt	しお	shio
pepper	こしょう	koshoo
soy sauce	しょうゆ	shooyu
fork	フォーク	fooku
knife	ナイフ	naifu
spoon	スプーン	supuun
chopsticks	はし	hashi
delicious	おいしい	oishii
sweet	あまい	amai
sour	すっぱい	suppai
bitter	にがい	nigai
spicy	からい	karai
It's spicy	からいです。	Karai desu.
It's not spicy.	からくありません。or から くないです。	Karaku arimasen. or Karaku nai desu.
It's not very spicy.	あまりからくありません。 or あまりからくないです。	Amari karaku arimasen. or Amari karaku nai desu.
Japanese tea	おちゃ	ocha
black tea	こうちゃ	koocha
coffee	コーヒー	koohii
milk	ミルク	miruku
sugar	さとう	satoo
check	おかいけい	okaikee

✎ Vocabulary Practice 2

Let's practice what you've learned! Match the Japanese in the left column with the English equivalent in the right.

1. はし hashi
2. おちゃ ocha
3. さとう satoo
4. しお shio
5. こうちゃ koocha
6. おかいけい okaikee
7. コーヒー koohii
8. ナイフ naifu
9. こしょう koshoo
10. フォーク fooku
11. しょうゆ shooyu
12. ミルク miruku

a. *milk*
b. *Japanese tea*
c. *salt*
d. *pepper*
e. *fork*
f. *soy sauce*
g. *sugar*
h. *chopsticks*
i. *black tea*
j. *coffee*
k. *check*
l. *knife*

ANSWER KEY

1. h; 2. b; 3. g; 4. c; 5. i; 6. k; 7. j; 8. l; 9. d; 10. e; 11. f; 12. a

Take It Further

Are you ready for katakana characters? As you already know, katakana characters are used mainly to write words of foreign origin, such as コンピューター **konpyuutaa** *computer* and テーブル **teeburu** *table*. Each of the 46 basic hiragana characters that you've learned has its corresponding katakana character. In this section, let's look at the first 25 basic characters.

アぎょう AGYOO *THE A-LINE*		
ア	a	アメリカ <u>a</u>merika *the United States*

アぎょう AGYOO *THE A-LINE*		
イ	i	インド *i*ndo *India*
ウ	u	マウス ma*u*su *computer mouse*
エ	e	エンジン *e*njin *engine*
オ	o	ラジオ raji*o* *radio*

カぎょう KAGYOO *THE KA-LINE*		
カ	ka	アメリカ ameri*ka* *the United States*
キ	ki	キーボード *ki*iboodo *keyboard*
ク	ku	クリスマス *ku*risumasu *Christmas*
ケ	ke	ケーキ *ke*eki *cake*
コ	ko	コンピューター *ko*npyuutaa *computer*

さぎょう SAGYOO *THE SA-LINE*		
サ	sa	サ<u></u>ラダ *sa*rada *salad*
シ	shi	シ<u></u>カゴ *shi*kago *Chicago*
ス	su	レ<u></u>ストラン re*su*toran *restaurant*
セ	se	セ<u></u>ーター *se*etaa *sweater*
ソ	so	ソ<u></u>フトウェア *so*futowea *software*

たぎょう TAGYOO *THE TA-LINE*		
タ	ta	カタ<u></u>カナ ka*ta*kana *katakana*
チ	chi	ブラ<u></u>ンチ buran*chi* *brunch*
ツ	tsu	ス<u></u>ポーツ supoo*tsu* *sports*
テ	te	テ<u></u>ニス *te*nisu *tennis*

タぎょう TAGYOO *THE TA-LINE*		
ト	to	フットボール fut*to*booru *football*

ナぎょう NAGYOO *THE NA-LINE*		
ナ	na	カタカナ kataka*na* *katakana*
ニ	ni	モニター mo*ni*taa *monitor*
ヌ	nu	ボジョレーヌーボー bojoree*nuu*boo *Beaujolais nouveau*
ネ	ne	インターネット intaa*ne*tto *internet*
ノ	no	ノート *no*oto *notebook*

As noted for hiragana, please follow the handwritten style when you practice writing katakana. You can find writing exercises in the *Guide to Reading and Writing Japanese*.

Great! In the next section, you'll learn the rest of the basic katakana characters!

Grammar Builder 2

7D Grammar Builder 2 (CD 2, Track 20)

The adjectives you've just learned for describing tastes—おいしい oishii (*delicious*), からい karai (*spicy*), すっぱい suppai (*sour*), あまい amai (*sweet*), and にがい nigai (*bitter*) —are all *i*-adjectives, which you learned about in Lesson 5. In this lesson, let's learn how to negate *i*-adjectives. There are two negative forms; you can use either one. With both negative forms, you replace the syllable い i with く ku, and then add either ありません arimasen or ないです nai desu. Note that *"very"* in Japanese is あまり amari, instead of とても totemo when used in a negative sentence.

It's sweet.	あまいです。	Amai desu.
It's not sweet.	あまくありません。or あまくないです。	Amaku arimasen. or Amaku nai desu.
It's not very sweet.	あまりあまくありません。or あまりあまくないです。	Amari amaku arimasen. or Amari amaku nai desu.

✎Work Out 1

7E Work Out 1 (CD 2, Track 21)

A. Let's practice using the new measure word はい hai and the Japanese native numbers to order drinks and food at a restaurant. Listen to the audio, and fill in the blanks with the words that you hear.

1. *Please give us two glasses of water.*

   Omizu o _____ kudasai.

   おみずを _____ ください。

2. *I'd like to have a glass of wine.*

   Wain o _____ **onegaishimasu.**

   ワインを _____おねがいします。

3. *Please give me a salad.*

   Sarada o _____ **kudasai.**

   サラダを _____ください。

B. Now let's practice the negative forms of *i*-adjectives.

   It's not bitter.

   Niga _____. or **Niga** _____

   _____.

   にが _____。 or にが _____。

   It's not sour.

   Suppa _____. or **Suppa** _____

   _____.

   すっぱ _____。 or にが _____。

   It's not very delicious.

   _____oishiku arimasen. or _____ oishiku nai desu.

   _____おいしくありません。 or_____おいしくないです。

   ANSWER KEY
   A. 1. nihai にはい; 2. ippai いっぱい; 3. hitotsu ひとつ
   B. 1. ku arimasen くありません, ku nai desu くないです; 2. ku arimasen くありません, ku nai desu くない
   です; 3. Amari あまり, Amari あまり

🎧 Bring It All Together

▶ 7F Bring It All Together (CD 2, Track 22)

Now let's listen in on a conversation in a restaurant.

A. Excuse me. We'd like to place an order, please.	すみません。ちゅうもんをおねがいします。	Sumimasen. Chuumon o onegaishimasu.
B. What would you like to drink?	おのみものはなにになさいますか。	Onomimono wa nani ni nasaimasu ka.
A. What kind of beer do you have?	ビールはなにがありますか。	Biiru wa nani ga arimasu ka.
B. We have Asahi and Kirin.	アサヒとキリンがございます。	Asahi to Kirin ga gozaimasu.
A. Two Asahis, please.	アサヒをふたつおねがいします。	Asahi o futatsu onegaishimasu.
B. What would you like to eat?	おしょくじはなにになさいますか。	Oshokuji wa nani ni nasaimasu ka.
A. One order of sashimi meal and one order of tempura meal, please.	さしみていしょくをひとつとてんぷらていしょくをひとつおねがいします。	Sashimi teeshoku o hitotsu to tenpura teeshoku o hitotsu onegaishimasu.
B. Certainly.	かしこまりました。	Kashikomarimashita.

Take It Further

You may have noticed that the waitress spoke a slightly different kind of Japanese than what you're already familiar with. She used honorific forms. Waiters, waitresses, and store clerks normally use extra polite language with honorifics to talk to their customers. At this point, you do not have to be able to use honorifics, but it is useful to be able to recognize them. Here are a few pointers: the honorific form of します shimasu, which means *to do*, is なさいます nasaimasu; the honorific form of あります arimasu is ございます gozaimasu; also, you'll sometimes hear an extra お o added to a noun, such as おのみもの onomimono instead of のみもの nomimono. With that in mind, let's look at the dialogue again, this time without its English translation.

A. すみません。ちゅうもんをおねがいします。	Sumimasen. Chuumon o onegaishimasu.
B. おのみものはなにになさいますか。	Onomimono wa nani ni nasaimasu ka.
A. ビールはなにがありますか。	Biiru wa nani ga arimasuka.
B. アサヒとキリンがございます。	Asahi to Kirin ga gozaimasu.
A. アサヒをふたつおねがいします。	Asahi o futatsu onegaishimasu.
B. おしょくじはなにになさいますか。	Oshokuji wa nani ni nasaimasu ka.
A. さしみていしょくをひとつとてんぷらていしょくをひとつおねがいします。	Sashimi teeshoku o hitotsu to tenpura teeshoku o hitotsu onegaishimasu.
B. かしこまりました。	Kashikomarimashita.

✎ Work Out 2
▶ 7G Work Out 2 (CD 2, Track 23)

Now let's practice some of what you've learned.

A. Translate the following sentences from Japanese to English.

1. おちゃをいっぱいください。

   Ocha o ippai kudasai.

   _____

At a Restaurant
At Work and School
Review Dialogues
Around Town
Everyday Life
Leisure

2. おさけはなにがありますか。

   Osake wa nani ga arimasu ka.

   _____

3. サラダをふたつおねがいします。

   Sarada o futatsu onegaishimasu.

   _____

4. あまいですか。

   Amai desu ka.

   _____

5. あまりあまくありません。

   Amari amaku arimasen.

   _____

B. Translate the following sentences from English to Japanese.

1. *Please give me a menu.*

   _____

2. *Is this spicy?*

   _____

3. *This is not spicy.*

   _____

4. *This salad is delicious.*

   _____

5. *Please give us two cups of coffee.*

_____

6. *I'd like milk and sugar, please.*

_____

ANSWER KEY

A. 1. *Please give me a cup of Japanese tea.* 2. *What kind of alcoholic beverages do you have?* 3. *Two orders of salad, please.* 4. *Is it sweet?* 5. *It's not very sweet.*
B. 1. **Menyuu o kudasai.** メニューをください。 2. **Kore wa karai desu ka.** これはからいですか。 3. **Kore wa karaku nai desu.** これはからくないです。 or **Kore wa karaku arimasen.** これはからくありません。
4. **Kono sarada wa oishii desu.** このサラダはおいしいです。 5. **Koohii o nihai kudasai.** コーヒーをにはい
ください。 6. **Miruku to satoo o onegaishimasu.** ミルクとさとうをおねがいします。

✎ Drive It Home

Complete the following sentences based on the English translations.

1. **Menyuu** _____. (*Please give me a menu.*)

   メニュー _____。

2. **Shooyu** _____. (*Please give me some soy sauce.*)

   しょうゆ _____。

3. **Hashi** _____. (*Please give me some chopsticks.*)

   はし _____。

4. **Supuun** _____. (*Please give me a spoon.*)

   スプーン _____。

5. **Omizu** _____ **ippai** _____. (*Please give me a glass of water.*)

   おみず _____ いっぱい _____。

6. **Koohii** _____ **nihai** _____ . *(Please give me a cup of coffee.)*

コーヒー _____ にはい _____ 。

ANSWER KEY
1.-4. o kudasai をください; 5-6. o を, kudasai ください

Parting Words

Well done. You've just finished your seventh lesson. You should now be able to:

☐ Make polite requests

☐ Use the particle を o

☐ Use a measure word that corresponds to *a glass/cup/bowl of*

☐ Use the negative forms of *i*-adjectives

☐ Recognize very polite language with some honorific forms

☐ Use what you've learned to order food and drinks at a restaurant

Take It Further

Let's end with a useful tip for when you go to a restaurant in Japan. Normally, your waiter or waitress will leave a check on your table after all the orders have been served. When you leave the table, take the check with you and go to the cashier where you pay. You do not have to tip in Japan.

Don't forget to practice and reinforce what you've learned by visiting **www.livinglanguage.com/languagelab** for flashcards, games, and quizzes!

Word Recall

1. ごはん gohan
2. だい dai
3. しお shio
4. きたがわ kita gawa
5. はし hashi
6. むすこ musuko
7. あまい amai
8. アパート apaato
9. さとう satoo
10. にじゅういち nijuu ichi
11. おかいけい okaikee
12. びょういん byooin

a. *measure word for cars, machines*
b. *salt*
c. *rice (cooked)*
d. *sweet*
e. *sugar*
f. *apartment*
g. *hospital*
h. *north side*
i. *son (one's own)*
j. *check*
k. *21*
l. *chopsticks*

ANSWER KEY
1. c; 2. a; 3. b; 4. h; 5. l; 6. i; 7. d; 8. f; 9. e; 10. k; 11. j; 12. g

Essential Japanese

Lesson 8: Everyday Life

Dai hachika: Mainichi no seekatsu

だいはちか：まいにちのせいかつ

こんにちは。だいはちかへようこそ。**Konnichi wa. Dai hachika e yookoso.** *Hello. Welcome to Lesson 8.* By the end of this lesson, you'll be able to:

☐ Ask for and tell the time

☐ Use verbs for daily activities

☐ Express what time you do various things

☐ Use the particle も mo

☐ Use what you've learned to talk about your daily routine
Let's get started with some expressions related to time.

Vocabulary Builder 1

▶ 8A Vocabulary Builder 1 (CD 2, Track 24)

now	いま	ima
what time	なんじ	nanji
What time is it now?	いまなんじですか。	**Ima nanji desu ka.**
one o'clock	いちじ	ichiji
two o'clock	にじ	niji
four o'clock	よじ	yoji
seven o'clock	しちじ	shichiji
nine o'clock	くじ	kuji
one minute	いっぷん	ippun
two minutes	にふん	nifun
three minutes	さんぷん	sanpun
four minutes	よんぷん or よんふん	yonpun or yonfun
five minutes	ごふん	gofun
six minutes	ろっぷん	roppun
seven minutes	ななふん	nanafun
eight minutes	はっぷん or はちふん	happun or hachifun
nine minutes	きゅうふん	kyuufun
ten minutes	じゅっぷん	juppun
a.m.	ごぜん	gozen
p.m.	ごご	gogo

✎ Vocabulary Practice 1

Let's practice the new vocabulary. Fill in what is missing in each of the following words.

1. _____ji *(one o'clock)*

   _____じ

2. _____ji *(nine o'clock)*

   ____じ

3. _____ji *(what time)*

   _____じ

4. **ip**_____ *(one minute)*

   いっ_____

5. **ni**_____ *(two minutes)*

   に_____

6. **san**_____ *(three minutes)*

   さん_____

7. **go**_____ *(five minutes)*

   ご_____

8. **rop**_____ *(six minutes)*

   ろっ_____

9. **nana**_____ *(seven minutes)*

   なな_____

10. hachi_____ (*eight minutes*)

はち_____

11. kyuu_____ (*nine minutes*)

きゅう_____

12. jup_____ (*ten minutes*)

じゅっ_____

ANSWER KEY
1. ichi いち; 2. ku く; 3. nan なん; 4. pun ぷん; 5. fun ふん; 6. pun ぷん; 7. fun ふん; 8. pun ぷん; 9. fun ふん; 10. fun ふん; 11. fun ふん; 12. pun ぷん

Take It Further

Here's another characters section! Let's learn the rest of the basic katakana characters.

ハぎょう HAGYOO *THE HA-LINE*		
ハ	ha	ハードウェア *ha*adowea *hardware*
ヒ	hi	コーヒー koo*hii* *coffee*
フ	fu	ナイフ nai*fu* *knife*
ヘ	he	ヘリコプター *he*rikoputaa *helicopter*
ホ	ho	ホテル *ho*teru *hotel*

Note that the katakana character ヘ **he** looks almost identical to its hiragana equivalent へ **he**. So it is fine for you to write those two characters the same way.

まぎょう MAGYOO *THE MA-LINE*		
マ	ma	マウス *mausu* *computer mouse*
ミ	mi	ミルク *miruku* *milk*
ム	mu	ゲーム *geemu* *game*
メ	me	イーメール *eemeeru* *e-mail*
モ	mo	モニター *monitaa* *monitor*

やぎょう YAGYOO *THE YA-LINE*		
ヤ	ya	タイヤ *taiya* *tire*
ユ	yu	ユタ *yuta* *Utah*
ヨ	yo	ヨーグルト *yooguruto* *yogurt*

らぎょう RAGYOO *THE RA-LINE*		
ラ	ra	サラダ **sa_ra_da** *salad*
リ	ri	アメリカ **ame_ri_ka** *the United States*
ル	ru	ホテル **hote_ru_** *hotel*
レ	re	レストラン **_re_sutoran** *restaurant*
ロ	ro	ロンドン **_ro_ndon** *London*

ワぎょう WAGYOO *THE WA-LINE*		
ワ	wa	ワイン **_wa_in** *wine*
ヲ	o	*n/a*

Please note that the katakana character ヲ **o** is not used in everyday modern Japanese language.

And then, just like hiragana, we have the last character:

ン	n	ワイン **wa_in_** *wine*

Great! You've learned the basic 46 katakana characters. Just as hiragana, you can use diacritics over katakana and also there are special katakana character combinations. We'll go through those in the following characters sections.

Grammar Builder 1

▶ 8B Grammar Builder 1 (CD 2, Track 25)

To express the time in Japanese, simply attach じ **ji** after the numbers 1 to 12 for hours, and ふん **fun** or ぷん **pun** for minutes. Pay attention to the special pronunciations of いっぷん **ippun** (*one minute*), ろっぷん **roppun** (*six minutes*), はっぷん **happun** (*eight minutes*), and じゅっぷん **juppun** (*ten minutes*). Half past the hour can be either さんじゅっぷん **sanjuppun** or はん **han**. はん **Han** literally means *half*. Note also that the words for a.m. and p.m. come before the time. Let's take a look at how this works when you put it all together.

11:03 a.m.	ごぜんじゅういちじさんぷん	gozen juuichiji sanpun
4:10 p.m.	ごごよじじゅっぷん	gogo yoji juppun
7:45 a.m.	ごぜんしちじよんじゅうごふん	gozen shichiji yonjuugofun
9:57 p.m.	ごごくじごじゅうななふん	gogo kuji gojuunanafun
3:19 a.m.	ごぜんさんじじゅうきゅうふん	gozen sanji juukyuufun
5:30 p.m.	ごごごじさんじゅっぷん or ごごごじはん	gogo goji sanjuppun or gogo goji han

To turn these into complete sentences, just add です **desu** at the end.

It's 7:45 a.m.	ごぜんしちじよんじゅうごふんです。	Gozen shichiji yonjuugofun desu.

| It's 5:30 p.m. | ごごごじさんじゅっぷんです。 | Gogo goji sanjuppun desu. |

Very good! Now let's add some more vocabulary so that you will be able to express what you do at these times.

Vocabulary Builder 2
▶ 8C Vocabulary Builder 1 (CD 2, Track 26)

What time do you … ?	なんじに〜ますか。	Nanji ni … masu ka.
to get up	おきます	okimasu
to eat	たべます	tabemasu
breakfast	ちょうしょく or あさごはん	chooshoku (fml.) or asagohan (infml.)
lunch	ちゅうしょく or ひるごはん	chuushoku (fml.) or hirugohan (infml.)
dinner	ゆうしょく or ゆうごはん	yuushoku (fml.) or yuugohan (infml.)
school	がっこう	gakkoo
work	しごと	shigoto
home	うち	uchi
to go home, to come home	うちにかえります	uchi ni kaerimasu
to study	べんきょうします	benkyooshimasu
Japanese (language)	にほんご	nihongo
English (language)	えいご	eego
to go to sleep/to sleep	ねます	nemasu
also/too	も	mo

✎ Vocabulary Practice 2

Let's practice what you've learned! Match the Japanese in the left column with the English equivalent in the right.

1. おきます okimasu   a. *to get up*
2. がっこう gakkoo   b. *English (language)*
3. たべます tabemasu   c. *dinner*
4. うち uchi   d. *lunch*
5. あさごはん asagohan   e. *Japanese (language)*
6. べんきょうします benkyooshimasu   f. *home*
7. ゆうごはん yuugohan   g. *to eat*
8. にほんご nihongo   h. *work*
9. ねます nemasu   i. *to study*
10. えいご eego   j. *school*
11. ひるごはん hirugohan   k. *to go to sleep/to sleep*
12. しごと shigoto   l. *breakfast*

ANSWER KEY

1. a; 2. j; 3. g; 4. f; 5. l; 6. i; 7. c; 8. e; 9. k; 10. b; 11. d; 12. h

Take It Further

Now it's **katakana** time! Do you remember the two kinds of diacritics, だくてん **dakuten** and はんだくてん **handakuten**? You can use them over **katakana**, too. Let's first look at the characters with だくてん **dakuten**:

カぎょう KAGYOO *THE KA-LINE* WITH だくてん DAKUTEN		サぎょう SAGYOO *THE SA-LINE* WITH だくてん DAKUTEN	
ガ	ga	ザ	za
ギ	gi	ジ	ji
グ	gu	ズ	zu
ゲ	ge	ゼ	ze
ゴ	go	ゾ	zo

タぎょう TAGYOO *THE TA-LINE* WITH だくてん DAKUTEN		ハぎょう HAGYOO *THE HA-LINE* WITH だくてん DAKUTEN	
ダ	da	バ	ba
ヂ	ji	ビ	bi
ヅ	zu	ブ	bu
デ	de	ベ	be
ド	do	ボ	bo

Now let's look at the five characters with はんだくてん handakuten:

ハぎょう HAGYOO *THE HA-LINE* WITH はんだくてん HANDAKUTEN	
パ	pa
ピ	pi
プ	pu
ペ	pe
ポ	po

Below are some katakana words that appear in *Essential Japanese* containing diacritics:

バッグ	*baggu*	*bag*
デパート	*depaato*	*department store*
ハードウェア	haadowea	*hardware*
ビール	*biiru*	*beer*
コンビニ	konbini	*convenience store*
ペン	*pen*	*pen*

Fantastic! Remember to refer to the *Japanese Script Guide,* which provides more in-depth guidance on Japanese characters along with reading and writing exercises.

Grammar Builder 2

▶ 8D Grammar Builder 2 (CD 2, Track 27)

You've just learned some new verbs and nouns to talk about your daily routine. You already know the verb いきます **ikimasu** (*to go*) from Lesson 6. So, you can use this verb and say しごとにいきます **shigoto ni ikimasu** (*I go to work*) or がっこうにいきます **gakkoo ni ikimasu** (*I go to school*). Don't forget to attach the particle に **ni** to the place you're going to. Here, the particle に **ni** plays a similar role to the word *to* in English. Note, however, that to say *I go home*, you need to use the expression うち にかえります **uchi ni kaerimasu**.

You will also use the particle に **ni** after a time expression to express what time you do certain things, such as eating breakfast or going to work. Here, the particle に **ni** plays a similar role to the word *at* in English. Let's listen to some examples.

| *I get up at seven.* | しちじにおきます。 | Shichiji ni okimasu. |
| *Mr./Ms. Yamada goes to work at 8:30.* | やまださんははちじはんにしごとにいきます。 | Yamada san wa hachiji han ni shigoto ni ikimasu. |

When asking what time something happens, you still need to use the particle に **ni** following なんじ **nanji** (*what time*). Let's listen to some examples of this. Note as well that the particle を **o** follows the object of the verb.

| *What time do you eat dinner?* | なんじにゆうしょくをたべますか。 | Nanji ni yuushoku o tabemasu ka. |
| *What time does Ms. Smith study Japanese?* | スミスさんはなんじににほんごをべんきょうしますか。 | Sumisu san wa nanji ni nihongo o benkyooshimasu ka. |

In *yes/no* questions and negative sentences, the particle を o is often replaced by the particle は wa.

I eat breakfast.	ちょうしょくをたべます。	Chooshoku o tabemasu.
Do you eat breakfast?	ちょうしょくはたべますか。	Chooshoku wa tabemasu ka.
I don't eat breakfast.	ちょうしょくはたべません。	Chooshoku wa tabemasen.

The particle も mo means *also* or *too*. The particle も mo can be used in various ways in a sentence, but in this lesson, let's learn how to use も mo by replacing the particle は wa with it.

Ms. Smith eats breakfast.	スミスさんはちょうしょくをたべます。	Sumisu san wa chooshoku o tabemasu.
Mr./Ms. Yamada eats breakfast, too.	やまださんもちょうしょくをたべます。	Yamada san mo chooshoku o tabemasu.
I eat breakfast, too.	わたしもちょうしょくをたべます。	Watashi mo chooshoku o tabemasu.

In the second and third examples, the particle も mo replaces the particle は wa, adding the information, "*Mr./Ms. Yamada, too*" and "*Me, too.*"

✎ Work Out 1
▶ 8E Work Out 1 (CD 2, Track 28)

Now, let's put everything you've learned so far together in a short comprehension practice. Listen to the audio, and fill in the blanks with the words that you hear.

1. *What time is it now?*

   Ima _____ desu ka.

   いま _____ ですか。

2. *It's 10:52 a.m.*

   _____ juuji gojuunifun desu.

   _____ じゅうじごじゅうにふんです。

3. *It's 12:26 p.m.*

   Gogo juuniji _____ desu.

   ごごじゅうにじ _____ です。

4. *I get up at 7:30.*

   _____ ni okimasu.

   _____ におきます。

5. *I eat breakfast at 8:00.*

   Hachiji ni chooshoku o _____.

   はちじにちょうしょくを _____ _____ 。

6. *What time do you go to work?*

   Nanji ni shigotoni _____.

   なんじにしごとに _____ 。

7. *I go to work at 9:00.*

   _____ shigoto ni ikimasu.

   _____ しごとにいきます。

8. *I go home at 5:00.*

   Goji ni uchi ni _____.

   ごじにうちに _____ 。

9. *My (older) brother goes home at 5:00, too.*

_____ goji ni uchi ni kaerimasu.

_____ごじにうちにかえります。

10. *I study Japanese at 6:00.*

Rokuji ni nihongo o _____.

ろくじににほんごを _____。

ANSWER KEY

1. nanji なんじ; 2. Gozen ごぜん; 3. nijuuroppun にじゅうろっぷん; 4. Shichiji han しちじはん or Shichiji sanjuppun しちじさんじゅっぷん; 5. tabemasu たべます; 6. ikimasu ka いきますか; 7. Kuji ni くじに; 8. kaerimasu かえります; 9. Ani mo あにも; 10. benkyooshimasu べんきょうします

🔊 Bring It All Together

▶ 8F Bring It All Together(CD 2, Track 29)

Let's bring it all together, and add a little bit more vocabulary and structure.

A. What time do you get up, Ms. Smith?	スミスさんはなんじにおきますか。	Sumisu san wa nanji ni okimasu ka.
B. I get up at 8:30. What about you, Mr. Yamada?	はちじはんにおきます。やまださんはどうですか。	Hachijihan ni okimasu. Yamada san wa doo desu ka.
A. I get up at 8:30, too.	わたしもはちじはんにおきますよ。	Watashi mo hachiji han ni okimasu yo.
B. What time do you go to school?	なんじにがっこうにいきますか。	Nanji ni gakkoo ni ikimasu ka.
A. I go to school at 8:45. I don't eat breakfast.	はちじよんじゅうごふんにいきますね。ちょうしょくはたべません。	Hachiji yonjuugofun ni ikimasu ne. Chooshoku wa tabemasen.

B. I go to work at 9:00. What time do you go home?	わたしはくじにしごとにいきますよ。やまださんはなんじにうちにかえりますか。	Watashi wa kuji ni shigoto ni ikimasu yo. Yamada san wa nanji ni uchi ni kaerimasu ka.
A. I go home at 4:00. And then I study English. What time do you go home?	よじにかえります。それからえいごをべんきょうをします。スミスさんはなんじにうちにかえりますか。	Yoji ni kaerimasu. Sore kara eego o benkyooshimasu. Sumisu san wa nanji ni uchi ni kaerimasu ka.
B. I go home at 6:00. My older sister comes home at 7:00. And then we eat dinner.	わたしはろくじにかえります。あねはしちじにかえりますね。それからゆうごはんをたべます。	Watashi wa rokuji ni kaerimasu. Ane wa shichiji ni kaerimasu ne. Sore kara yuugohan o tabemasu.
A. What time do you study Japanese?	なんじににほんごをべんきょうしますか。	Nanji ni nihongo o benkyooshimasu ka.
B. I study at 8:00.	はちじにべんきょうします。	Hachiji ni benkyooshimasu.

Take It Further

You may have noticed a new particle in the dialogue: ね ne, as in はちじよんじゅうごふんにいきますね Hachi ji yonjuugofun ni ikimasu ne (*I go to school at 8:45*) and あねはしちじにかえりますね Ane wa shichiji ni kaerimasu ne (*My older sister comes home at 7:00*). Just as with the particle よ yo, which you learned in Lesson 5, the particle ね ne comes at the end of a sentence. The particle ね ne is sometimes used when answering a question as a way of eliciting agreement. Like the particle よ yo, the particle ね ne is used very often in colloquial Japanese, and adds a natural flow to a conversation.

✎ Work Out 2

▶ 8G Work Out 2 (CD XX, Track XX)

Let's work it out with a translation exercise.

A. Translate the following sentences from Japanese to English.

1. ごぜんじゅうじはっぷんです。

   Gozen juuji happun desu.

   _____

2. じゅうにじにちゅうしょくをたべます。

   Juuniji ni chuushoku o tabemasu.

   _____

3. さんじにべんきょうします。

   Sanji ni benkyooshimasu.

   _____

4. じゅういちじにねます。

   Juuichiji ni nemasu.

   _____

5. やまださんもじゅういちじにねます。

   Yamada san mo juuichiji ni nemasu.

   _____

B. Translate the following sentences from English to Japanese.

1. *What time is it?*

_____

2. *It's 7:07 p.m.*

_____

3. *I will not eat lunch.*

_____

4. *I go home at 9:30.*

_____

5. *I study Japanese at 3:00.*

_____

ANSWER KEY
A. 1. *It's 10:08 a.m.* 2. *I eat lunch at 12:00.* 3. *I study at 3:00.* 4. *I go to sleep at 11:00.* 5. *Mr./Ms. Yamada goes to sleep at 11:00, too.*
B. 1. **Nanji desu ka.** なんじですか。 2. **Gogo shichiji nanafun desu.** ごごしちじななふんです。
3. **Chuushoku (or Hirugohan) wa tabemasen.** ちゅうしょく(or ひるごはん)はたべません。 4. **Kuji han ni uchi ni kaerimasu. or Kuji sanjuppun ni uchi ni kaerimasu.** くじはんにうちにかえります。or くじさんじゅっぷんにうちにかえります。 5. **Sanji ni nihongo o benkyooshimasu.** さんじににほんごをべんきょうします。

✎ Drive It Home

Complete the following sentences by inserting appropriate particles.

1. Yamada san _____ hachiji han _____ chooshoku _____ tabemasu.

   (Mr./Ms. Yamada eats breakfast at 8:30.)

   やまださん _____ はちじはん _____ ちょうしょく _____ たべます。

2. Nanji _____ chooshoku _____ tabemasu _____.

   (What time do you eat breakfast?)

   なんじ_____ちょうしょく_____たべます_____。

3. Sumisu san _____ nanji _____ chooshoku _____ tabemasu _____.

   (What time does Ms. Smith eat breakfast?)

   スミスさん _____なんじ _____ちょうしょく _____たべます_____。

4. Chooshoku _____ tabemasu. *(I eat breakfast.)*

   ちょうしょく _____たべます。

5. Chooshoku _____ tabemasu _____. *(Do you eat breakfast?)*

   ちょうしょく _____たべます _____。

6. Chooshoku _____ tabemasen. *(I don't eat breakfast.)*

   ちょうしょく _____たべません。

7. Watashi _____ chooshoku _____ tabemasu. *(I eat breakfast, too.)*

   わたし _____ちょうしょく _____たべます。

ANSWER KEY
1. wa は, ni に, o を 2. ni に, o を, ka か; 3. wa は, ni に, o を, ka か; 4. o を 5. wa は, ka か; 6. wa は;
7. mo も, o を

Parting Words

よくできました！Yokudekimashita! *Well done!* In this lesson, you learned the basic vocabulary you need to describe a few aspects of your everyday life. You should now be able to:

☐ Ask for and tell the time

☐ Use verbs for daily activities

☐ Express what time you do various things

☐ Use the particle も **mo**

☐ Use what you've learned to talk about your daily routine

Take It Further

▶ 8H Take It Further (CD 2, Track 31)

Here are some more verbs that may come in handy:

to come	きます	kimasu
to exercise	うんどうします	undooshimasu
to rest	やすみます	yasumimasu
to speak	はなします	hanashimasu
to do	します	shimasu
to listen	พี่きます	kikimasu
to watch	みます	mimasu
to read	よみます	yomimasu
to make	つくります	tsukurimasu
to buy	かいます	kaimasu

You will practice using some of these verbs in Lesson 10. You're almost there!

Don't forget to practice and reinforce what you've learned by visiting **www.livinglanguage.com/languagelab** for flashcards, games, and quizzes!

Word Recall

1. たべます tabemasu

2. いもうと imooto

3. がっこう gakkoo

4. みせ mise

5. にほんご nihongo

6. さつ satsu

7. しごと shigoto

8. パン pan

9. くじ kuji

10. ひゃく hyaku

11. さかな sakana

12. わたしのペン watashi no pen

a. *bread*

b. *nine o'clock*

c. *school*

d. *my pen*

e. *fish*

f. *hundred*

g. *Japanese (language)*

h. *younger sister (one's own)*

i. *to eat*

j. *measure word for books, photo albums, magazines*

k. *work*

l. *store*

ANSWER KEY
1. i; 2. h; 3. c; 4. l; 5. g; 6. j; 7. k; 8. a; 9. b; 10. f; 11. e; 12. d

Lesson 9: At Work and School

Dai kyuuka: Shokuba ya gakkoo de

だいきゅうか：しょくばやがっこうで

In this lesson, you'll learn vocabulary related to your work and school life. By the end of this lesson, you'll be able to:

☐ Express the names of some professions and fields of study

☐ Express the days of the week

☐ Use other time expressions such as *morning, today,* and *next week*

☐ Talk about your weekly routines and what you're planning to do

Vocabulary Builder 1

▶ 9A Vocabulary Builder 1 (CD 3, Track 1)

occupation	しょくぎょう	shokugyoo
medical doctor	いしゃ	isha
nurse	かんごし	kangoshi
police officer	けいさつかん	keesatsukan
firefighter	しょうぼうし	shoobooshi
office worker	かいしゃいん	kaishain
store clerk	てんいん	ten-in
college	だいがく	daigaku
college student	だいがくせい	daigakusee
high school	こうこう	kookoo
high school student	こうこうせい	kookoosee
economics	けいざいがく	keezaigaku
literature	ぶんがく	bungaku

✎ Vocabulary Practice 1

Let's practice what you've learned! Match the Japanese in the left column with
the English equivalent in the right.

1. けいさつかん keesatsukan   a. nurse

2. けいざいがく keezaigaku   b. office worker

3. しょうぼうし shoobooshi   c. economics

4. しょくぎょう shokugyoo   d. high school student

5. てんいん ten-in   e. high school

6. こうこうせい kookoosee   f. police officer

7. いしゃ isha   g. occupation

8. ぶんがく bungaku   h. literature

9. だいがく daigaku   i. *college*

10. かいしゃいん kaishain   j. *medical doctor*

11. かんごし kangoshi   k. *firefighter*

12. こうこう kookoo   l. *store clerk*

ANSWER KEY
1. f; 2. c; 3. k; 4. g; 5. l; 6. d; 7. j; 8. h; 9. i; 10. b; 11. a; 12. e

Take It Further

Welcome to another katakana section! We're now ready to look at glides.
Every glide represented by hiragana has its katakana counterpart.

	K	S	T	N	H	M	R
ya	キャ kya	シャ sha	チャ cha	ニャ nya	ヒャ hya	ミャ mya	リャ rya
yu	キュ kyu	シュ shu	チュ chu	ニュ nyu	ヒュ hyu	ミュ myu	リュ ryu
yo	キョ kyo	ショ sho	チョ cho	ニョ nyo	ヒョ hyo	ミョ myo	リョ ryo

	G	Z	D	B	P
ya	ギャ gya	ジャ ja	ヂャ ja	ビャ bya	ピャ pya
yu	ギュ gyu	ジュ ju	ヂュ ju	ビュ byu	ピュ pyu
yo	ギョ gyo	ジョ jo	ヂョ jo	ビョ byo	ピョ pyo

Below are some katakana words that appear in *Essential Japanese*
containing glides:

シャツ	*shatsu*	*shirt*
ジャズ	*jazu*	*jazz*
コンピューター	**konpyuutaa**	*computer*
ジョギング	*jogingu*	*jogging*

Wonderful! In the next character section, we'll look at double consonants in katakana.

Grammar Builder 1

▶ 9B Grammar Builder 1 (CD 3, Track 2)

You've just learned the words for various occupations in Japanese. You also already know せんせい sensee (*teacher*), which is also an occupation. If you want to further modify *teacher* to clarify what type of teacher, you can use the particle の no, which connects two nouns.

school teacher	がっこうのせんせい	gakkoo no sensee
English (language) teacher	えいごのせんせい	eego no sensee
dance teacher	ダンスのせんせい	dansu no sensee

Likewise, with the expression てんいん ten-in (*store clerk*), you can make it more specific by saying スーパーのてんいん suupaa no ten-in (*supermarket clerk*) or ほんやのてんいん honya no ten-in (*bookstore clerk*). To say *college student* or *high school student*, you would use fixed expressions in Japanese— だいがくせい daigakusee (*college student*) and こうこうせい kookoosee (*high school student*)— without the particle の no. If you wanted to say *economics student* or *literature student*, however, you can use の no and say けいざいがくのがくせい keezaigaku no gakusee and ぶんがくのがくせい bungaku no gakusee.

Vocabulary Builder 2

▶ 9C Vocabulary Builder 2 (CD 3, Track 3)

Now let's look at some more expressions of time.

Monday	げつようび	getsuyoobi
Tuesday	かようび	kayoobi
Wednesday	すいようび	suiyoobi
Thursday	もくようび	mokuyoobi
Friday	きんようび	kin-yoobi
Saturday	どようび	doyoobi
Sunday	にちようび	nichiyoobi
when	いつ	itsu
what day of the week	なんようび	nan-yoobi
from ... to ...	～から～まで	... kara ... made
morning	あさ	asa
noon	ひる	hiru
afternoon	ごご	gogo
evening	ゆうがた	yuugata
night	よる	yoru
today	きょう	kyoo
tomorrow	あした	ashita
this week	こんしゅう	konshuu
next week	らいしゅう	raishuu

✎ Vocabulary Practice 2

Let's practice what you've learned! Match the Japanese in the left column with the English equivalent in the right.

1. きんようび kin-yoobi

2. にちようび nichiyoobi

3. よる yoru

4. げつようび getsuyoobi

a. Saturday

b. night

c. this week

d. Monday

5. どようび doyoobi   e. *Tuesday*

6. きょう kyoo   f. *Wednesday*

7. すいようび suiyoobi   g. *Sunday*

8. こんしゅう konshuu   h. *today*

9. らいしゅう raishuu   i. *tomorrow*

10. かようび kayoobi   j. *Thursday*

11. あした ashita   k. *next week*

12. もくようび mokuyoobi   l. *Friday*

ANSWER KEY
1. l; 2. g; 3. b; 4. d; 5. a; 6. h; 7. f; 8. c; 9. k; 10. e; 11. i; 12. j

Take It Further

Now let's look at double consonants in katakana. The rule of double consonants for katakana is the same as that of hiragana. Double consonants are written with a small ツ tsu placed immediately before the consonant to be doubled. Let's look at some examples:

ロック	**ro*kk*u**	*rock (music)*
クラシック	**kurashi*kk*u**	*classical (music)*
フットボール	**fu*tt*obooru**	*football*
インターネット	**intaane*tto***	*internet*
バスケットボール	**basuke*tt*obooru**	*basketball*
バッグ	**ba*gg*u**	*bag*
ポップス	**po*pp*usu**	*pop (music)*
ヒップホップ	**hi*pp*uho*pp*u**	*hip-hop*

As noted for hiragana, keep in mind that double **n** are not considered as double consonants. This is because the first **n** is represented by the character ン **n**, as illustrated in the following examples:

カンヌ	ka<u>n</u>nu	*Cannes (French city)*
トンネル	to<u>n</u>neru	*tunnel*

Wonderful! You have only two more character sections to go. You're almost there!

Grammar Builder 2

▶ 9D Grammar Builder 2 (CD 3, Track 4)

You've just learned various additional expressions used to describe time. Let's look further at how these expressions are used in sentences.

On what day of the week are you going?	なんようびにいきますか。	**Nan-yoobi ni ikimasu ka.**
I'm going on Monday.	げつようびにいきます。	**Getsuyoobi ni ikimasu.**
When are you going?	いついきますか。	**Itsu ikimasu ka.**
I'm going in the morning.	あさいきます。 or あさにいきます。	**Asa ikimasu. or Asa ni ikimasu.**
I'm going today.	きょういきます。	**Kyoo ikimasu.**
I'm going next week.	らいしゅういきます。	**Raishuu ikimasu.**
I go to work from Monday to Friday.	げつようびからきんようびまでしごとにいきます。	**Getsuyoobi kara kinyoobi made shigoto ni ikimasu.**

The particle に **ni** follows the days of the week, and is something like the English *on* as in げつようびに **getsuyoobi ni** (*on Monday*). With いつ **itsu** (*when*), きょう **kyoo** (*today*), あした **ashita** (*tomorrow*), こんしゅう **konshuu** (*this week*), and らいしゅう **raishuu** (*next week*), you do not use に **ni**. For あさ **asa** (*morning*), ひる **hiru** (*noon*), ごご **gogo** (*afternoon*), ゆうがた **yuugata** (*evening*), and よる **yoru** (*night*), the particle に **ni** is optional. Lastly, when you use 〜から 〜まで … **kara** … **made** (*from … to …*), the particle に **ni** does not follow even when you're talking about days of the week.

If you want to use two different time expressions together, such as *Monday morning* and *tomorrow afternoon*, use the particle の **no** to connect the two expressions.

Thursday morning	もくようびのあさ	mokuyoobi no asa
tomorrow afternoon	あしたのごご	ashita no gogo
this Thursday	こんしゅうのもくようび	konshuu no mokuyoobi
next Thursday	らいしゅうのもくようび	raishuu no mokuyoobi

The use of the particle に **ni** after a combined expression depends on the second expression. So you do not have to use に **ni** after もくようびのあさ **mokuyoobi no asa** because the second expression is あさ **asa**. On the other hand, you have to use に **ni** after らいしゅうのもくようび **raishuu no mokuyoobi** because the second expression is もくようび **mokuyoobi**.

✎ Work Out 1
▶ 9E Work Out 1 (CD 3, Track 5)

Let's practice the time expressions you've just learned in some complete sentences. Listen to the audio, and fill in the blanks with the words that you hear.

1. *I'm going to a restaurant on Tuesday.*

   _____ resutoran ni ikimasu.

   _____ レストランにいきます。

2. *I study Japanese in the morning.*

   _____ nihongo o benkyooshimasu.

   _____ にほんごをべんきょうします。

3. *I'm going to a party on Friday night.*

   _____ paatii ni ikimasu.

   _____パーティーにいきます。

4. *I'm going to the department store tomorrow afternoon.*

   _____ depaato ni ikimasu.

   _____デパートにいきます。

5. *I'm going to a concert this Saturday.*

   Konshuu no _____ konsaato ni ikimasu.

   こんしゅうの _____コンサートにいきます。

6. *I'm going to the hospital next week.*

   _____ byooin ni ikimasu.

   _____びょういんにいきます。

7. *I go to the supermarket on Wednesday and Saturday.*

   _____ doyoobi ni suupaa ni ikimasu.

   _____どようびにスーパーにいきます。

8. *I eat brunch on Sunday.*

   _____ buranchi o tabemasu.

   _____ブランチをたべます。

9. *On what days of the week do you go to work?*

_____ shigoto ni ikimasu ka.

_____しごとにいきますか。

ANSWER KEY

1. **Kayoobi ni** かようびに; 2. **Asa (ni)** あさ(に); 3. **Kin-yoobi no yoru (ni)** きんようびのよる(に); 4. **Ashita no gogo (ni)** あしたのごご(に); 5. **doyoobi ni** どようびに; 6. **Raishuu** らいしゅう; 7. **Suiyoobi to** すいようびと; 8. **Nichiyoobi ni** にちようびに; 9. **Nan-yoobi ni** なんようびに

🔊 Bring It All Together

▶ 9F Bring It All Together (CD 3, Track 6)

Let's bring it all together, and add a little bit more vocabulary and structure.

A. What's your father's occupation, Ms. Smith?	スミスさんのおとうさんのしょくぎょうはなんですか。	Sumisu san no otoosan no shokugyoo wa nan desu ka.
B. My father is a police officer.	ちちはけいさつかんですよ。	Chichi wa keesatsukan desu yo.
A. When does your father go to work?	おとうさんはいつしごとにいきますか。	Otoosan wa itsu shigoto ni ikimasu ka.
B. From Monday to Wednesday, my father goes to work in the morning. And on Friday and Saturday, he goes to work in the evening.	ちちはげつようびからすいようびまであさしごとにいきます。それからきんようびとどようびにゆうがたしごとにいきます。	Chichi wa getsuyoobi kara suiyoobi made asa shigoto ni ikimasu. Sore kara kinyoobi to doyoobi ni yuugata shigoto ni ikimasu.
A. Is that so? What time does he go to work in the evening?	そうですか。ゆうがたなんじにしごとにいきますか。	Soo desu ka. Yuugata nanji ni shigoto ni ikimasu ka.
B. He goes to work at 5:00. He comes back home at 2:00 a.m.	ごじにいきます。ごぜんにじにうちにかえりますよ。	Goji ni ikimasu. Gozen niji ni uchi ni kaerimasu yo.

✎ Work Out 2

▶ 9G Work Out 2 (CD 3, Track 7)

Now let's practice some of what you've learned.

A. Translate the following sentences from Japanese to English.

1. きょうさかなをたべます。

   Kyoo sakana o tabemasu.

   _____

2. げつようびのあさにうちにかえります。

   Getsuyoobi no asa ni uchi ni kaerimasu.

   _____

3. こんしゅうのどようびにしごとにいきます。

   Konshuu no doyoobi ni shigoto ni ikimasu.

   _____

4. げつようびからきんようびまでだいがくにいきます。

   Getsuyoobi kara kin-yoobi made daigaku ni ikimasu.

   _____

5. なんようびにスーパーにいきますか。

   Nan-yoobi ni suupaa ni ikimasu ka.

   _____

B. Translate the following sentences from English to Japanese.

1. *I'm going to the department store on Sunday.*

   _____

2. *I'm going to the park tomorrow.*

   _____

3. *I'm going to a restaurant on Wednesday night.*

   _____

4. *I'm going to a concert next Tuesday.*

   _____

5. *When are you going to the hospital?*

   _____

ANSWER KEY
A. 1. *I'm going to eat fish today.* 2. *I'll go home on Monday morning.* 3. *I'll go to work this Saturday.*
4. *I go to college from Monday to Friday.* 5. *On what days of the week do you go to the supermarket?*
B. 1. **Nichiyoobi ni depaato ni ikimasu.** にちようびにデパートにいきます。 2. **Ashita kooen ni ikimasu.** あ
したこうえんにいきます。 3. **Suiyoobi no yoru resutoran ni ikimasu.** すいようびのよるレストランにいきま
す。 or **Suiyoobi no yoru ni resutoran ni ikimasu.** すいようびのよるにレストランにいきます。 4. **Raishuu
no kayoobi ni konsaato ni ikimasu.** らいしゅうのかようびにコンサートにいきます。 5. **Itsu byooin ni
ikimasu ka.** いつびょういんにいきますか。

✎ Drive It Home

Complete the following phrases and sentences by inserting appropriate particles.
If no particle is possible, write "X" instead.

1. **Suiyoobi** _____ **doyoobi** _____ **suupaa** _____ **ikimasu.**

   (I go to the supermarket on Wednesday and Saturday.)

   すいようび _____ どようび _____ スーパー _____ いきます。

2. **dansu** _____ **sensee** (*dance teacher*)

   ダンス _____せんせい

3. **raishuu** _____**mokuyoobi** (*next Thursday*)

   らいしゅう _____もくようび

4. **Getsuyoobi** _____ **ikimasu.** (*I'm going on Monday.*)

   げつようび _____いきます。

5. **Itsu** _____ **ikimasu** _____. (*When are you going?*)

   いつ _____いきます _____。

6. **suupaa** _____**ten-in** (*supermarket clerk*)

   スーパー _____てんいん

7. **Kyoo** _____ **ikimasu.** (*I'm going today.*)

   きょう _____いきます。

8. **ashita** _____**gogo** (*tomorrow afternoon*)

   あした_____ごご

9. **Raishuu** _____ **byooin** _____ **ikimasu.** (*I'm going to the hospital next week.*)

   らいしゅう _____びょういん _____いきます。

ANSWER KEY
1. to と, ni に, ni に; 2. no の; 3. no の; 4. ni に; 5. X, ka か; 6. no の; 7. X; 8. no の; 9. X, ni に

Parting Words

よくできました！**Yoku dekimashita!** *Well done!* Now you can talk even more about time in Japanese, as well as various professions. You should now be able to:

- ☐ Express the names of some professions and fields of study
- ☐ Express the days of the week
- ☐ Use other time expressions such as *morning, today,* and *next week*
- ☐ Talk about your weekly routines and what you're planning to do

Take It Further

▶ 9H Take It Further (CD 3, Track 8)

You might also want to add the months of the year to your vocabulary. They are easy to remember: simply attach がつ **gatsu** to the numbers 1 to 12:

January	いちがつ	ichigatsu
February	にがつ	nigatsu
March	さんがつ	sangatsu
April	しがつ	shigatsu
May	ごがつ	gogatsu
June	ろくがつ	rokugatsu
July	しちがつ	shichigatsu
August	はちがつ	hachigatsu
September	くがつ	kugatsu
October	じゅうがつ	juugatsu
November	じゅういちがつ	juuichigatsu
December	じゅうにがつ	juunigatsu

Don't forget to practice and reinforce what you've learned by visiting **www.livinglanguage.com/languagelab** for flashcards, games, and quizzes!

Word Recall

1. いしゃ isha

2. しちにん shichinin

3. えいご eego

4. しょうぼうし shoobooshi

5. とてもおおきい totemo ookii

6. こうこうせい kookoosee

7. おねえさん oneesan

8. やさい yasai

9. よる yoru

10. やっつ yattsu

11. どこ doko

12. ごぜん gozen

a. *very big*

b. *medical doctor*

c. *where*

d. *vegetable*

e. *seven people*

f. *older sister (someone else's)*

g. *English (language)*

h. *night*

i. *8 (native Japanese number)*

j. *high school student*

k. *firefighter*

l. *a.m.*

ANSWER KEY
1. b; 2. e; 3. g; 4. k; 5. a; 6. j; 7. f; 8. d; 9. h; 10. i; 11. c; 12. l

Lesson 10: Leisure

Dai jukka: Yoka
だいじゅっか：よか

Hello. こんにちは。**Konnichi wa.** You made it to the last lesson! In this final lesson, we'll talk about all the things that you like to do for fun. By the end of this lesson, you'll be able to:

☐ Use vocabulary to describe what you do in your free time

☐ Ask somebody about their weekend plan

☐ Make a suggestion by saying *Let's …* and *Why don't we … ?*

☐ Express likes and dislikes

☐ Ask somebody what kind of music and sports they like

☐ Use what you've learned to talk about hobbies and recreational activities
   はじめましょう！**Hajimemashoo!** *Let's begin!*

Vocabulary Builder 1

▶ 10A Vocabulary Builder 1 (CD 3, Track 9)

weekend	しゅうまつ	shuumatsu
this weekend	こんしゅうまつ	konshuumatsu
to do	します	shimasu
to read	よみます	yomimasu
to read a book	ほんをよみます	hon o yomimasu
to listen	ききます	kikimasu
music	おんがく	ongaku
to listen to music	おんがくをききます	ongaku o kikimasu
to watch	みます	mimasu
movie	えいが	eega
to watch a movie	えいがをみます	eega o mimasu
shopping	かいもの	kaimono
to go shopping	かいものにいきます	kaimono ni ikimasu
to play sports	スポーツをします	supootsu o shimasu
to play football	フットボールをします	futtobooru o shimasu
to stay home	うちにいます	uchi ni imasu
Let's ...	～ましょう。	... mashoo.
Why don't we ...?	～ませんか。	... masen ka.
together	いっしょに	issho ni

✎ Vocabulary Practice 1

Let's practice what you've learned! Match the Japanese in the left column with the English equivalent in the right.

1. よみます yomimasu   a. *together*
2. みます mimasu   b. *this weekend*
3. かいもの kaimono   c. *to do*
4. いっしょに issho ni   d. *shopping*
5. します shimasu   e. *to stay home*
6. うちにいます uchi ni imasu   f. *movie*
7. ききます kikimasu   g. *to watch*
8. こんしゅうまつ konshuumatsu h. *to read*
9. おんがく ongaku   i. *to listen*
10. えいが eega   j. *weekend*
11. しゅうまつ shuumatsu   k. *music*

ANSWER KEY
1. h; 2. g; 3. d; 4. a; 5. c; 6. e; 7. i; 8. b; 9. k; 10. f; 11. j

Take It Further

Let's now learn how long vowels are represented in katakana. One major difference between hiragana and katakana usage is in the representation of long vowels. Any vowel may be elongated by writing a dash (ー) after it. Below are some examples showing the contrast between long bowels in hiragana and katakana:

ひらがな HIRAGANA WORD CONTAINING A LONG VOWEL			カタカナ KATAKANA WORD CONTAINING A LONG VOWEL		
おかあさん	*okaa*san	*mother (someone else's)*	スカート	*sukaato*	*skirt*
いいえ	*iie*	*no*	イーメール	*iimeeru*	*e-mail*

ひらがな HIRAGANA **WORD CONTAINING A LONG VOWEL**			カタカナ KATAKANA **WORD CONTAINING A LONG VOWEL**		
じゅう	*juu*	ten	ジュース	**juusu**	*juice*
れい	*ree*	zero	チョコレート	**chokoreeto**	*chocolate*
おとうさん	*otoosan*	*father (someone else's)*	トークショー	**tookushoo**	*talk show*

Great! In the next and the last character section, we'll look at some katakana-specific combination characters in an effort to approximate the pronunciation of foreign words.

Grammar Builder 1

▶ 10B Grammar Builder 1 (CD 3, Track 10)

You've just learned a lot of vocabulary to describe what you do in your free time. To ask somebody what he or she is going to do this weekend, say こんしゅうまつになにをしますか。**Konshuumatsu ni nani o shimasu ka.** (*What are you going to do this weekend?*), or しゅうまつになにをしますか。**Shuumatsu ni nani o shimasu ka.** (*What are you going to do for the weekend?*). Remember that the particle に **ni** follows こんしゅうまつ **konshuumatsu** (*this weekend*) and しゅうまつ **shuumatsu** (*weekend*). As you already know, Japanese verbs do not make a distinction between present tense and future tense. So しゅうまつになにをしますか **Shuumatsu ni nani o shimasu ka** can be a question about what somebody usually does on a weekend, or what somebody is going to do for the upcoming weekend. It all depends on context.

To make a suggestion such as *Let's watch a movie*, change the verb-ending from ます **masu** to ましょう **mashoo**. Alternatively, you can change the verb-ending to ませんか **masen ka**, which is similar to the English expression *Why don't we ...*

? You can also use the expression いっしょに issho ni—meaning *together*—in your sentences with ましょう mashoo and ませんか masen ka.

Let's watch a movie.	えいがをみましょう。	Eega o mimashoo.
Why don't we watch a movie?	えいがをみませんか。	Eega o mimasen ka.
Let's watch a movie together.	いっしょにえいがをみましょう。	Issho ni eega o mimashoo.
Why don't we watch a movie together?	いっしょにえいがをみませんか。	Issho ni eega o mimasen ka.

Vocabulary Builder 2

▶ 10C Vocabulary Builder 2 (CD 3, Track 11)

to like ...	〜がすきです。	... ga suki desu.
to not like ...	〜はすきではありません。	... wa suki de wa arimasen.
to like very much	〜がとてもすきです。	... ga totemo suki desu.
to not like very much	〜はあまりすきではありません。	... wa amari suki de wa arimasen.
Do you like ... ?	〜はすきですか。	... wa suki desu ka.
what kind of ...	どんな	donna
What kind of sports do you like?	どんなスポーツがすきですか。	Donna supootsu ga suki desu ka.
baseball	やきゅう	yakyuu
basketball	バスケットボール	basukettobooru
football	フットボール	futtobooru
What kind of music do you like?	どんなおんがくがすきですか。	Donna ongaku ga suki desu ka.
rock	ロック	rokku

pop	ポップス	**poppusu**
hip-hop	ヒップホップ	**hippuhoppu**
classical	クラシック	**kurashiiku**
jazz	ジャズ	**jazu**
Japan	にほん	**nihon**
the United States	アメリカ	**amerika**

✎ Vocabulary Practice 2

Let's practice the new vocabulary. Fill in the missing Japanese in each of the following phrases and sentences.

1. _____ ga suki desu. (*I like baseball.*)

   _____がすきです。

2. _____ ga suki desu. (*I like basketball.*)

   _____がすきです。

3. _____ ga suki desu. (*I like football*)

   _____がすきです。

4. _____ ongaku ga suki desu ka. (*What kind of music do you like?*)

   _____おんがくがすきですか。

5. _____ ga suki desu. (*I like rock.*)

   _____がすきです。

6. _____ ga suki desu. (*I like pop.*)

   _____がすきです。

7. _____ ga suki desu. (*I like hip-hop.*)

   _____ がすきです。

8. _____ ga suki desu. (*I like classical.*)

   _____ がすきです。

9. _____ ga suki desu. (*I like jazz.*)

   _____ がすきです。

10. _____ to _____ (*Japan and the United States.*)

    _____ と _____

ANSWER KEY
1. **Yakyuu** やきゅう; 2. **Basukettobooru** バスケットボール; 3. **Futtobooru** フットボール; 4. **Donna** どんな;
5. **Rokku** ロック; 6. **Poppusu** ポップス; 7. **Hippuhoppu** ヒップホップ; 8. **Kurashikku** クラシック; 9. **Jazu** ジャズ; 10. **nihon** にほん, **amerika** アメリカ

Take It Further

Here's our last katakana section. You've come a long way!

In order to approximate the pronunciation of foreign words, the following combinations are commonly used. Note that these combinations are not used in hiragana.

ウィ wi	ウィンドーショッピング	<u>wi</u>ndooshoppingu	*window shopping*
ウェ we	ウェイトレス	<u>we</u>itoresu	*waitress*
ウォ wo	ウォール	<u>wo</u>oru	*Wall*
シェ she	シェパード	<u>she</u>paado	*Shepherd*
チェ che	チェーン	<u>che</u>en	*chain*
ティ ti	パーティー	paa<u>ti</u>i	*party*

ファ fa	ファックス	*fakkusu*	*fax*
フィ fi	フィンランド	*finrando*	*Finland*
フェ fe	フェンス	*fensu*	*fence*
フォ fo	フォーク	*fooku*	*fork*
ジェ je	ジェーン	*jeen*	*Jane*
ディ di	ディスプレイ	*disupurei*	*display*
デュ du	デューク	*duuku*	*Duke*

Remember that the second character of each of the above combinations must be written small.

おめでとうございます! **Omedetoogozaimasu!** Congratulations! You've reached the end of the character lessons for *Essential Japanese*! You've learned all the hiragana, katakana, and special character combinations. If you'd like to learn more about the Japanese script or practice reading and writing, please use the *Guide to Reading and Writing Japanese*. Just remember that it takes a lot of practice to be able to read and write Japanese, but the experience of learning Japanese will be so much more rewarding if you put the extra effort into learning how to read and write. Best of luck!

Grammar Builder 2

▶ 10D Grammar Builder 2 (CD 3, Track 12)

You've just learned how to talk about your likes and dislikes using the Japanese expressions すきです **suki desu** and すきではありません **suki de wa arimasen**. To say that you like something, you will say the name of the thing you like, plus the particle が **ga**, followed by すきです **suki desu**.

I like sports.	スポーツがすきです。	Supootsu ga suki desu.

If you want to ask a question with a specific answer, you will retain this formula, but use the word for *what kind of*—どんな donna—and end with the question particle か ka.

What kind of sports do you like?	どんなスポーツがすきですか。	Donna supootsu ga suki desu ka.
I like basketball.	バスケットボールがすきです。	Basukettobooru ga suki desu.

To say you don't like something, you will use the expression すきではありません Suki de wa arimasen. In negative sentences, the particle は wa replaces the particle が ga.

I don't like sports.	スポーツはすきではありません。	Supootsu wa suki de wa arimasen.

The particle は wa also replaces the particle が ga in *yes/no* questions.

Do you like basketball?	バスケットボールはすきですか。	Basukettobooru wa suki desu ka.

To say you like something very much, use the expression とても totemo, which you already know how to use with *i*-adjectives.

I like basketball very much.	バスケットボールがとてもすきです。	Basukettobooru ga totemo suki desu.

In a negative sentence, use あまり amari instead of とても totemo.

I don't like basketball very much.	バスケットボールはあまりすきではありません。	Basukettobooru wa amari suki de wa arimasen.

✎ Work Out 1

▶ 10E Work Out 1 (CD 3, Track 13)

Let's practice the time expressions you've just learned in some complete sentences. Listen to the audio, and fill in the blanks with the words that you hear.

1. *What are you going to do for the weekend?*

   _____ nani o shimasu ka.

   _____なにをしますか。

2. *I'll play baseball.*

   _____ shimasu.

   _____します。

3. *What are you going to do this weekend?*

   Konshuumatsu ni _____.

   こんしゅうまつに _____。

4. *I'll stay home.*

   _____imasu.

   _____います。

5. *What kind of music do you like?*

   _____ ongaku ga suki desu ka.

   _____おんがくがすきですか。

6. *I like Japanese pop music.*

   Nihon no poppusu ga _____.

   にほんのポップスが _____。

7. *Do you like jazz?*

   Jazu wa _____.

   ジャズは _____。

8. *No, I don't like jazz very much.*

   Iie, jazu wa amari _____.

   いいえ、ジャズはあまり _____。

9. *Why don't we go shopping together?*

   _____ **kaimono ni ikimasen ka.**

   _____かいものにいきませんか。

10. *Let's play basketball.*

    Basukettobooru o _____.

    バスケットボールを _____。

ANSWER KEY

1. **Shuumatsu ni** しゅうまつに; 2. **Yakyuu o** やきゅうを; 3. **nani o shimasu ka** なにをしますか; 4. **Uchi ni** うちに; 5. **Donna** どんな; 6. **suki desu** すきです; 7. **suki desu ka** すきですか; 8. **suki de wa arimasen** すきではありません; 9. **Issho ni** いっしょに; 10. **shimashoo** しましょう

Bring It All Together

▶ 10F Bring It All Together (CD 3, Track 14)

Let's bring it all together, and add a little bit more vocabulary and structure.

A. Ms. Smith, what do you do on a weekend?	スミスさんはしゅうまつになにをしますか。	Sumisu san wa shuumatsu ni nani o shimasu ka.
B. I watch movies.	えいがをみます。	Eega o mimasu.
A. What kind of movies do you like?	どんなえいががすきですか。	Donna eega ga suki desu ka.
B. I like Japanese movies. I like Kurosawa movies very much.	にほんのえいががすきです。くろさわのえいががとてもすきですね。	Nihon no eega ga suki desu. Kurosawa no eega ga totemo suki desu ne.
A. Is that so? I like American movies.	そうですか。わたしはアメリカのえいががすきですよ。	Soodesuka. Watashi wa amerika no eega ga suki desu yo.
B. Do you play any sports, Mr. Yamada?	やまださんはスポーツはしますか。	Yamada san wa supootsu wa shimasu ka.
A. No, I don't play sports. But I watch sports. I like football and baseball.	いいえ、スポーツはしませんね。でもスポーツをみますよ。フットボールとやきゅうがすきです。	Iie, supootsu wa shimasen ne. Demo supootsu o mimasu yo. Futtobooru to yakyuu ga suki desu.
B. What are you going to do this weekend, Mr. Yamada?	やまださんはこんしゅうまつになにをしますか。	Yamada san wa konshuumatsu ni nani o shimasu ka.

| A. I'll watch baseball. And then I'll go to a restaurant. What about you, Ms. Smith? | やきゅうをみます。それからレストランにいきますよ。スミスさんは？ | Yakyuu o mimasu. Sore kara resutoran ni ikimasu yo. Sumisu san wa? |
| B. I'll stay home. I'll watch a DVD. | うちにいます。DVDをみますよ。 | Uchi ni imasu. Diibuidii o mimasu yo. |

✎ Work Out 2

▶ 10G Work Out 2 (CD 3, Track 15)

Now let's practice some of what you've learned.

A. Translate the following sentences from Japanese to English.

1. こんしゅうまつにえいがはみますか。

   Konshuumatsu ni eega wa mimasu ka.

   _____

2. やきゅうをしましょう。

   Yakyuu o shimashoo.

   _____

3. どんなおんがくがすきですか。

   Donna ongaku ga suki desu ka.

   _____

4. どんなほんをよみますか。

   Donna hon o yomimasu ka.

   _____

5. ロックとヒップホップがとてもすきです。

Rokku to hippuhoppu ga totemo suki desu.

_____

B. Change the following likes to dislikes, or vice versa.

Example: おんがくがすきです。**Ongaku ga suki desu.** ⊠ おんがくはすきではありま
せん。**Ongaku wa suki de wa arimasen.**

1. やきゅうがすきです。

Yakyuu ga suki desu.

_____

2. クラシックがすきです。

Kurashikku ga suki desu.

_____

3. ジャズがすきです。

Jazu ga suki desu.

_____

4. フットボールはすきではありません。

Futtobooru wa suki de wa arimasen.

_____

5. えいがはすきではありません。

Eega wa suki de wa arimasen.

_____

ANSWER KEY

A. 1. *Are you going to watch a movie this weekend?* 2. *Let's play baseball.* 3. *What kind of music do you like?* 4. *What kind of books do you read?* or *What kind of books are you going to read?* 5. *I like rock and hip-hop very much.*

B. 1. **Yakyuu wa suki de wa arimasen.** やきゅうはすきではありません。 2. **Kurashikku wa suki de wa arimasen.** クラシックはすきではありません。 3. **Jazu wa suki de wa arimasen.** ジャズはすきではありません。 4. **Futtobooru ga suki desu.** フットボールがすきです。 5. **Eega ga suki desu.** えいががすきです。

✎ Drive It Home

Complete the following sentences by inserting appropriate particles.

1. Uchi _____ imasu. (*I'm staying at home.*)

   うち _____います。

2. Eega _____ mimasen _____. (*Why don't we watch a movie?*)

   えいが _____みません _____。

3. Donna supootsu _____ suki desu _____. (*What kind of sports do you like?*)

   どんなスポーツ _____すきです _____。

4. Kaimono_____ ikimasu. (*I'm going to go shopping.*)

   かいもの _____いきます。

5. Supootsu _____suki de wa arimasen. (*I don't like sports.*)

   スポーツ _____すきではありません。

6. Ongaku _____ kikimasu. (*I listen to music.*)

   おんがく _____ききます。

7. Basukettobooru _____ suki desu _____. (*Do you like basketball?*)

   バスケットボール _____すきです _____。

8. **Shuumatsu** _____ **nani** _____ **shimasu** _____. (*What are you going to do for the weekend?*)

しゅうまつ _____ なに _____ します _____ 。

9. **Nihon** _____ **eega** _____ **suki desu.** (*I like Japanese movies.*)

にほん _____ えいが _____ すきです。

ANSWER KEY
1. ni に; 2. o を, ka か; 3. ga が, ka か; 4. ni に; 5. wa は; 6. o を; 7. wa は, ka か; 8. ni に, o を, ka か; 9. no の, ga が

Parting Words

おめでとうございます！ **Omedetoo gozaimasu!** *Congratulations!* You've finished the final lesson. You should now be able to:

☐ Use vocabulary to describe what you do in your free time

☐ Ask somebody about their weekend plan

☐ Make a suggestion by saying *Let's …* and *Why don't we …?*

☐ Express likes and dislikes

☐ Ask somebody what kind of music and sports they like

☐ Use what you've learned to talk about hobbies and recreational activities

Take It Further

▶ 10H Take It Further (CD 3, Track 16)

You may want to extend your vocabulary with some more popular activities:

jog, jogging	ジョギング	jogingu
to jog	ジョギングをします	jogingu o shimasu
ski, skiing	スキー	sukii
to ski	スキーをします	sukii o shimasu

game	ゲーム	geemu
to play a game	ゲームをします	geemu o shimasu
dance, dancing	ダンス	dansu
to dance	おどります	odorimasu
cooking	りょうり	ryoori
to cook	りょうりをします	ryoori o shimasu

Don't forget to practice and reinforce what you've learned by visiting **www.livinglanguage.com/ languagelab** for flashcards, games, and quizzes!

Word Recall

1. にほん nihon
2. このペン kono pen
3. おきます okimasu
4. 〜のとなり … no tonari
5. やきゅう yakyuu
6. おいしい oishii
7. ちゅうしょく chuushoku
8. おとうとさん otootosan
9. てんいん ten-in
10. とお too
11. かいもの kaimono
12. よにん yonin

a. *to get up*
b. *this pen (close to the speaker)*
c. *store clerk*
d. *baseball*
e. *Japan*
f. *delicious*
g. *next to …*
h. *four people*
i. *shopping*
j. *younger brother (someone else's)*
k. *lunch*
l. *10 (native Japanese number)*

ANSWER KEY
1. e; 2. b; 3. a; 4. g; 5. d; 6. f; 7. k; 8. j; 9. c; 10. l; 11. i; 12. h

Quiz 2
テスト 2

Now let's review! In this section you'll find a final quiz testing what you learned in Lessons 1-10. Once you've completed it, score yourself to see how well you've done. If you find that you need to go back and review, please do so before continuing on to the final section with review dialogues and comprehension questions.

A. Match the Japanese words on the left to the correct English translations on the right.

1. みぎ migi   a. *store clerk*
2. やさい yasai   b. *sweet*
3. あまい amai   c. *right*
4. てんいん ten-in   d. *movie*
5. えいが eega   e. *vegetable*

B. Rewrite the following times using numbers instead of words. For example, you might write 7 pm, 2:25 pm, 9:47 am, etc.

1. ごぜんろくじです。 **Gozen rokuji desu.** _____

2. ごごくじはんです。 **Gogo kuji han desu.** _____

3. よじはっぷんです。 **Yoji happun desu.** _____

4. しちじごじゅうろっぷんです。 **Shichiji gojuuroppun desu.** _____

5. じゅういちじじゅっぷんです。 **Juuichiji juppun desu.** _____

C. Fill in the blanks with the appropriate Japanese adjectives in the correct form.

1. **Yamada san no ie wa** _____ **desu.** (*Mr./Ms. Yamada's house is big.*)

   やまださんのいえは _____ です。

2. **Watashi no tokee wa** _____ **desu.**

   (*My clock is not old.*)

   わたしのとけいは _____ です。

3. **Kore wa** _____ **kuruma desu.** (*This is an expensive car.*)

   これは _____ くるまです。

4. **Kono baggu wa** _____ **arimasen.** (*This bag is not cheap.*)

   このバッグは _____ ありません。

5. **Kore wa** _____ **hon de wa arimasen.**

   (*This is not a new book.*)

   これは _____ ほんではありません。

D. Complete the following phrases and sentences by inserting appropriate particles.

1. **Ongaku** _____ **kikimasu.** (*I listen to music.*)

   おんがく _____ ききます。

2. **Kooen** _____ **ikimasu.** (*I'm going to the park.*)

   こうえん _____ いきます。

3. **raishuu** _____ **kayoobi** (*next Tueday*)

   らいしゅう _____ かようび

4. **hoteru** _____ **mukai gawa** (*across from the hotel*)

   ホテル _____ むかいがわ

5. Rokuji _____ tabemashoo. (*Let's eat at six o'clock.*)

ろくじ _____ たべましょう。

E. Fill in the blanks with the appropriate Japanese verbs in the correct form.

1. Hon o _____. (*I read books.*)

ほんを _____ 。

2. Depaato ni_____.

(*Are you going to the department store?*)

デパートに _____ 。

3. Niku wa _____. (*I don't eat meat.*)

にくは_____ 。

4. Konsaato ni _____. (*Why don't we go to a concert?*)

コンサートに _____ 。

5. Yakyuu o _____. (*Let's play baseball.*)

やきゅうを _____ 。

F. Fill in the blanks with the appropriate expression.

1. _____ desu ka. (*What is it?*)

_____ですか。

2. _____ ongaku desu ka. (*What kind of music is it?*)

_____ おんがくですか。

3. _____ desu ka. (*Where is it?*)

_____ですか。

4. _____ arimasu ka. *(What is there?)*

   _____ ありますか。

5. _____ desu ka. *(What time is it?)*

   _____ ですか。

ANSWER KEY
A. 1. c; 2. e; 3. b; 4. a; 5. d
B. 1. 6 am; 2. 9:30 pm; 3. 4:08; 4. 7:56; 5. 11:10
C. 1. ookii おおきい; 2. furuku nai ふるくない; 3. takai たかい; 4. yasuku やすく; 5. atarashii あたらしい
D. 1. o を; 2. ni に; 3. no の; 4. no の; 5. ni に
E. 1. yomimasu よみます; 2. ikimasu ka いきますか; 3. tabemasen たべません;
4. ikimasen ka いきませんか; 5. shimashoo しましょう
F. 1. Nan なん; 2. Donna どんな; 3. Doko どこ; 4. Nani ga なにが; 5. Nanji なんじ

How Did You Do?

Give yourself a point for every correct answer, then use the following key to determine whether or not you're ready to move on:

0-11 points: It's probably best to go back and study the lessons again. Take as much time as you need to. Review the vocabulary lists and carefully read through each Grammar Builder section.

12-24 points: If the questions you missed were in sections A or B, you may want to review the vocabulary again; if you missed answers mostly in sections C through F, check the Grammar Builder sections to make sure you have grammar basics down.

25-30 points: Feel free to move on to the Review Dialogues! Great job!

[ ][ ] **Points**

Review Dialogues

Here's your chance to practice all the vocabulary and grammar you've mastered in ten lessons of *Essential Japanese* with these five dialogues.

You'll hear each dialogue first in Japanese at a conversational pace. Listen carefully for meaning. Can you get the gist of the conversation? Next, you'll hear each sentence individually, first in Japanese and then in English. This should help fill in any gaps in understanding you had the first time. Finally, you'll do some role-play by taking part in the same conversation. You'll first hear the native speaker say a line from the dialogue, then you'll respond appropriately based on the English prompt in the pause provided. You'll hear the correct response in Japanese, which you should repeat for practice.

DIALOGUE 1

Japanese Only - 11A (CD 3, Track 17); Japanese and English - 11B (CD 3, Track 18); Role Play Exercise - 11C (CD 3, Track 19)

かぞくについてはなす
KAZOKU NI TSUITE HANASU
TALKING ABOUT THE FAMILY

こばやし: すずきさん、おかあさんはおげんきですか。

Kobayashi: Suzuki san, okaasan wa ogenki desu ka.

Ms. Suzuki, is your mother well?

すずき: はい、おかげさまで。ありがとうございます。

Suzuki: Hai, okagesama de. Arigatoo gozaimasu.

Yes, she's well. Thank you.

こばやし:	すずきさんはごきょうだいはいますか。
Kobayashi:	**Suzuki san wa gokyoodai wa imasu ka.**
	Do you have any siblings, Ms. Suzuki?
すずき:	はい、あにとあねがいます。こばやしさんは？
Suzuki:	**Hai, ani to ane ga imasu. Kobayashi san wa?**
	Yes, I have an older brother and an older sister. How about you, Mr. Kobayashi?
こばやし:	おとうとがひとりいます。おとうとはがくせいです。
Kobayashi:	**Otooto ga hitori imasu. Otooto wa gakusee desu.**
	I have one younger brother. He is a student.
すずき:	おとうとさんはだいがくせいですか。
Suzuki:	**Otooto san wa daigakusee desu ka.**
	Is he a college student?
こばやし:	はい、そうです。
Kobayashi:	**Hai, soo desu.**
	Yes, that's right.
すずき:	そうですか。わたしのあにはだいがくのせんせいですよ。
Suzuki:	**Watashi no ani wa daigaku no sensee desu yo.**
	My older brother is a college professor.
こばやし:	どこのだいがくのせんせいですか。
Kobayashi:	**Doko no daigaku no sensee desu ka.**
	Where is he a college professor?
すずき:	にほんだいがくです。けいざいがくのせんせいです。
Suzuki:	**Nihon daigaku desu. Keezaigaku no sensee desu.**
	Nihon University. He's a professor of economics.
こばやし:	ほんとうですか。おとうとはにほんだいがくのがくせいです！
Kobayashi:	**Hontoo desu ka. Otooto wa nihon daigaku no gakusee desu!**
	Really? My younger brother is a student at Nihon University!
すずき:	それはぐうぜんですね！けいざいがくのがくせいですか。
Suzuki:	**Sore wa guuzen desu ne! Keezaigaku no gakusee desu ka.**
	That's a coincidence, isn't it? Is he an economics student?

こばやし: いいえ、ぶんがくです。

Kobayashi: Iie, bungaku desu.

No, he's a literature student.

すずき: いいですね。ぶんがくはおもしろいですね。

Suzuki: Ii desune. Bungaku wa omoshiroi desu ne.

That's nice. Literature is interesting, isn't it?

こばやし: すずきさんのおねえさんのしょくぎょうはなんですか。

Kobayashi: Suzuki san no oneesan no shokugyoo wa nan desu ka.

What's your older sister's profession?

すずき: あねはかんごしです。しごとはとてもいそがしいです。

Suzuki: Ane wa kangoshi desu. Shigoto wa totemo isogashii desu.

She's a nurse. The work is very busy.

こばやし: おねえさんはなんじにうちにかえりますか。

Kobayashi: Oneesan wa nanji ni uchi ni kaerimasu ka.

What time does she come home?

すずき: ごごじゅうじにうちにかえります。

Suzuki: Gogo juuji ni uchi ni kaerimasu.

She comes home at 10 p.m.

こばやし: おそいですね。あさははやいですか。

Kobayashi: Osoi desu ne. Asa wa hayai desu ka.

That's late. Is she up early in the morning?

すずき: あまりはやくありません。じゅういちじにしごとにいきます。

Suzuki: Amari hayaku arimasen. Juuichiji ni shigoto ni ikimasu.

Not very early in the morning. She goes to work at eleven.

✎ Dialogue 1 Practice

Now let's check your comprehension of the dialogue and review what you learned in Lessons 1-10.

A. Is each of the following statements true or false?

1. すずきさんはおにいさんといもうとさんがいます。

   Suzuki san wa oniisan to imootosan ga imasu.

   _____

2. こばやしさんのおとうとさんはだいがくせいです。

   Kobayashi san no otootosan wa daigakusee desu.

   _____

3. すずきさんのおにいさんはぶんがくのせんせいです。

   Suzuki san no oniisan wa bungaku no sensee desu.

   _____

4. すずきさんのおねえさんはかんごしです。

   Suzuki san no oneesan wa kangoshi desu.

   _____

5. かんごしはとてもいそがしいです。

   Kangoshi wa totemo isogashii desu.

   _____

B. Answer the following questions in Japanese.

1. こばやしさんはいもうとさんがいますか。

   Kobayashi san wa imootosan wa imasu ka.

   _____

2. こばやしさんのおとうとさんはどこのだいがくのがくせいですか。

   Kobayashi san no otootosan wa doko no daigaku no gakusee desu ka.

   _____

3. すずきさんのおねえさんはなんじにうちにかえりますか。

   Suzuki san no oneesan wa nanji ni uchi ni kaerimasu ka.

   _____

4. すずきさんのおねえさんはなんじにしごとにいきますか。

   Suzuki san no oneesan wa nanji ni shigoto ni ikimasu ka.

   _____

ANSWER KEY
A. 1. False; 2. True; 3. False; 4. True; 5. True
B. 1. いいえ、いもうとさんはいません。Iie, imootosan wa imasen. 2. にほんだいがくのがくせいです。Nihon daigaku no gakusee desu. 3. ごごじゅうじにうちにかえります。Gogo juuji ni uchi ni kaerimasu. 4. じゅういちじにしごとにいきます。Juuichiji ni shigoto ni ikimasu.

◀) Dialogue 2

▶ Japanese Only - 12A (CD 3, Track 20); Japanese and English - 12B (CD 3, Track 21); Role Play Exercise - 12C (CD 3, Track 22)

ゆうじんのうちをたずねる

YUUJIN NO UCHI O TAZUNERU

VISITING A FRIEND'S HOUSE

なかむら:	こんにちは。
Nakamura:	**Konnichi wa.**
	Hello.
さとう:	こんにちは。ようこそ、なかむらさん。
Satoo:	**Konnichiwa. Yookoso, Nakamura san.**
	Hello. Welcome, Mr. Nakamura.
なかむら:	おじゃまします。
Nakamura:	**Ojamashimasu.**
	Pardon the intrusion. (polite expression on entering someone's house)
さとう:	こうちゃとケーキはどうですか。
Satoo:	**Koocha to keeki wa doo desu ka.**
	How about some black tea and cake?
なかむら:	すみません。おねがいします。
Nakamura:	**Sumimasen. Onegaishimasu.**
	Sorry for the trouble. Yes, please.
さとう:	どんなケーキがすきですか。チョコレートケーキと、チーズケーキと、ショートケーキがあります。
Satoo:	**Donna keeki ga suki desu ka. Chokoreeto keeki to chiizu keeki to shooto keeki ga arimasu.**
	What kind of cake do you like? I have chocolate cake, cheesecake, and shortcake.

なかむら: そうですね・・・チョコレートケーキをおねがいします。

Nakamura: Soo desu ne … Chokoreeto keeki o onegaishimasu.

Let's see… I'd like chocolate cake.

さとう: こうちゃとチョコレートケーキです。どうぞ。

Satoo: Koocha to chokoreeto keeki desu. Doozo.

Tea and a piece of chocolate cake. Here you go.

なかむら: ありがとうございます。おおきいケーキですね！

Nakamura: Arigatoogozaimasu. Ookii keeki desu ne!

Thank you. A big piece of cake!

さとう: どうですか。

Satoo: Doo desu ka.

How is it?

なかむら: とてもおいしいです！

Nakamura: Totemo oishii desu!

Very delicious!

さとう: それはよかった。

Satoo: Sore wa yokatta.

I'm glad to hear that.

なかむら: これはいいテーブルですね。

Nakamura: Kore wa ii teeburu desu ne.

This is a good table.

さとう: ありがとうございます。でも、たかくないですよ。

Satoo: Arigatoogozaimasu. Demo, takaku nai desu yo.

Thank you. But it's not expensive.

なかむら: おおきいテレビですね！なんインチですか。

Nakamura: Ookii terebi desu ne! Nan inchi desu ka.

That's a big TV! How many inches is it?

さとう:	ごじゅうインチです。このテレビはあたらしいですよ。
Satoo:	**Gojuu inchi desu. Kono terebi wa atarashii desu yo.**
	Fifty inches. This TV is new.
なかむら:	テレビはなんだいありますか。
Nakamura:	**Terebi wa nandai arimasu ka.**
	How many TVs do you have?
さとう:	えっと･･･さんだいありますね。このテレビはおおきいです。でも、にだいはちいさいです。
Satoo:	**Etto … sandai arimasu ne. Kono terebi wa ookii desu. Demo nidai wa chiisai desu.**
	Let's see … I have three. This TV is big. But the other two are small.
なかむら:	そうですか。わたしはコンピューターがさんだいあります。でもテレビはいちだいですよ。あまりおおきくありません。
Nakamura:	**Soo desu ka. Watashi wa konpyuutaa ga sandai arimasu. Demo terebi wa ichidai desu yo. Amari ookiku arimasen.**
	Is that so? I have three computers. But I have one TV. It's not very big.
さとう:	なかむらさん、おんがくをききませんか。どんなおんがくがすきですか。
Satoo:	**Nakamura san, ongaku o kikimasen ka. Donna ongaku ga suki desu ka.**
	Mr. Nakamura, why don't we listen to some music? What kind of music do you like?
なかむら:	ジャズがすきです。
Nakamura:	**Jazu ga suki desu.**
	I like jazz.
さとう:	それではジャズをききましょう！
Satoo:	**Sorede wa jazu o kikimashoo!**
	Then let's listen to jazz!

✏ Dialogue 2 Practice

A. Is each of the following statements true or false?

1. ここはなかむらさんのうちです。

   _____

   Koko wa Nakamura san no uchi desu.

2. なかむらさんはチョコレートケーキがすきです。

   Nakamura san wa chokoreeto keeki ga suki desu.

   _____

3. さとうさんのテーブルはたかいです。

   Satoosan no teeburu wa takai desu.

   _____

4. さとうさんはテレビがよんだいあります。

   Satoo san wa terebi ga yondai arimasu.

   _____

5. なかむらさんはコンピューターがさんだいあります。

   Nakamura san wa konpyuutaa ga sandai arimasu.

   _____

B. Answer the following questions in Japanese.

1. キャロットケーキはありますか。

   Kyarotto keeki wa arimasu ka.

   _____

2. さとうさんのテレビはなんインチですか。

   Satoo san no terebi wa nan inchi desu ka.

   _____

3. なかむらさんはおおきいテレビはありますか。

   Nakamura san wa ookii terebi wa arimasu ka.

   _____

4. なかむらさんはどんなおんがくがすきですか。

   Nakamura san wa donna ongaku ga suki desu ka.

   _____

ANSWER KEY
A. 1. False; 2. True; 3. False; 4. False; 5. True
B. 1. いいえ、ありません。Iie, arimasen. 2. ごじゅうインチです。Gojuu inchi desu. 3. いいえ、ありませ
ん。Iie, arimasen. 4. ジャズがすきです。Jazu ga suki desu.

💬 Dialogue 3

▶ Japanese Only - 13A (CD 3, Track 23); Japanese and English - 13B (CD 3, Track 24); Role
Play Exercise - 13C (CD 3, Track 25)

とうきょうにつく
TOOKYOO NI TSUKU
ARRIVING IN TOKYO

いとう:	こんにちは。はじめまして。わたしはツアーガイドのいとうです。
Itoo:	**Konnichi wa. Hajimemashite. Watashi wa tsuaagaido no Itoo desu.**
	Hello. How do you do? I am Ito, the tour guide.
わたなべ:	わたなべです。どうぞよろしく。
Watanabe:	**Watanabe desu. Doozo yoroshiku.**
	I'm Watanabe. Nice to meet you.

いとう: とうきょうにようこそ。

Itoo: **Tookyoo ni yookoso.**

Welcome to Tokyo.

わたなべ: とうきょうえきはおおきいですね！

Watanabe: **Tookyoo eki wa ookii desu ne!**

Tokyo Station is big!

いとう: そうですね。レストランもデパートもありますよ。

Itoo: **Soo desu ne. Resutoran mo depaato mo arimasu yo.**

Isn't it? It even has restaurants and a department store.

わたなべ: ホテルはここからとおいですか。

Watanabe: **Hoteru wa koko kara tooi desu ka.**

Is the hotel far from here?

いとう: とおくありません。くるまがあります。じゅうごふんですね。ちいさいホテルです。でも、いいホテルですよ。

Itoo: **Tooku arimasen. Kuruma ga arimasu. Juugofun desu ne. Chiisai hoteru desu. Demo, ii hoteru desu yo.**

It's not far. I have a car. It's 15 minutes. It's a small hotel. But it's a good hotel.

わたなべ: くるまはどこですか。

Watanabe: **Kuruma wa doko desu ka.**

Where is the car?

いとう: えきのむかいがわです。くろいくるまです。

Itoo: **Eki no mukai gawa desu. Kuroi kuruma desu.**

It's across from the station. It's a black car.

わたなべ: ああ、あそこですね。いとうさん、ゆうしょくパーティーはなんじですか。

Watanabe: **Aa, asoko desu ne. Itoo san, yuushoku paatii wa nanji desu ka.**

Ah, it's over there, isn't it? What time is the dinner party, Mr. Ito?

いとう：	しちじです。レストランはホテルのとなりですよ。
Itoo:	**Shichiji desu. Resutoran wa hoteru no tonari desu yo.**
	Seven o'clock. The restaurant is next to the hotel.
わたなべ：	いま、よじですね。ゆうしょくまでホテルにいます。すこしねます。
Watanabe:	**Ima, yoji desu ne. Yuushoku made hoteru ni imasu. Sukoshi nemasu.**
	It's four o'clock now, right? I'll stay at the hotel until dinner. I'm going to sleep a little.
いとう：	それはいいですね。
Itoo:	**Sore wa ii desu ne.**
	That's good.
わたなべ：	ホテルのちょうしょくはなんじですか。
Watanabe:	**Hoteru no chooshoku wa nanji desu ka.**
	What time is breakfast at the hotel?
いとう：	ろくじからじゅうじまでです。
Itoo:	**Rokuji kara juuji made desu.**
	From six to ten o'clock.
わたなべ：	それではしちじはんにちょうしょくをたべます。
Watanabe:	**Sorede wa shichiji han ni chooshoku o tabemasu.**
	Then I'll have breakfast at seven thirty.
いとう：	それではあした、はちじはんにあいますか。
Itoo:	**Sorede wa ashita, hachiji han ni aimasu ka.**
	Then shall we meet at eight thirty tomorrow?
わたなべ：	いいですね。そうしましょう。
Watanabe:	**Ii desu ne. Soo shimashoo.**
	Sounds good. Let's do that.

✎ Dialogue 3 Practice

A. Is each of the following statements true or false?

1. ここはとうきょうえきです。

   Koko wa Tookyoo eki desu.

   _____

2. いとうさんはツアーガイドです。

   Itoo san wa tsuaagaido desu.

   _____

3. いとうさんのくるまはしろいです。

   Itoo san no kuruma wa shiroi desu.

   _____

4. ゆうしょくパーティーはしちじです。

   Yuushoku paatii wa shichiji desu.

   _____

5. ホテルのちょうしょくはろくじからくじまでです。

   Hoteru no chooshoku wa rokuji kara kuji made desu.

   _____

B. Answer the following questions in Japanese.

1. ホテルはとうきょうえきからとおいですか。

   Hoteru wa Tookyoo eki kara tooi desu ka.

   _____

2. いとうさんのくるまはどこですか。

Itoo san no kuruma wa doko desu ka.

_____

3. レストランはどこですか。

Resutoran wa doko desu ka.

_____

4. わたなべさんはあしたなんじにちょうしょくをたべますか。

Watanabe san wa ashita nanji ni chooshoku o tabemasu ka.

_____

ANSWER KEY
A. 1. True; 2. True; 3. False; 4. True; 5. False
B. 1. いいえ、とおくありません。**Iie, tooku arimasen.** 2. えきのむかいがわです。**Eki no mukai gawa desu.**
3. ホテルのとなりです。**Hoteru no tonari desu.** 4. しちじはんにちょうしょくをたべます。**Shichiji han ni chooshoku o tabemasu.**

◀ Dialogue 4

▶ Japanese Only - 14A (CD 3, Track 26); Japanese and English - 14B (CD 3, Track 27); Role Play Exercise - 14C (CD 3, Track 28)

レストランで
RESUTORAN DE
AT A RESTAURANT

おとこのひと：	すみません。ちゅうもんをおねがいします。
Otoko no hito:	**Sumimasen. Chuumon o onegaishimasu.**
	Excuse me. I'd like to place an order, please.
ウェイトレス：	かしこまりました。おのみものはなにになさいますか。
Weitoresu:	**Kashikomarimashita. Onomimono wa nani ni nasaimasu ka.**
	Certainly. What would you like to drink?

おとこのひと: 　ワインをいっぱいおねがいします。

Otoko no hito: **Wain o ippai onegaishimasu.**

I'd like to have a glass of wine.

ウェイトレス: 　かしこまりました。おしょくじはなにになさいますか。

Weitoresu: **Kashikomarimashita. Oshokuji wa nani ni nasaimasu ka.**

Certainly. What would you like to eat?

おとこのひと: 　サラダはなにがありますか。

Otoko no hito: **Sarada wa nani ga arimasu ka.**

What kind of salad do you have?

ウェイトレス: 　グリーンサラダとチキンサラダとシーフードサラダとミックスサラダがございます。

Weitoresu: **Guriin sarada to chikin sarada to shiifuudo sarada to mikkusu sarada ga gozaimasu.**

We have Green Salad, Chicken Salad, Seafood Salad, and Mixed Salad.

おとこのひと: 　それではグリーンサラダをおねがいします。

Otoko no hito: **Sore de wa guriin sarada o onegaishimasu.**

Then I'd like a Green Salad.

ウェイトレス: 　グリーンサラダをおひとつですね。

Weitoresu: **Guriin sarada o ohitotsu desu ne.**

One Green Salad, it is.

おとこのひと: 　それから、トマトとなすのスパゲッティをおねがいします。

Otoko no hito: **Sore kara, tomato to nasu no supagetti o onegaishimasu.**

And also, I'd like Spaghetti with Tomato and Eggplant, please.

ウェイトレス: 　かしこまりました。ワインとグリーンサラダとトマトとなすのスパゲッティですね。

Weitoresu: **Kashikomarimashita. Wain to guriin sarada to tomato to nasu no supagetti desu ne.**

A glass of wine, a Green Salad, and Spaghetti with Tomato and Eggplant.

～さんじゅっぷんご～
~Sanjuppun go~
~thirty minutes later~

ウェイトレス:　デザートはいかがですか。
Weitoresu:　**Dezaato wa ikaga desu ka.**
　　　　　　　How about some dessert?
おとこのひと:　けっこうです。コーヒーをいっぱいください。
Otoko no hito:　**Kekkoo desu. Koohii o ippai kudasai.**
　　　　　　　No, thank you. Please give me a cup of coffee.
ウェイトレス:　かしこまりました。
Weitoresu:　**Kashikomarimashita.**
　　　　　　　Certainly.

✎ Dialogue 4 Practice

A. Is each of the following statements true or false?

1. ここはレストランです。

   Koko wa resutoran desu.

2. おとこのひとはビールをのみます。

   Otoko no hito wa biiru o nomimasu.

3. おとこのひとはチキンサラダをたべます。

   Otoko no hito wa chikin sarada o tabemasu.

4. おとこのひとはトマトとなすのスパゲッティをたべます。

Otoko no hito wa tomato to nasu no supagetti o tabemasu.

5. おとこのひとはこうちゃをのみます。

Otoko no hito wa koocha o nomimasu.

B. Answer the following questions in Japanese.

1. どんなサラダがありますか。

Donna sarada ga arimasu ka.

2. おとこのひとはどんなサラダをたべますか。

Otoko no hito wa donna sarada o tabemasu ka.

3. おとこのひとはデザートはたべますか。

Otoko no hito wa dezaato wa tabemasu ka.

ANSWER KEY
A. 1. True; 2. False; 3. False; 4. True; 5. False
B. 1. グリーンサラダとチキンサラダとシーフードサラダとミックスサラダがあります。Guriin sarada to chikin sarada to shiifuudo sarada to mikkusu sarada ga arimasu. 2. グリーンサラダをたべます。Guriin sarada o tabemasu. 3. いいえ、デザートはたべません。Iie, dezaato wa tabemasen.

Dialogue 5

Japanese Only - 15A (CD 3, Track 29); Japanese and English - 15B (CD 3, Track 30); Role Play Exercise - 15C (CD 3, Track 31)

しゅうまつのけいかく
SHUUMATSU NO KEEKAKU
WEEKEND PLANS

さいとう：　たかはしさん、それはあたらしいくつですか。
Saitoo:　**Takahashi san, sore wa atarashii kutsu desu ka.**
Ms. Takahashi, are those new shoes?

たかはし：　はい、そうです。
Takahashi:　**Hai, soo desu.**
Yes, they are.

さいとう：　いいくつですね！
Saitoo:　**Ii kutsu desu ne!**
Nice shoes!

たかはし：　ありがとうございます。
Takahashi:　**Arigatoogozaimasu.**
Thank you.

さいとう：　わたしのくつはふるいです。にちようびにくつのかいものにいきます。
Saitoo:　**Watashi no kutsu wa furui desu. Nichiyoobi ni kutsu no kaimono ni ikimasu.**
My shoes are old. I'm going shoe shopping on Sunday.

たかはし：　どこにかいものにいきますか。
Takahashi:　**Doko ni kaimono ni ikimasu ka.**
Where are you going shopping?

さいとう：　デパートにいきます。
Saitoo:　**Depaato ni ikimasu.**
I'm going to the department store.

たかはし:	わたしもにちようびにデパートにいきますよ。
Takahashi:	**Watashi mo nichiyoobi ni depaato ni ikimasu yo.**
	I'm going to the department store on Sunday, too.
さいとう:	なにをかいますか。
Saitoo:	**Nani o kaimasu ka.**
	What are you going to buy?
たかはし:	バッグをかいます。
Takahashi:	**Baggu o kaimasu.**
	I'm going to buy a bag.
さいとう:	いいですね。いっしょにデパートにいきませんか。
Saitoo:	**Ii desu ne. Issho ni depaato ni ikimasen ka.**
	Nice. Why don't we go to the department store together?
たかはし:	そうしましょう！にじはどうですか。
Takahashi:	**Soo shimashoo! Niji wa doo desu ka.**
	Let's do that! How about two o'clock?
さいとう:	いいですよ。たかはしさんはどようびになにをしますか。
Saitoo:	**Ii desu yo. Takahashi san wa doyoobi ni nani o shimasu ka.**
	Sounds good. What are you going to do on Saturday, Ms. Takahashi?
たかはし:	うちにいます。えいごのべんきょうをします。らいしゅうのすいようびにしけんがあります。
Takahashi:	**Uchi ni imasu. Eego no benkyoo o shimasu. Raishuu no suiyoobi ni shiken ga arimasu.**
	I'm staying home. I'm studying English. I have an exam next Wednesday.
さいとう:	むずかしいですか。
Saitoo:	**Muzukashii desu ka.**
	Is it difficult?
たかはし:	むずかしいです！さいとうさんはらいしゅうしけんはありますか。
Takahashi:	**Muzukashii desu! Saitoo san wa raishuu shiken wa arimasu ka.**
	It is difficult! Do you have an exam next week, Mr. Saitoo?

さいとう:	ありません！
Saitoo:	**Arimasen!**
	No, I don't!
たかはし:	それはいいですね。どようびになにをしますか。
Takahashi:	**Sore wa ii desu ne. Doyoobi ni nani o shimasu ka.**
	That's nice. What are you going to do on Saturday?
さいとう:	やきゅうをします。でもべんきょうもしますよ。
Saitoo:	**Yakyuu o shimasu. Demo benkyoo mo shimasu yo.**
	I'm playing baseball. But I'll study, too.
たかはし:	それではにちようびのにじにあいましょう。
Takahashi:	**Sorede wa nichiyoobi no niji ni aimashoo.**
	Then let's meet at two on Sunday.
さいとう:	さようなら。
Saitoo:	**Sayoonara.**
	Goodbye.

✎ Dialogue 5 Practice

A. Is each of the following statements true or false?

1. たかはしさんのくつはあたらしいです。

   Takahashi san no kutsu wa atarashii desu.

   _____

2. さいとうさんのくつはふるいです。

   Saitoo san no kutsu wa furui desu.

   _____

3. さいとうさんとたかはしさんはいちじにいっしょにデパートにいきます。

   Saitoo san to Takahashi san wa ichiji ni issho ni depaato ni ikimasu.

   _____

4. たかはしさんはすいようびにえいごのしけんがあります。

Takahashi san wa suiyoobi ni eego no shiken ga arimasu.

_____

5. さいとうさんもすいようびにしけんがあります。

Saitoo san mo suiyoobi ni shiken ga arimasu.

_____

B. Answer the following questions in Japanese.

1. さいとうさんとたかはしさんはなんようびにデパートにいきますか。

Saitoo san to Takahashi san wa nan-yoobi ni depaato ni ikimasu ka.

_____

2. たかはしさんはなにをかいますか。

Takahashi san wa nani o kaimasu ka.

_____

3. たかはしさんはどようびになにをしますか。

Takahashi san wa doyoobi ni nani o shimasu ka.

_____

4. さいとうさんはどようびになにをしますか。

Saitoo san wa doyoobi ni nani o shimasu ka.

_____

ANSWER KEY
A. 1. True; 2. True; 3. False; 4. True; 5. False
B. 1. にちようびにデパートにいきます。Nichiyoobi ni depaato ni ikimasu. 2. バッグをかいます。Baggu o kaimasu. 3. えいごのべんきょうをします。Eego no benkyoo o shimasu. 4. やきゅうをします。べんきょうもします。Yakyuu o shimasu. Benkyoo mo shimasu.

Don't forget to practice and reinforce what you've learned by visiting **www.livinglanguage.com/languagelab** for flashcards, games, and quizzes!

Glossary

Note that the following abbreviations will be used in this glossary: (m.) = masculine, (f.) = feminine, (sg.) = singular, (pl.) = plural, (fml.) = formal/polite, (infml.) = informal/familiar. If a word has two grammatical genders, (m./f.) or (f./m.) is used.

Japanese-English

A

aa ああ *ah, oh*

achira あちら *that, that way (far from both the speaker and the listener) (polite)*

ageru, agemasu あげる、あげます *to give*

  ... te ageru, ... te agemasu ～てあげる、～てあげます *to give a favor of ... ing*

(... to ... no) aida (～と～の)間 *between (... and ...)*

aisukuriimu アイスクリーム *ice cream*

aka 赤 *red (noun)*

aka wain 赤ワイン *red wine*

akai 赤い *red (adjective)*

akarui 明るい *bright*

akeru, akemasu 開ける、開けます *to open (transitive verb)*

aki 秋 *fall, autumn*

amai 甘い *sweet*

ame 雨 *rain*

  Ame desu. 雨です。 *It's raining.*

  Ame ga futte imasu. 雨が降っています。 *It's raining.*

amerika アメリカ *the United States*

amerikajin アメリカ人 *American (person)*

anata あなた *you (sg.) (subject pronoun)*

  anatagata あなた方 *you (pl.) (subject pronoun)*

  anata no あなたの *your (sg.)*

  anatatachi あなた達 *you (pl.) (subject pronoun)*

ane 姉 *older sister (one's own)*

ani 兄 *older brother (one's own)*

a(n)mari (+ negative) あ(ん)まり *not so often, not so much*

ano あの *that (far from both the speaker and the listener)*

  ano pen あのペン *that pen*

anoo あのう *Well ...*

ao 青 *blue (noun)*

aoi 青い *blue (adjective)*

apaato アパート *apartment*

arau, araimasu 洗う、洗います *to wash*

are あれ *that (far from both the speaker and the listener)*

arerugii アレルギー *allergy*

Arigatoo gozaimashita. ありがとうございました。 *Thank you.*

  Arigatoo gozaimasu. ありがとうございます。 *Thank you.*

  Doomo arigatoo gozaimashita. どうもありがとうございました。 *Thank you very much.*

  Doomo arigatoo gozaimasu. どうもありがとうございます。 *Thank you very much.*

aru, arimasu ある、あります *there is ... / to have ... (inanimate)*

aruku, arukimasu 歩く、歩きます *to walk*

  aruite gofun 歩いて五分 *five minute walk*

asa 朝 *morning*

asagohan 朝ご飯 *breakfast (infml.)*

asatte あさって *the day after tomorrow*

ashi 足 *foot*

ashi 脚 *leg*

ashisutanto アシスタント *assistant*

ashita 明日 *tomorrow*

asobu, asobimasu 遊ぶ、遊びます *to play (a game)*

asoko あそこ *there (far from both the speaker and the listener)*

asu 明日 *tomorrow*

atama 頭 *head*

  atama ga itai, atama ga itai desu 頭が痛い、頭が痛いです *to have a headache*

atarashii 新しい *new*

atatakai 暖かい *warm*

atesaki 宛先 *(sent) to*

ato de 後で *later, after*

resutoran o deta ato de レストランを出た後で
 after leaving a restaurant
atsui 暑い *hot (weather, room temperature)*
atsui 熱い *hot (to the touch)*
au, aimasu 会う、会います *to meet*
au, aimasu 合う、合います *to match*
 jiinzu ni au ジーンズに合う *to match with jeans*
azukaru, azukarimasu 預かる、預かります
 to keep
baa バー *bar*
baggu バッグ *bag*
baiorin バイオリン *violin*
ban バン *van*
ban 晩 *evening, night*
 konban 今晩 *tonight*
 maiban 毎晩 *every night*
bareebooru バレーボール *volleyball*
basu バス *bus*
basukettobooru バスケットボール *basketball*
basutee バス停 *bus stop*
bataa バター *butter*
batto バット *bat*
beddo ベッド *bed*
bengoshi 弁護士 *lawyer*
benkyoosuru, benkyooshimasu 勉強する、
 勉強します *to study*
benri 便利 *convenient*
besuto ベスト *vest, best*
biichi ビーチ *beach*
biiru ビール *beer*
 biiru ken ビール券 *beer gift coupon*
bikkurisuru, bikkurishimasu びっくりする、
 びっくりします *to be surprised, to be scared*
bin 瓶 *bottle*
biru ビル *high-rise building*
bitaminzai ビタミン剤 *vitamin supplement*
biyooin 美容院 *beauty salon*
biyooshi 美容師 *hair dresser*
bojoreenuuboo ボジョレーヌーボー *Beaujolais
 nouveau*
boku (used only by male speakers) 僕 *I*
booeki 貿易 *trade, export and import business*
booekigaisha 貿易会社 *trading company*
booru ボール *ball*
boorupen ボールペン *ballpoint pen*
bu 部 *set, copy (counter for written materials)*
buchoo 部長 *division manager*
bukka 物価 *prices (of commodities)*

bungaku 文学 *literature*
buranchi ブランチ *brunch*
burausu ブラウス *blouse*
buta 豚 *pig*
butaniku 豚肉 *pork*
byakuya 白夜 *white night*
byooin 病院 *hospital*
byooki 病気 *illness*
canada カナダ *Canada*
chairo 茶色 *brown (noun)*
chairoi 茶色い *brown (adjective)*
… chaku 〜着 *arriving…*
 Naha chaku 那覇着 *arriving in Naha*
chansu チャンス *chance*
chanto ちゃんと *properly, exactly, accurately
 (infml.)*
cheen チェーン *chain*
chero チェロ *cello*
chichi 父 *father (one's own)*
chichi no hi 父の日 *father's day*
chiisai 小さい *small*
chiizu チーズ *cheese*
chikai 近い *close*
chikaku 近く *nearby*
chikatetsu 地下鉄 *subway*
chikin sarada チキンサラダ *chicken salad*
chokoreeto チョコレート *chocolate*
choo 腸 *intestine*
choomiryoo 調味料 *seasoning*
chooshoku 朝食 *breakfast (fml.)*
chotto ちょっと *a little*
chuugakkoo 中学校 *junior high school*
chuugoku 中国 *China*
chuugokugo 中国語 *Chinese (language)*
chuugokujin 中国人 *Chinese (person)*
chuumon 注文 *order*
chuumonsuru, chuumonshimasu 注文する、
 注文します *to order*
chuusha 注射 *injection, shot*
chuushasuru, chuushashimasu 注射する、
 注射します *to give an injection*
chuushoku 昼食 *lunch (fml.)*
da, desu だ、です *to be*
daasu ダース *dozen*
dai 台 *counter for mechanical items*
daidokoro 台所 *kitchen*
daigaku 大学 *college, university*
daigakuin 大学院 *graduate school*

daigakuinsee 大学院生 *graduate school student*
daigakusee 大学生 *college student*
daijoobu 大丈夫 *all right*
daisuki da, daisuki desu 大好きだ、大好きです
to like very much, to like a lot
dake だけ *only*
dansu ダンス *dance, dancing*
dare 誰 *who*
dare ka 誰か *someone*
dare mo (+ negative) 誰も *no one, nobody*
daroo, deshoo だろう、でしょう *will probably*
… te (mo) ii deshoo ka. 〜て(も)いいでしょ
うか。 *May I … ? (polite)*
… te (mo) yoroshii deshoo ka. 〜て(も)よろしい
でしょうか。 *May I … ? (polite)*
de で *particle (marks a place where some action
takes place; marks means and instruments)*
dekakeru, dekakemasu 出掛ける、出掛けます *to
go out*
kamera o motte dekakemasu カメラを持って出
掛けます *to go out with a camera*
dekiru, dekimasu できる、できます *can do*
demo でも *however, but*
… demo 〜でも *… or something like that*
koohii demo コーヒーでも *coffee or something
like that*
denki gishi 電気技師 *electrical engineer*
densha 電車 *train*
denshirenji 電子レンジ *microwave oven*
(o)denwa (お)電話 *telephone (polite with o)*
(o)denwabangoo (お)電話番号 *telephone number
(polite with o)*
denwasuru, denwashimasu 電話する、電話し
ます *to make a phone call*
depaato デパート *department store*
deru, demasu 出る、出ます *to leave, to attend*
dete iru, dete imasu 出ている、出ています
to have left
… ni deru 〜に出る *to attend …*
… o deru 〜を出る *to leave …*
deshi 弟子 *disciple*
dewa では *then*
dezaato デザート *dessert*
dezain デザイン *design*
diizeru ディーゼル *diesel*
disupuree ディスプレイ *display*
do 度 *degree*
sanjuuhachi do 三十八度 *38 degrees*

dochira どちら *where, which one, which way
(polite)*
dochira no hoo どちらの方 *which one*
doitsu ドイツ *Germany*
doitsugo ドイツ語 *German (language)*
doitsujin ドイツ人 *German (person)*
doko どこ *where*
doko ka どこか *somewhere*
doko mo (+ negative) どこも *nowhere*
doku 毒 *poison*
dokusho 読書 *reading books*
donata どなた *who (polite)*
donna どんな *what kind of*
dono どの *which (one)*
dono pen どのペン *which pen*
dono gurai どのぐらい *how long, how much*
doo どう *how*
Doo deshita ka. どうでしたか。 *How was it?*
Doo desu ka. どうですか。 *How is it?/
What about … ?/How about … ?*
Doo nasaimashita ka. どうなさいましたか。
What's the matter? (polite)
Doo shimashita ka. どうしましたか。 *What's
the matter?*
doo yatte どうやって *how*
dooitsu 同一 *identical*
dookoo 同行 *accompaniment*
dooshite どうして *why*
Doozo. どうぞ。 *Here you go./Please.*
Doozo yoroshiku. どうぞよろしく。 *Nice to
meet you.*
dore どれ *which one*
doresshingu ドレッシング *dressing*
doyoobi 土曜日 *Saturday*
e 絵 *drawing, painting*
e へ *particle (marks the goal of movement)*
ebi えび *shrimp*
ee ええ *yes (infml.)*
eega 映画 *movie*
eega kanshoo 映画鑑賞 *seeing movies (lit., movie
appreciation)*
eegakan 映画館 *movie theater*
eego 英語 *English (language)*
eegyoo hookokusho 営業報告書 *business report*
eki 駅 *station*
en 円 *yen*
ichiman en 一万円 *10,000 yen*
sen en 千円 *1,000 yen*

enjin エンジン *engine*
enjinia エンジニア *engineer*
enpitsu 鉛筆 *pencil*
ensoosuru, ensooshimasu 演奏する、演奏します
　to perform (music)
etto えっと *Well ...*
fakkusu ファックス *fax*
fensu フェンス *fence*
finrando フィンランド *Finland*
fonto フォント *font*
fooku フォーク *fork*
fuben 不便 *inconvenient*
fujisan 富士山 *Mt. Fuji*
fukee 父兄 *fathers and eldest sons (fml.)*
fuku, fukimasu 吹く、吹きます *to play (a wind
　instruments)*
fukumu, fukumimasu 含む、含みます *to be
　included*
fukutsuu 腹痛 *stomachache*
fuminshoo 不眠症 *insomnia*
　fuminshoo da, fuminshoo desu 不眠症だ、
　　不眠症です *to suffer from insomnia*
fumon 不問 *passing over a matter*
furansu フランス *France*
furansu ryoori フランス料理 *French cuisine*
furansugo フランス語 *French (language)*
furansujin フランス人 *French (person)*
furu, furimasu 降る、降ります *to fall,
　to come down*
　Ame ga futte imasu. 雨が降っています。
　　It's raining.
　Yuki ga futte imasu. 雪が降っています。
　　It's snowing.
furui 古い *old*
furuuto フルート *flute*
futa 蓋 *lid*
futari 二人 *two people*
futatsu 二つ *two (native Japanese number)*
futsuka 二日 *second (day of the month)*
futtobooru フットボール *football*
(go)fuufu (ご)夫婦 *married couple (polite
　with go)*
fuyu 冬 *winter*
ga が *particle (marks a subject)*
ga が *but*
ga 蛾 *moth*
gaarufurendo ガールフレンド *girlfriend*
gakki 楽器 *musical instrument*

gakkoo 学校 *school*
gakusee 学生 *student*
gan 癌 *cancer*
geemu ゲーム *game*
genkan 玄関 *entrance hall*
genki 元気 *vigorous*
　Genki desu. 元気です。 *I'm fine.*
　Ogenki desu ka. お元気ですか。 *How are you?*
genkin 現金 *cash*
geri 下痢 *diarrhea*
　geri o suru, geri o shimasu 下痢をする、
　　下痢をします *to have diarrhea*
getsuyoobi 月曜日 *Monday*
ginkoo 銀行 *bank*
ginkooin 銀行員 *bank clerk*
gishi 技師 *engineer*
go 五 *five*
go 後 *later, after*
　sanjuppun go 三十分後 *30 minutes later*
gobyuu 誤びゅう *error (fml.)*
gofun 五分 *five minutes*
gogatsu 五月 *May*
gogo 午後 *afternoon, p.m.*
gohan ご飯 *cooked rice, meal*
goji 五時 *five o'clock*
gojitsu 後日 *later, some other day*
gojuu 五十 *fifty*
gokai 五階 *fifth floor*
gokyoodai ご兄弟 *siblings (someone else's)*
Gomennasai. ごめんなさい。 *I'm sorry.*
goran ni naru, goran ni narimasu ご覧になる、
　ご覧になります *to see, to look, to watch
　(honorific)*
goro 頃 *about, approximately*
gorufu ゴルフ *golf*
goshujin ご主人 *husband (someone else's)*
gozaimasu ございます *to exist, there is, to have
　(polite)*
　... de gozaimasu. ～でございます。 *to be ...
　　(polite)*
gozen 午前 *morning, a.m.*
gruupu happyoo グループ発表 *group
　presentation*
gurai ぐらい *about, approximately*
guree グレー *grey (noun)*
guriin sarada グリーンサラダ *green salad*
guuzen 偶然 *coincidence*
gyaku 逆 *opposite*

gyuuniku 牛肉 *beef*
ha 歯 *tooth*
haadowea ハードウェア *hardware*
haato ハート *heart*
hachi 八 *eight*
hachifun 八分 *eight minutes*
hachigatsu 八月 *August*
hachiji 八時 *eight o'clock*
hachijuu 八十 *eighty*
hade 派手 *showy, loud*
haha 母 *mother (one's own)*
hai はい *yes*
hai 杯 *counter for liquid in cups/glasses/bowls*
hai 肺 *lung*
haikensuru, haikenshimasu 拝見する、
    拝見します *to see, to look, to watch (humble)*
hairu, hairimasu 入る、入ります *to enter, to join*
    haitte iru, haitte imasu 入っている、
        入っています *to have entered, to belong*
    ofuro ni hairu, ofuro ni hairimasu お風呂に入
        る、お風呂に入ります *to take a bath*
Hajimemashite. はじめまして。 *How do you do?*
hajimete 初めて *first time, for the first time*
hakaru, hakarimasu 測る、測ります *to measure*
    netsu o hakaru, netsu o hakarimasu 熱を測
        る、熱を測ります *to check one's temperature*
hakike 吐き気 *nausea*
    hakike ga suru, hakike ga shimasu 吐き気がす
        る、吐き気がします *to feel like vomiting*
hakka 発火 *ignition*
haku 泊 *staying over night*
    nihaku 二泊 *two nights*
    nihaku mikka 二泊三日 *two nights three days*
hamu ハム *ham*
han 半 *half, half past the hour*
    goji han 五時半 *five thirty*
hana 花 *flower*
hana 鼻 *nose*
hanasu, hanashimasu 話す、話します *to speak*
hanbun 半分 *half*
hankachi ハンカチ *handkerchief*
hantoshi 半年 *half a year*
    hantoshikan 半年間 *for half a year*
happun 八分 *eight minutes*
happyoo 発表 *presentation*
hara 腹 *belly, abdomen*
harau, haraimasu 払う、払います *to pay*
hare 晴れ *sunny*

Hare desu. 晴れです。 *It's sunny.*
Harete imasu. 晴れています。 *It's sunny.*
haru 春 *spring*
hashi 箸 *chopsticks*
hashiru, hashirimasu 走る、走ります *to run*
hataraku, hatarakimasu 働く、働きます
    to work
… hasu ～発 *leaving …*
    Haneda hatsu 羽田発 *leaving Haneda*
hatsuka 二十日 *twentieth (day of the month)*
hayabaya 早々 *promptly*
hayai 早い *early*
hayaku 早く *early, quickly*
hayashi 林 *woods*
Hee. へえ。 *Well … /Wow./I see.*
heejitsu 平日 *weekday*
heta 下手 *unskillful, poor at*
heya 部屋 *room*
hi 日 *day*
hidari 左 *left*
hidarigawa 左側 *left side*
hidoi ひどい *terrible, severe*
higashigawa 東側 *east side*
hiki 匹 *counter for animal*
hikkosu, hikkoshimasu 引っ越す、引っ越します
    to move (to a new location)
hikooki 飛行機 *airplane*
hiku, hikimasu 弾く、弾きます *to play (piano)*
hikui 低い *low*
hima 暇 *be free (having a lot of free time)*
hin 品 *dignity*
hinketsu 貧血 *anemia*
hippuhoppu ヒップホップ *hip-hop*
hiragana 平仮名 *hiragana characters*
hiroi 広い *spacious*
hiroo 疲労 *exhaustion, fatigue*
hiroshima 広島 *Hiroshima*
(o)hiru (お)昼 *noon (polite with o)*
hirugohan 昼ご飯 *lunch (infml.)*
hisabisa 久々 *long-absence*
Hisashiburi desu ne. 久しぶりですね。
    Long time no see.
hito 人 *person*
    onna no hito 女の人 *woman*
    otoko no hito 男の人 *man*
hitori 一人 *one person*
hitorikko 一人っ子 *only child*
hitotsu 一つ *one (native Japanese number)*

hiyaku 飛躍 *leap*
hiyoo 費用 *cost, expense*
  kootsuuhi 交通費 *transportation costs*
hoka 他 *other*
hoken 保険 *insurance*
  shakaihoken 社会保険 *social insurance*
hokenshoo 保険証 *health insurance card*
hon 本 *book*
hon 本 *counter for long cylindrical objects*
hone 骨 *bone*
  hone o oru, hone o orimasu 骨を折る、骨を折り
  ます *to break a bone*
honkon 香港、ホンコン *Hong Kong*
hontoo 本当 *true*
  Hontoo desu ka. 本当ですか。 *Really?/Is that
  true?*
  hontoo ni 本当に *really*
hon-ya 本屋 *book store*
hoo 方 *direction, side*
  dochira no hoo どちらの方 *which one*
  ~ nai hoo ga ii desu. 〜ない方がいいです。 *You'd
  better not …*
  … (ta/da) hoo ga ii desu. 〜(た/だ)方がいい
  です。 *You'd better …*
hookoo 方向 *direction*
hooritsu 法律 *law*
hooritsu jimusho 法律事務所 *law firm*
hoshii, hoshii desu 欲しい、欲しいです *to want*
  hoshigatte iru, hoshigatte imasu 欲しがってい
  る、欲しがっています *(Someone) wants*
  hotate 帆立 *scallop*
hoteru ホテル *hotel*
hyaku 百 *hundred*
hyakupaasento 100パーセント *hundred percent*
  uuru hyakupaasento ウール100パーセント
  100% wool
hyoogen 表現 *expression*
i 胃 *stomach*
ichi 一 *one*
  ichiman 一万 *ten thousand*
  ichiman en 一万円 *ten thousand yen*
  ichiban 一番 *number one, the most*
  ichiban ii 一番いい *the best*
  ichido 一度 *once*
  ichido mo (+negative) 一度も *never*
  moo ichido もう一度 *once more*
  ichigatsu 一月 *January*
  ichiji 一時 *one o'clock*

ie 家 *house*
igirisu イギリス *England*
igirisujin イギリス人 *English (person)*
ii いい *good*
  emu de ii エムでいい *medium is okay*
  Junbi wa ii desu ka. 準備はいいですか。
  Are you ready?
  moshi yokattara もし良かったら *if it's okay,
  if you like*
  Sore wa yokatta. それはよかった。 *I'm glad to
  hear that.*
  … te (mo) ii?/… te (mo) ii desu ka./… te
  (mo) ii deshoo ka. 〜て(も)いい?/〜て(も)いい
  ですか。/〜て(も)いいでしょうか。 *May I … ?*
iie いいえ *no*
iimeeru イーメール *e-mail*
ijoo 以上 *more than*
ika いか *cuttlefish, squid*
ikaga いかが *how (polite)*
  Ikaga deshita ka. いかがでしたか。 *How was
  it? (polite)*
  Ikaga desu ka. いかがですか。 *How is it?
  (polite)*
  … wa ikaga desu ka. 〜はいかがですか。
  How about … ? (polite)
iku, ikimasu 行く、行きます *to go*
  itte iru, itte imasu 行っている、行っています
  to have gone
(o)ikura (polite with o) （お）いくら *how much*
(o)ikutsu (polite with o) （お）いくつ *how many,
how old*
ima 今 *now*
ima 居間 *living room*
ima made ni 今までに *up to now*
imi 意味 *meaning*
imooto 妹 *younger sister (one's own)*
imootosan 妹さん *younger sister (someone else's)*
inchi インチ *inch*
indo インド *India*
intaanetto インターネット *internet*
inu 犬 *dog*
ippai 一杯 *full*
ipponjooshi 一本調子 *monotonous*
ippun 一分 *one minute*
Irasshaimase. いらっしゃいませ。 *Welcome
  (to our store).*

irassharu, irasshaimasu いらっしゃる、いらっしゃいます *to go, to come, to exist, there is (honorific)*

ireru, iremasu 入れる、入れます *to put into*

sarada ni ireru, sarada ni iremasu サラダに入れる、サラダに入れます *to put into a salad*

iru, imasu いる、います *to have … /there is … (animate)*

uchi ni iru, uchi ni imasu 家にいる、家にいます *to stay home*

isha 医者 *medical doctor*

isogashii 忙しい *busy*

issho ni 一緒に *together*

isu 椅子 *chair*

itadaku, itadakimasu いただく、いただきます *to eat, to drink, to receive (humble)*

… te itadaku, … te itadakimasu 〜ていただく、〜ていただきます *to receive a favor of … ing (humble)*

itai 痛い *painful*

atama ga itai, atama ga itai desu 頭が痛い、頭が痛いです *to have a headache*

nodo ga itai, nodo ga itai desu 喉が痛い、喉が痛いです *to have a sore throat*

onaka ga itai, onaka ga itai desu お腹が痛い、お腹が痛いです *to have a stomachache*

itaria イタリア *Italy*

itaria ryoori イタリア料理 *Italian cuisine*

itariago イタリア語 *Italian (language)*

itasu, itashimasu いたす、いたします *to do (humble)*

itoko 従兄弟 *cousin*

itsu いつ *when*

itsuka 五日 *fifth (day of the month)*

itsumo いつも *always*

itsutsu 五つ *five (native Japanese number)*

iu, iimasu 言う、言います *to say*

izen 以前 *before*

ja(a) じゃ(あ) *then*

jagaimo じゃがいも *potato*

jama 邪魔 *obstruction*

Ojamashimasu. お邪魔します。 *Pardon the intrusion.*

jazu ジャズ *jazz*

jiinzu ジーンズ *jeans*

jikan 時間 *time, hour(s)*

nijikan 二時間 *two hours*

jimi 地味 *sober, quiet (color)*

jimu 事務 *office (clerical) work*

jimusho 事務所 *office*

jinja 神社 *shrine*

jinjibu 人事部 *human resources department*

jisho 辞書 *dictionary*

jitsu wa 実は *actually*

jiyuu 自由 *freedom*

jiyuu 自由 *free*

jiyuujikan 自由時間 *free time*

jogingu ジョギング *jog, jogging*

joozu 上手 *skillful, good at*

jugyoo 授業 *class*

junbi 準備 *preparation*

Junbi wa ii desu ka. 準備はいいですか。 *Are you ready?*

juppun 十分 *ten minutes*

juu 十 *ten*

juu 銃 *gun*

juudoo 柔道 *judo*

juugatsu 十月 *October*

juugo 十五 *fifteen*

juuhachi 十八 *eighteen*

juuichi 十一 *eleven*

juuichigatsu 十一月 *November*

juuichiji 十一時 *eleven o'clock*

juuji 十時 *ten o'clock*

juuku 十九 *nineteen*

juukyuu 十九 *nineteen*

juunana 十七 *seventeen*

juuni 十二 *twelve*

juunigatsu 十二月 *December*

juuniji 十二時 *twelve o'clock*

juuroku 十六 *sixteen*

juusan 十三 *thirteen*

juushi 十四 *fourteen*

juushichi 十七 *seventeen*

juusu ジュース *juice, soft drink*

juuyon 十四 *fourteen*

ka か *particle (marks a question; used to express surprise)*

ka 蚊 *mosquito*

ka か *or*

kaado カード *card, credit card*

kaato カート *shopping cart*

kaban かばん *bag*

kabushikigaisha 株式会社 *joint-stock cooperation*

kachoo 課長 *section manager*

kado 角 *corner*

kaeru, kaerimasu 帰る、帰ります *to go back, to return, to go home, to come home*

kafeore カフェオレ *café au lait*

kagu 家具 *furniture*

kai 貝 *shellfish*

kaidan 階段 *stairs*

kaigi 会議 *meeting*

kaii moji 会意文字 *compound ideographic characters*

kaimono 買い物 *shopping*

kaisha 会社 *company*

kaishain 会社員 *office worker, company employee*

kakaru, kakarimasu かかる、かかります *to take (time)*

kakijun 書き順 *stroke order*

kaku 画 *stroke (for writing characters)*

kaku, kakimasu 書く、書きます *to write*

kakushu 各種 *various*

kakusuu 画数 *number of strokes*

kamau, kamaimasu 構う、構います *to mind*
　… te (mo) kamaimasen ka. 〜て（も）構いませんか。 *Do you mind … ing?*

kamera カメラ *camera*

kami 紙 *paper*

kami 髪 *hair (on the head)*

kami no ke 髪の毛 *hair (on the head)*

kamoshirenai, kamoshiremasen かもしれない、かもしれません *may (conjecture)*

… kana(a) 〜かな(あ) *I wonder …*

kanadajin カナダ人 *Canadian (person)*

kanai 家内 *wife (one's own)*

kanbi 完備 *fully furnished*

kangae 考え *idea*

kangoshi 看護師 *nurse*

kanja 患者 *patient*

kanji 漢字 *Chinese characters*

kankoku 韓国 *Korea*

kankoo 観光 *sightseeing*

kannu カンヌ *Cannes*

kanojo 彼女 *she*
　kanojo no 彼女の *her*
　kanojora 彼女ら *they (people, feminine)*
　kanojotachi 彼女達 *they (people, feminine)*

kansuru 関する *concerning, regarding*

kantan 簡単 *easy, simple*

kao 顔 *face*

kaoiro 顔色 *complexion*
　kaoiro ga warui, kaoiro ga warui desu 顔色が悪い、顔色が悪いです *to look pale*

kapuchiino カプチーノ *cappuccino*

kara から *from*
　… kara … made 〜から〜まで *from … to …*

kara から *because, so*

karaa カラー *hair dye, hair color*

karada 体、身体 *body*

karai 辛い *spicy*

kare 彼 *he*
　kare no 彼の *his*
　karera 彼ら *they (people)*

karee カレー *curry*

kariru, karimasu 借りる、借ります *to borrow*
　karate iru, karate imasu 借りている、借りています *to have borrowed*

karui 軽い *light*

Kashikomarimashita. かしこまりました。 *Certainly. (polite)*

… kashira. 〜かしら。 *I wonder …*

kashu 歌手 *singer*

kasu, kashimasu 貸す、貸します *to lend*
　kashite iru, kashite imasu 貸している、貸しています *to have lent*

kata 方 *person (polite)*

kata 肩 *shoulders*
　kata ga kotte iru, kata ga kotte imasu 肩が凝っている、肩が凝っています *to have stiff shoulders*

katakana 片仮名 *katakana characters*

katsu かつ *cutlet*

katsute かつて *formerly*

katte 勝手 *selfish*

katto カット *haircut*

kau, kaimasu 買う、買います *to buy*

kawa 川 *river*

kawaii かわいい *cute*

kawaru, kawarimasu 代わる、代わります *to replace (a person), to transfer (a phone line)*

kawaru, kawarimasu 変わる、変わります *to change*

kayoobi 火曜日 *Tuesday*

kaze 風 *wind*

kaze 風邪 *cold*
　kaze o hiku, kaze o hikimasu 風邪をひく、風邪をひきます *to catch a cold*

(go)kazoku (polite with go) （ご）家族 *family*

gonin kazoku 五人家族 *five people in a family*
ke 毛 *hair*
kedo けど *but*
kee-eegaku 経営学 *business management*
keekaku 計画 *plan*
keeken 経験 *experience*
keeki ケーキ *cake*
keeri 経理 *accounting*
keesatsu 警察 *police*
keesatsukan 警察官 *police officer*
keesee moji 形声文字 *phonetic-ideographic characters*
keetai (denwa) 携帯(電話) *cell phone*
keezai 経済 *economy*
keezaigaku 経済学 *economics*
kega 怪我 *injury*
  kega o suru, kega o shimasu 怪我をする、怪我をします *to get injured*
Kekkoo desu. 結構です。 *No, thank you.*
ken 件 *matter, case*
ken 券 *coupon, voucher*
  biiru ken ビール券 *beer gift coupon*
kendoo 剣道 *kendo*
kenmee 件名 *subject (letter, e-mail)*
kensa 検査 *examination*
kensasuru, kensashimasu 検査する、検査します *to examine*
kesa 今朝 *this morning*
ketsuatsu 血圧 *blood pressure*
  ketsuatsu ga takai, ketsuatsu ga takai desu 血圧が高い、血圧が高いです *to have high blood pressure*
  ketsuatsu ga hikui, ketsuatsu ga hikui desu 血圧が低い、血圧が低いです *to have low blood pressure*
ki 木 *tree*
kibun 気分 *feeling*
  kibun ga warui, kibun ga warui desu 気分が悪い、気分が悪いです *to feel sick*
kichinto きちんと *properly, exactly, accurately*
kiiboodo キーボード *keyboard*
kiiro 黄色 *yellow (noun)*
kiiroi 黄色い *yellow (adjective)*
kikai 機会 *chance*
kiku, kikimasu 聞く、聞きます *to listen, to inquire*
kiku, kikimasu 聴く、聴きます *to listen (with focus, such as listening to music)*

kinmu 勤務 *work (fml.)*
  kinmuchi 勤務地 *place of work*
kinoo 昨日 *yesterday*
kin-yoobi 金曜日 *Friday*
kinyuusuru, kinyuushimasu 記入する、記入します *to fill out (a form)*
kirai da, kirai desu 嫌いだ、嫌いです *to dislike*
kiree きれい *beautiful, pretty, clean*
kiru, kirimasu 切る、切ります *to cut*
kissaten 喫茶店 *coffee shop*
kitagawa 北側 *north side*
kitanai 汚い *dirty*
kiyaku 規約 *agreement, rules*
kiyoo 起用 *promotion, appointment*
kochira こちら *this, this way (polite)*
kodomo 子供 *child*
kodomosan 子供さん *child (somebody else's)*
kokage 木陰 *tree shadow*
koko ここ *here*
kokonoka 九日 *ninth (day of the month)*
kokonotsu 九つ *nine (native Japanese number)*
kokoro 心 *heart*
komu, komimasu 混む、混みます *to get crowded*
  konde iru, konde imasu 混んでいる、混んでいます *to be crowded*
komugi 小麦 *wheat*
konban 今晩 *tonight*
Konban wa. こんばんは。 *Good evening.*
konbini コンビニ *convenience store*
kondo 今度 *next time, this time, shortly*
Konnichi wa. こんにちは。 *Hello./Good afternoon.*
konnyaku こんにゃく *konnyaku potato*
kono この *this*
  kono hen ni この辺に *in this area*
  kono pen このペン *this pen*
konpyuutaa コンピューター *computer*
konsaato コンサート *concert*
konshuu 今週 *this week*
konshuumatsu 今週末 *this weekend*
kooban 交番 *police booth*
koobe 神戸 *Kobe*
koocha 紅茶 *black tea*
kooen 公園 *park*
koohii コーヒー *coffee*
kooka 効果 *effect*
kookoku 広告 *advertisement*
kookoo 高校 *high school*

kookoosee 高校生 *high school student*
koosaten 交差点 *intersection*
kootsuu 交通 *transportation*
  kootsuuhi 交通費 *transportation costs*
kopii コピー *copy*
kopiisuru, kopiishimasu コピーする、コピーします *to copy*
kore これ *this*
kore made ni これまでに *up to now*
korokke コロッケ *croquette*
koru, korimasu 凝る、凝ります *to get stiff*
  kata ga kotte iru, kata ga kotte imasu 肩が凝っている、肩が凝っています *to have stiff shoulders*
koshi 腰 *waist, hip*
koshoo 胡椒 *pepper*
kossetsusuru, kossetsushimasu 骨折する、骨折します *to break a bone*
kotae 答え *answer*
koto こと *thing*
  … koto ga aru, … koto ga arimasu 〜ことがある、〜ことがあります *to have done …, to have an experience of … ing*
  taberu koto to nomu koto 食べることと飲むこと *eating and drinking*
kotoba 言葉 *word, language*
kotoshi 今年 *this year*
ku 九 *nine*
kubaru, kubarimasu 配る、配ります *to distribute*
kuchi 口 *mouth*
kudasaru, kudasaimasu くださる、くださいます *to give (honorific)*
  … naide kudasai 〜ないでください。 *Please don't …*
  … o kudasai. 〜をください。 *Please give me …*
  … te kudasai 〜てください。 *Please …*
  … te kudasaru, … te kudasaimasu 〜てくださる、〜てくださいます *to give a favor of … ing (honorific)*
kugatsu 九月 *September*
kuji 九時 *nine o'clock*
kukkii クッキー *cookie*
kumori 曇り *cloudy*
  Kumori desu. 曇りです。 *It's cloudy.*
kuni 国 *country, nation*
kurabu クラブ *club*
kurai 暗い *dark*

kurarinetto クラリネット *clarinet*
kurashikku クラシック *classical*
kurasu クラス *class*
kurasumeeto クラスメート *classmate*
kurejitto kaado クレジットカード *credit card*
kureru, kuremasu くれる、くれます *to give*
  … te kureru, … te kuremasu 〜てくれる、〜てくれます *to give a favor of … ing*
kurisumasu クリスマス *Christmas*
kuroi 黒い *black*
kuru, kimasu 来る、来ます *to come*
  kite iru, kite imasu 来ている、来ています *to have come, to be here*
kuruma 車 *car*
kuruujingu クルージング *cruise*
kusuri 薬 *medicine*
kutsu 靴 *shoes*
kuuki 空気 *air*
kyabetsu キャベツ *cabbage*
kyaku 客 *customer, guest*
kyappu キャップ *cap*
kyonen 去年 *last year*
kyoo 今日 *today*
kyoodai 兄弟 *siblings (one's own)*
  sannin kyoodai 三人兄弟 *three children in a family*
kyookasho 教科書 *textbook*
kyooshi 教師 *teacher*
kyooto 京都 *Kyoto*
kyuu 九 *nine*
kyuubo 急募 *immediate opening*
kyuufun 九分 *nine minutes*
kyuujin (kookoku) 求人(広告) *job posting*
kyuujuu 九十 *ninety*
kyuuri きゅうり *cucumber*
(o)kyuuryoo (polite with o) (お)給料 *salary*
kyuuyo 給与 *salary*
maa maa まあまあ *so so*
maaketingu マーケティング *marketing*
machi 町 *town*
machiaishitsu 待合室 *waiting room*
mada まだ *still, yet (in negative)*
made まで *until*
  … kara … made 〜から〜まで *from … to …*
mado 窓 *window*
(… no) mae (〜の)前 *in front of …*
  mae ni 前に *before*

paatii e iku mae ni パーティーへ行く前に *before going to the party*

magaru, magarimasu 曲がる、曲がります *to turn*

mai 枚 *counter for thin flat objects*

maiban 毎晩 *every night*

mainichi 毎日 *every day*

mairu, mairimasu 参る、参ります *to go, to come (humble)*

majime 真面目 *earnest*

maku, makimasu 蒔く、蒔きます *to plant (seeds)*

mannenhitsu 万年筆 *fountain pen*

manshon マンション *condominium*

… masen ka. ～ませんか。 *Why don't we … ?*

… mashoo. ～ましょう。 *Let's …*

… mashoo ka. ～ましょうか。 *Shall we … ?*

massugu まっすぐ *straight*

mata また *again*

mataseru, matasemasu 待たせる、待たせます *to keep someone waiting*

　Omatase itashimashita. お待たせいたしました。 *I have kept you waiting. (polite)*

matsu, machimasu 待つ、待ちます *to wait*

　Omachi kudasai. お待ちください。 *Please wait. (polite)*

　Omachishite orimasu. お待ちしております。 *I/We will be waiting for you. (polite)*

matto マット *mat*

mausu マウス *mouse*

(… no) mawari (～の)まわり *around …*

mazui まずい *bad (taste)*

me 目 *eye*

… me ～目 *the … th/the … rd*

　futatsume 二つ目 *second*

　hitotsume 一つ目 *first*

　ichinichime 一日目 *the first day*

　mittsume 三つ目 *third*

medium エム *medium (size)*

　emu de ii エムでいい *medium is okay*

mee 名 *counter for customers in restaurants, clubs, bars (polite)*

　nimeesama 二名様 *two people (polite)*

meeru メール *e-mail*

meetoru メートル *meter*

mekishiko メキシコ *Mexico*

mekishiko ryoori メキシコ料理 *Mexican cuisine*

mekishikojin メキシコ人 *Mexican (person)*

memai めまい *dizziness*

memai ga suru, memai ga shimasu めまいがする、めまいがします *to feel dizzy*

men 綿 *cotton*

mensetsu 面接 *interview*

menyuu メニュー *menu*

meotojawan 夫婦茶碗 *"his and hers" rice bowl set*

meshiagaru, meshiagarimasu 召し上がる、召し上がります *to eat, to drink (honorific)*

michi 道 *street, road*

midori 緑 *green (noun)*

mieru, miemasu 見える、見えます *to be able to be seen, to be visible*

migaku, migakimasu 磨く、磨きます *to brush, to polish*

migi 右 *right*

migigawa 右側 *right side*

miitingu ミーティング *meeting*

mijikai 短い *short*

mikka 三日 *third (day of the month)*

mikkusu sarada ミックスサラダ *mixed salad*

mimi 耳 *ear*

minamigawa 南側 *south side*

minasan 皆さん *everyone (polite)*

minna みんな *everyone*

miru, mimasu 見る、見ます *to watch, to look*

miru, mimasu 診る、診ます *to check, to examine*

… te miru, … te mimasu ～てみる、～てみます *to try … ing*

miruku ミルク *milk*

mise 店 *store*

miso 味噌 *soy bean paste*

(o)misoshiru (polite with o) (お)味噌汁 *miso soup*

mittsu 三つ *three (native Japanese number)*

(o) mizu (polite with o) (お)水 *water*

mo も *also, too, both … and*

modoru, modorimasu 戻る、戻ります *to return*

　modotte iru, modotte imasu 戻っている、戻っています *to have returned*

mokuyoobi 木曜日 *Thursday*

mondai 問題 *problem*

monitaa モニター *monitor*

mono 者 *person (humble)*

　tantoo no mono 担当の者 *a person in charge*

moo もう *already*

　moo ichido もう一度 *once more*

　moo sukoshi もう少し *a little more*

Mooshiwake arimasen. 申し訳ありません *to* nekutai ネクタイ

Mooshiwake arimasen. 申し訳ありません。
I'm very sorry. (polite)

Mooshiwake gozaimasen. 申し訳ございません。
I'm very sorry. (polite)

moosu, mooshimasu 申す、申します *to say*
(humble)

morau, moraimasu もらう、もらいます *to receive*
… te morau, … te moraimasu 〜てもらう、〜て
もらいます *to receive a favor of … ing*

mori 森 *forest*

moshi もし *if, in case*
moshi yokattara もし良かったら *if it's okay, if*
you like

moshi moshi もしもし *hello (on the phone)*

motsu, mochimasu 持つ、持ちます *to hold,*
to own
kamera o motte dekakeru, kamera o motte
dekakemasu カメラを持って出掛ける、カメラを
持って出掛けます *to go out with a camera*
motte iru, motte imasu 持っている、持ってい
ます *to have*
omochi desu ka. お持ちですか。 *Do you have …*
? (polite)

motte iku, motte ikimasu 持って行く、持って行き
ます *to take something (inanimate object)*

motte kuru, motte kimasu 持って来る、持って来
ます *to bring something (inanimate object)*

motto もっと *more*

muika 六日 *sixth (day of the month)*

muji 無地 *solid (color)*

(… no) mukai (gawa) (〜の)向かい(側) *across*
from …

mukashimukashi 昔々 *once upon a time*

mune 胸 *chest*

musuko 息子 *son (one's own)*

musukosan 息子さん *son (someone else's)*

musume 娘 *daughter (one's own)*

musumesan 娘さん *daughter (someone else's)*

muttsu 六つ *six (native Japanese number)*

muurugai ムール貝 *mussel*

muzukashii 難しい *difficult*

myaku 脈 *pulse*

myoo 妙 *strange*

nagai 長い *long*

naifu ナイフ *knife*

(… no) naka (〜の)中 *inside …, among …*

nakanaka なかなか *not easily, not readily (in*
negative); quite (in affirmative)

nakanaka ii なかなかいい *quite good*

nakanaka konai, nakanaka kimasen なかなか来
ない、なかなか来ません *to not come readily*

… nakereba ikenai, … nakereba ikemasen 〜
なければいけない、〜なければいけません
to have to …

… nakereba naranai, … nakereba narimasen
〜なければならない、〜なければなりません *to*
have to …

… nakute wa ikenai, … nakute wa ikemasen
〜なくてはいけない、〜なくてはいけません *to have*
to …

… nakute wa naranai, … nakute wa
narimasen 〜なくてはならない、〜なくてはなりま
せん *to have to …*

(o)namae (polite with o) (お)名前 *name*
Onamae wa? お名前は？ *What's your name?*

nan(i) 何 *what*
nani ka 何か *something*
nani mo (+ negative) 何も *nothing*

nana 七 *seven*

nanafun 七分 *seven minutes*

nanajuu 七十 *seventy*

nanatsu 七つ *seven (native Japanese number)*

nande なんで *why (infml.)*

nando ka 何度か *several times*

nando mo 何度も *many times*

nanji 何時 *what time*

nanoka 七日 *seventh (day of the month)*

narau, naraimasu 習う、習います *to take lessons*
on

naru, narimasu なる、なります *to become*
natte iru, natte imasu なっている、なってい
ます *to have become*
oyasuku natte imasu お安くなっています *has*
been priced down (polite)

nasaru, nasaimasu なさる、なさいます *to do*
(honorific)

nasu なす *eggplant*

natsu 夏 *summer*

natsu yasumi 夏休み *summer vacation*

naze なぜ *why*

ne ね *particle (used to seek agreement; express*
agreement; confirm information)

nedan 値段 *price*

nekki 熱気 *hot air*

neko 猫 *cat*

nekutai ネクタイ *necktie*

nen 年 *year*
  ichinenkan 一年間 *for a year*
nenree 年齢 *age*
nenzasuru, nenzashimasu 捻挫する、捻挫します *to have a sprain*
neru, nemasu 寝る、寝ます *to go to sleep, to sleep*
netsu 熱 *fever*
  netsu ga aru, netsu ga arimasu 熱がある、熱があります *to have a fever*
  netsu o hakaru, netsu o hakarimasu 熱を測る、熱を測ります *to check one's temperature*
netsuki 寝つき *wake-to-sleep transition*
ni 二 *two*
ni に *particle (marks a location; marks time, day, month; marks a purpose, goal)*
nichiyoobi 日曜日 *Sunday*
nifun 二分 *two minutes*
nigai 苦い *bitter*
nigate 苦手 *poor at*
nigatsu 二月 *February*
nigiyaka 賑やか *lively*
nihon 日本 *Japan*
nihongo 日本語 *Japanese (language)*
nihonjin 日本人 *Japanese (person)*
nihonshu 日本酒 *sake*
niji 二時 *two o'clock*
nijuu 二十 *twenty*
niku 肉 *meat*
nin 人 *counter for people*
ninki 人気 *popularity*
  ninki ga aru, ninki ga arimasu 人気がある、人気があります *to be popular*
nishigawa 西側 *west side*
niwa 庭 *garden, yard*
nizakana 煮魚 *boiled fish*
no の *particle (connects nouns)*
no の *one (indefinite pronoun)*
  amerika no アメリカの *the American one*
  muji no 無地の *the one in solid color*
node ので *because, since*
nodo 喉 *throat*
  nodo ga itai, nodo ga itai desu 喉が痛い、喉が痛いです *to have a sore throat*
nomimono 飲み物 *drink*
noo 脳 *brain*
nooto ノート *notebook*
noru, norimasu 乗る、乗ります *to ride, to get on*

noru, norimasu 載る、載ります *to get into, to be put on*
  notte iru, notte imasu 載っている、載っています *to have been put on*
  nugu, nugimasu 脱ぐ、脱ぎます *to take off (shoes, clothes)*
nyoo 尿 *urine*
nyuugakusuru, nyuugakushimasu 入学する、入学します *to enter school*
nyuuinsuru, nyuuinshimasu 入院する、入院します *to be hospitalized*
nyuuyooku ニューヨーク *New York*
o を *particle (marks a direct object)*
obaasan おばあさん *grandmother (someone else's)*
ocha お茶 *Japanese tea*
odoru, odorimasu 踊る、踊ります *to dance*
ofisu オフィス *office*
ofuro お風呂 *bath*
  ofuro ni hairu, ofuro ni hairimasu お風呂に入る、お風呂に入ります *to take a bath*
ogawa 小川 *stream*
Ohayoo gozaimasu. おはようございます。 *Good morning.*
oishii おいしい *delicious*
ojiisan おじいさん *grandfather (someone else's)*
ojoosan お嬢さん *daughter (someone else's)*
okaasan お母さん *mother (someone else's)*
okaeshi お返し *return, change (polite)*
Okagesama de. おかげさまで。 *I'm fine. (polite)*
okaikee お会計 *check*
okane お金 *money*
okazu おかず *dish eaten with cooked rice*
okinawa 沖縄 *Okinawa*
okiru, okimasu 起きる、起きます *to get up*
okosan お子さん *child (someone else's)*
oku, okimasu 置く、置きます *to put*
  ... te oku, ... te okimasu 〜ておく、〜ておきます *to do ... beforehand*
okureru, okuremasu 遅れる、遅れます *to be late*
okusan 奥さん *wife (someone else's)*
okyakusan, okyakusama お客さん、お客さま *customer, guest (polite)*
ome ni kakaru, ome ni kakarimasu お目にかかる、お目にかかります *to see, to meet (humble)*
Omedetoo gozaimasu. おめでとうございます。 *Congratulations.*
omoi 重い *heavy*

omoshiroi 面白い *interesting*
omou, omoimasu 思う、思います *to think*
onaji 同じ *same*
onaka お腹 *belly, abdomen*
  onaka ga itai, onaka ga itai desu お腹が痛い、お腹が痛いです *to have a stomachache*
oneesan お姉さん *older sister (someone else's)*
onegaisuru, onegaishimasu お願いする、お願いします *to ask for*
  Onegaishimasu. お願いします。 *Please. (asking for a favor)*
  … o onegaishimasu. 〜をお願いします。 *I'd like to have …*
ongaku 音楽 *music*
oniisan お兄さん *older brother (someone else's)*
onna 女 *female*
  onna no hito 女の人 *woman*
oobo 応募 *application*
ooi 多い *many, much, a lot*
ookii 大きい *big*
oosaka 大阪 *Osaka*
oosama 王様 *king*
opushonaru tsuaa オプショナルツアー *optional tour*
orenji オレンジ *orange*
oriru, orimasu 降りる、降ります *to get off*
  orite iru, orite imasu 降りている、降りています *to have gotten off, to be off*
oru, orimasu おる、おります *to exit, there is (humble)*
oshieru, oshiemasu 教える、教えます *to teach, to tell*
osoi 遅い *late*
ossharu, osshaimasu おっしゃる、おっしゃいます *to say (honorific)*
otearai お手洗い *restroom*
otoko 男 *male*
  otoko no hito 男の人 *man*
otoosan お父さん *father (someone else's)*
otooto 弟 *younger brother (one's own)*
otootosan 弟さん *younger brother (someone else's)*
ototoi おととい *the day before yesterday*
otsuri お釣り *change*
otto 夫 *husband (one's own)*
Oyasuminasai. おやすみなさい。 *Good night.*
oyogu, oyogimasu 泳ぐ、泳ぎます *to swim*
paama パーマ *perm*

paatii パーティー *party*
pan パン *bread*
panda パンダ *panda*
pantsu パンツ *pants*
pasokon パソコン *personal computer*
pen ペン *pen*
piano ピアノ *piano*
pin ピン *pin*
pinku ピンク *pink (noun)*
piza ピザ *pizza*
poppusu ポップス *pop*
porutogarugo ポルトガル語 *Portuguese (language)*
puuru プール *pool*
rainen 来年 *next year*
raishuu 来週 *next week*
raito ライト *light*
rajio ラジオ *radio*
ree 零 *zero*
reezooko 冷蔵庫 *refrigerator*
renrakusuru, renrakushimasu 連絡する、連絡します *to contact*
renshuusuru, renshuushimasu 練習する、練習します *to practice*
repooto レポート *report*
resutoran レストラン *restaurant*
retasu レタス *lettuce*
ringo りんご *apple*
rinku リンク *link, rink*
rirakkusususu, rirakkusushimasu リラックスする、リラックスします *to relax*
rirekisho 履歴書 *curriculum vitae, resume*
riyuu 理由 *reason*
rokku ロック *rock*
roku 六 *six*
rokugatsu 六月 *June*
rokuji 六時 *six o'clock*
rokujuu 六十 *sixty*
rooka 廊下 *hallway*
rooma ローマ *Rome*
roosoku 蝋燭 *candle*
roppun 六分 *six minutes*
ryakugo 略語 *abbreviation*
ryokoo 旅行 *travel*
ryokoosha 旅行社 *travel company*
ryoo 量 *amount*
ryoori 料理 *cooking, cuisine*

ryoori o suru, ryoori o shimasu 料理をする、料理をします *to cook*
(go)ryooshin (polite with go) (ご)両親 *parents*
ryuu 竜 *dragon*
ryuugakusuru, ryuugakushimasu 留学する、留学します *to study abroad*
sagasu, sagashimasu 探す、探します *to look for*
saikin 最近 *recently*
saizu サイズ *size*
sakana 魚 *fish*
(o)sake (polite with o) (お)酒 *alcoholic beverage*
sakkaa サッカー *soccer*
sama 様 *Mr., Ms. (polite)*
samui 寒い *cold (weather, room temperature)*
samuke 寒気 *chill*
　samuke ga suru, samuke ga shimasu 寒気がする、寒気がします *to have chills*
san さん *Mr., Ms.*
san 三 *three*
sangatsu 三月 *March*
sanji 三時 *three o'clock*
sanjuppun 三十分 *thirty minutes*
sanjuu 三十 *thirty*
sanpun 三分 *three minutes*
sarada サラダ *salad*
sashiageru, sashiagemasu さしあげる、さしあげます *to give (humble)*
　… te sashiageru, … te sashiagemasu ～てさしあげる、～てさしあげます *to give a favor of … ing (humble)*
sashimi 刺身 *sliced raw fish*
satoo 砂糖 *sugar*
satsu 冊 *counter for bound objects*
Sayoonara. さようなら。 *Goodbye.*
seekatsu 生活 *everyday life*
seetaa セーター *sweater*
seeyakugaisha 製薬会社 *pharmaceutical company*
semai 狭い *narrow*
seminaa セミナー *seminar*
sen 千 *thousand*
　sen en 千円 *thousand yen*
senjitsu 先日 *the other day*
senmenjo 洗面所 *area with a wash stand*
sensee 先生 *teacher*
　Tanaka sensee 田中先生 *Prof./Dr. Tanaka*
senshuu 先週 *last week*
sentakuki 洗濯機 *washing machine*

setsumee 説明 *description*
shaabetto シャーベット *sherbet*
shachoo 社長 *president of a company*
shain 社員 *company employee*
shakai 社会 *society*
　shakaihoken 社会保険 *social insurance*
shakoo dansu 社交ダンス *ballroom daincing*
shashin 写真 *photograph, photography*
shatsu シャツ *shirt*
shawaa シャワー *shower*
　shawaa o abiru, shawaa o abimasu シャワーを浴びる、シャワーを浴びます *to take a shower*
sheedo シェード *shade*
shepaado シェパード *Shepherd*
shi 四 *four*
shiai 試合 *game (of sport)*
shibaraku しばらく *for a while*
shichi 七 *seven*
shichigatsu 七月 *July*
shichiji 七時 *seven o'clock*
shigatsu 四月 *April*
(o)shigoto (polite with o) (お)仕事 *job, work*
(o)shiharai (polite with o) (お)支払い *payment*
shiifuudo sarada シーフードサラダ *seafood salad*
shiji moji 指示文字 *indicative characters*
shika (+ negative) しか *only*
shikago シカゴ *Chicago*
shikaku 資格 *qualification*
shiken 試験 *exam*
shikyuusuru, shikyuushimasu 支給する、支給します *to provide, to cover*
shima 縞 *stripes*
… te shimau, … te shimaimasu ～てしまう、～てしまいます *to finish … ing, to have done …*
shimeru, shimemasu 閉める、閉めます *to close (transitive verb)*
shinbun 新聞 *newspaper*
shingoo 信号 *traffic light*
　shingoo no temae 信号の手前 *before the traffic light*
shinkansen 新幹線 *Japanese bullet train*
shinrigaku 心理学 *psychology*
shinryoojo 診療所 *clinic*
shinsatsu 診察 *medical consultation*
shinsatsushitsu 診察室 *medical consulting room*
(go)shinseki (polite with go) (ご)親戚 *relatives*
shinsetsu 親切 *kind, generous*
shinshitsu 寝室 *bedroom*

shinu, shinimasu 死ぬ、死にます *to die*
  shinde iru, shinde imasu 死んでいる、死んでいます *to be dead*
shinzoo 心臓 *heart*
shio 塩 *salt*
shiokarai 塩辛い *salty*
shiro wain 白ワイン *white wine*
shiroi 白い *white*
shiru, shirimasu 知る、知ります *to know*
  shitteimasu 知っています *I know*
  shirimasen 知りません *I don't know*
(… no) shita (〜の)下 *under …*
shitee 師弟 *teacher and student*
shitee 子弟 *children (fml.)*
shitsumon 質問 *question*
shitsuree 失礼 *impoliteness, rudeness*
  Shitsuree itashimasu 失礼いたします。 *Good-bye. (polite)*
  Shitsureeshimasu. 失礼します。 *Good-bye. (polite)*
shizuka 静か *quiet*
shokugyoo 職業 *occupation*
shokuji 食事 *meal*
shokuyoku 食欲 *appetite*
  shokuyoku ga aru, shokuyoku ga arimasu 食欲がある、食欲があります *to have an appetite*
shoobooshi 消防士 *firefighter*
shoogakkoo 小学校 *elementary school*
shookee moji 象形文字 *pictorial characters*
shookyuu 昇給 *salary increase*
shoorai 将来 *future*
shoosetsu 小説 *novel*
shooshoo 少々 *a few, a little*
shooto keeki ショートケーキ *shortcake*
shooyo 賞与 *bonus, reward*
shooyu 醤油 *soy sauce*
shoshin 初診 *the first medical consultation*
shucchoo 出張 *business trip*
shufu 主婦 *housewife*
shujin 主人 *husband (one's own)*
shujutsu 手術 *operation, surgery*
shujutsusuru, shujutsushimasu 手術する、手術します *to operate*
shukudai 宿題 *homework*
shumi 趣味 *hobby*
(go)shusshin (polite with go) (ご)出身 *place of origin, hometown*
shuu 週 *week*

isshuukan 一週間 *a week*
shuumatsu 週末 *weekend*
sobo 祖母 *grandmother (one's own)*
sochira そちら *that, that way (far from the speaker but close to the listener) (polite)*
sofaa ソファー *sofa*
sofu 祖父 *grandfather (one's own)*
sofuto ソフト *software*
sofutowea ソフトウェア *software*
soko そこ *there (far from the speaker but close to the listener)*
sono その *that (far from the speaker but close to the listener); its*
  sono pen そのペン *that pen*
soo そう *so*
  Soo da naa. そうだなあ。 *Let me see.*
  Soo desu. そうです。 *That's right.*
  Soo desu ka. そうですか。 *Is that so?/Really? (rising intonation)/I see. (falling intonation)*
  Soo desu ne. そうですね。 *Yes, it is./Let me see./That's right. (falling intonation)/Right? (rising intonation)*
  Soo desu yo. そうですよ。 *That's right.*
  Soo ka. そうか。 *I see.*
  Soo shimashoo! そうしましょう！ *Let's do that!*
  soo suru, soo shimasu そうする、そうします *to do so*
soojisuru, soojishimasu 掃除する、掃除します *to clean*
sooshinsha 送信者 *(sent) from*
soosoo 早々 *promptly*
sora 空 *sky*
sore それ *that (far from the speaker but close to the listener); it (subject pronoun)*
  sorera それら *they (inanimate)*
sorede それで *so, for that reason*
sorede wa それでは *then*
  Sorede wa mata. それではまた。 *See you then./See you later.*
  sore ja(a) それじゃ(あ) *then (infml.)*
  Sore ja(a) mata. それじゃ(あ)また。 *See you then./See you later. (infml.)*
sorekara それから *and then*
soshite そして *and, and then*
sotsugyoo 卒業 *graduation*
sotsugyoosuru, sotsugyooshimasu 卒業する、卒業します *to graduate*
sugiru, sugimasu すぎる、すぎます *too, too much*

sugoi すごい *amazing*
suiee 水泳 *swimming*
suimin 睡眠 *sleep*
　suimin o toru, suimin o torimasu 睡眠をとる、睡眠をとります *to get some sleep*
suiyoobi 水曜日 *Wednesday*
sukaafu スカーフ *scarf*
sukaato スカート *skirt*
sukejuuru スケジュール *schedule*
suki da, suki desu 好きだ、好きです *to like*
sukii スキー *ski, skiing*
sukoshi 少し *a little*
　moo sukoshi もう少し *a little more*
Sumimasen. すみません。 *Excuse me./I'm sorry./Sorry for the trouble.*
sumoo 相撲 *sumo wrestling*
supagetti スパゲッティ *spaghetti*
supein スペイン *Spain*
supein ryoori スペイン料理 *Spanish cuisine*
supeingo スペイン語 *Spanish (language)*
supeinjin スペイン人 *Spanish (person)*
supootsu スポーツ *sport*
　suppootsu o suru, supootsu o shimasu スポーツをする、スポーツをします *to play sports*
suppai すっぱい *sour*
supuun スプーン *spoon*
suru, shimasu する、します *to do*
　… ni suru, … ni shimasu ～にする、～にします *to decide on …*
sushi 寿司 *sushi*
sutoresu ストレス *stress*
　sutoresu ga tamatte iru, sutoresu ga tamatte imasu ストレスが溜まっている、ストレスが溜まっています *to be under a lot of stress*
suu, suimasu 吸う、吸います *to inhale*
　tabako o suu, tabako o suimasu 煙草を吸う、煙草を吸います *to smoke a cigarette*
suugaku 数学 *mathematics*
suupaa スーパー *supermarket*
suutsukeesu スーツケース *suitcase*
suwaru, suwarimasu 座る、座ります *to sit down*
suzushii 涼しい *cool*
tabako 煙草 *tobacco, cigarette*
　tabako o suu, tabako o suimasu 煙草を吸う、煙草を吸います *to smoke a cigarette*
tabemono 食べ物 *food*
taberu, tabemasu 食べる、食べます *to eat*
tabun 多分 *perhaps, probably*

tai, tai desu たい、たいです *to want to*
taiboku 大木 *big tree*
taifuu 台風 *typhoon*
taiguu 待遇 *treatment, labor conditions*
taihen 大変 *hard, very*
taiinsuru, taiinshimasu 退院する、退院します *to leave the hospital, to be released from hospital*
taimuzu sukuea タイムズスクエア *Times Square*
taisetsu 大切 *important*
takai 高い *high, tall, expensive*
tako たこ *octopus*
takusan たくさん *a lot, many, much*
takushii タクシー *taxi*
tamago 卵 *egg*
tamanegi たまねぎ *onion*
tamani たまに *once in a while*
tamaru, tamarimasu 溜まる、溜まります *to accumulate*
　sutoresu ga tamatte iru, sutoresu ga tamatte imasu ストレスが溜まっている、ストレスが溜まっています *to be under a lot of stress*
tane 種 *seed*
tanjoobi 誕生日 *birthday*
tanoshii 楽しい *enjoyable, fun*
tanoshimi ni suru, tanoshimi ni shimasu 楽しみにする、楽しみにします *to look forward*
tansu たんす *chest of drawers*
tantoo 担当 *being in charge*
　tantoo no mono 担当の者 *a person in charge*
tara たら *if, when (conjunction)*
tarinai, tarimasen 足りない、足りません *to be insufficient, to be short*
tataku, tatakimasu たたく、たたきます *to play (a percussion instrument)*
tatemono 建物 *building*
tatsu, tachimasu 立つ、立ちます *to stand up*
tazuneru, tazunemasu 訪ねる、訪ねます *to visit*
te 手 *hand*
teeburu テーブル *table*
teeshoku 定食 *prefix meal*
tegami 手紙 *letter*
temae 手前 *before, this side*
　shingoo no temae 信号の手前 *before the traffic light*
ten-in 店員 *store clerk*
tenisu テニス *tennis*
tenisu kooto テニスコート *tennis court*
tenjoo 天井 *ceiling*

Glossary

231

tenjooin 添乗員 *tour guide*
tenpura 天ぷら *tempura*
tenpusuru, tenpushimasu 添付する、添付します
　to attach (a document)
(o)tera (polie with o) (お)寺 *temple*
terebi テレビ *television*
tiishatsu ティーシャツ（Tシャツ）　*T-shirt*
to と　*and, with; when, if; that (conjunction)*
tochi 土地　*land*
(o)toiawase (polite wih o)
　(お)問い合わせ　*inquiry*
toire トイレ　*toilet*
tokee 時計　*watch, clock*
toki 時　*when (conjunction)*
tokidoki 時々　*sometimes*
tokoro 所　*place*
toku 徳　*virtue*
toku ni 特に　*especially*
tokugi 特技　*special ability, special skill*
tokui 得意　*good at*
tomato トマト　*tomato*
tomodachi 友達　*friend*
(… no) tonari (〜の)隣　*next to …*
tonneru トンネル　*tunnel*
too 十　*ten (native Japanese number)*
tooi 遠い　*far*
tooka 十日　*tenth (day of the month)*
tookushoo トークショー　*talk show*
Tookyoo 東京　*Tokyo*
toonyuu 豆乳　*soy milk*
toriniku 鶏肉　*chicken*
toru, torimasu 撮る、撮ります　*to take (photos)*
toshokan 図書館　*library*
totemo とても　*very, very much*
tsuaagaido ツアーガイド　*tour guide*
tsuchi 土　*soil*
tsuitachi 一日　*first (day of the month)*
(… ni) tsuite (〜に) ついて　*about …*
tsukau, tsukaimasu 使う、使います　*to use*
tsukeru, tsukemasu 点ける、点けます　*to light*
tsuki 月　*moon*
tsuku, tsukimasu 着く、着きます　*to arrive*
tsukue 机　*desk*
tsukuru, tsukurimasu 作る、作ります　*to make*
tsuma 妻　*wife (one's own)*
tsumaranai つまらない　*boring*
tsumetai 冷たい　*cold (to the touch)*

tsurete iku, tsurete ikimasu 連れて行く、連れて
　行きます　*to take someone or animal*
tsurete kuru, tsurete kimasu 連れて来る、連れて
　来ます　*to bring someone or animal*
tsuyoi 強い　*strong*
uchi 家　*house, one's home, one's family*
　uchi ni iru, uchi ni imasu 家にいる、家にい
　　ます　*to stay home*
ude 腕　*arm*
(… no) ue (〜の)上　*on, above …*
ueru, uemasu 植える、植えます　*to plant*
ukeru, ukemasu 受ける、受けます　*to take*
　shinsatsu o ukeru, shinsatsu o ukemasu 診
　　察を受ける、診察を受けます　*to take a medical
　　consultation, to consult a physician*
uketsuke 受付　*reception desk, information desk,
　front desk*
uketsukegakari 受付係　*receptionist*
umi 海　*ocean*
un うん　*yes (infml.)*
unagi うなぎ　*eel*
unajuu うな重　*broiled eel on rice*
undoo 運動　*exercise*
undoosuru, undooshimasu 運動する、運動し
　ます　*to exercise*
urusai うるさい　*noisy*
(… no) ushiro (〜の)後ろ　*behind …*
uso 嘘　*lie*
　uso o tsuku, uso o tsukimasu 嘘をつく、嘘をつ
　　きます　*to tell a lie*
uun ううん　*Well …*
uuru ウール　*wool*
　uuru hyakupaasento ウール100パーセント
　　100% wool
wa は　*particle (marks a topic)*
waapuro ワープロ　*word processor*
wafuu 和風　*Japanese style*
wain ワイン　*wine*
　aka wain 赤ワイン　*red wine*
　shiro wain 白ワイン　*white wine*
wakai 若い　*young*
wakaru, wakarimasu 分かる、分かります
　to understand
　Wakarimashita. 分かりました。　*I got it.*
warui 悪い　*bad*
wataru, watarimasu 渡る、渡ります　*to cross*
watashi 私　*I*
　watashi no 私の　*my*

watashitachi 私達 *we*

webudezainaa ウェブデザイナー *web designer*

weeruzu ウェールズ *Wales*

weitoresu ウエイトレス *waitress*

windooshoppingu ウィンドーショッピング *window shopping*

ya や *and*

yakizakana 焼き魚 *broiled fish*

yakyuu 野球 *baseball*

yama 山 *mountain*

yappari やっぱり *after all, as expected*

yaru, yarimasu やる、やります *to give (to a plant, an animal), to do (infml.)*

yasai 野菜 *vegetable*

yasashii 易しい *easy*

yasashii 優しい *kind, gentle*

yasui 安い *cheap*
　oyasuku nattte imasu お安くなっています *has been priced down (polite)*

yasumi 休み *day off, holiday, vacation*

yasumu, yasumimasu 休む、休みます *to take some rest, to be absent, to take a day off*
　kaisha o yasumu, kaisha o yasumimasu 会社を休む、会社を休みます *to take a day off from work*

yattsu 八つ *eight (native Japanese number)*

yo よ *particle (used to make an assertion)*

yobu, yobimasu 呼ぶ、呼びます *to call*

yoji 四時 *four o'clock*

yokka 四日 *fourth (day of the month)*

(... no) yoko (〜の)横 *the side of ...*

yoku よく *often, well*
　Yoku dekimashita. よくできました。 *Well done.*

yokushitsu 浴室 *bathroom*

yomu, yomimasu 読む、読みます *to read*

yon 四 *four*

yonfun 四分 *four minutes*

yonjuu 四十 *forty*

yonpun 四分 *four minutes*

yoochien 幼稚園 *kindergarden*

yoofuu 洋風 *Western style*

yooi 用意 *preparation*

yooka 八日 *eighth (day of the month)*

Yookoso. ようこそ。 *Welcome.*

yooshi 用紙 *form (to fill out)*

... yori ...〜より〜 *more ... than ...*

yorokonde ... 喜んで〜 *to be glad to ...*

yoroshii よろしい *good (polite)*

... te (mo) yoroshii deshoo ka. 〜て(も)よろしいでしょうか。 *May I ... ? (polite)*

... te (mo) yoroshii desu ka. 〜て(も)よろしいですか。 *May I ... ? (polite)*

yoroshii desu ka. よろしいですか。 *Is it okay? (polite)*

yoroshikattara よろしかったら *if it's okay, if you like (polite)*

yoru 夜 *evening, night*

yottsu 四つ *four (native Japanese number)*

yoyaku 予約 *appointment, reservation*

yoyakusuru, yoyakushimasu 予約する、予約します *to make an appointment, to make a reservation*

yudetamago ゆで卵 *boiled egg*

yuki 雪 *snow*
　Yuki desu. 雪です。 *It's snowing.*
　Yuki ga futte imasu. 雪が降っています。 *It's snowing.*

yukkuri ゆっくり *slowly*

yuubinkyoku 郵便局 *post office*

yuugata 夕方 *early evening*

yuugohan 夕ご飯 *dinner (infml.)*

yuuhan 夕飯 *dinner*

yuujin 友人 *friend (fml.)*

yuumee 有名 *famous*

yuushoku 夕食 *dinner (fml.)*

yuusoosuru, yuusooshimasu 郵送する、郵送します *to mail*

zangyoosuru, zangyooshimasu 残業する、残業します *to work overtime*

zasshi 雑誌 *magazine*

zehi 是非 *by all means, at any cost*

zen 禅 *zen*

zenbu 全部 *all*
　zenbu de 全部で *all together*

zenzen (+ negative) 全然 *not at all*

zero ゼロ *zero*

zubon ズボン *pants*

zutsu ずつ *each*

zutsuu 頭痛 *headache*
　zutsuu ga suru, zutsuu ga shimasu 頭痛がする、頭痛がします *to have a headache*

English-Japanese
A

a few *shooshoo* 少々

a little *chotto, shooshoo, sukoshi* ちょっと、少々、少し

a little more *moo sukoshi* もう少し

a lot *ooi, takusan* 多い、たくさん

a.m. *gozen* 午前

abbreviation *ryakugo* 略語

abdomen *hara, onaka* 腹、お腹

able (to be) *mieru, miemasu* 見える、見えます

about *goro, gurai* 頃、ぐらい

　about... *(... ni) tsuite* (〜に)ついて

above... *(... no) ue* (〜の)上

absent (to be) *yasumu, yasumimasu* 休む、休みます

accompaniment *dookoo* 同行

accounting *keeri* 経理

accumulate (to) *tamaru, tamarimasu* 溜まる、溜まります

across from... *(... no) mukai (gawa)* (〜の)向かい(側)

actually *jitsu wa* 実は

advertisement *kookoku* 広告

after *ato de, go* 後で、後

　after leaving a restaurant *resutoran o deta ato de* レストランを出た後で

after all *yappari* やっぱり

afternoon *gogo* 午後

again *mata* また

age *nenree* 年齢

agreement *kiyaku* 規約

ah *aa* ああ

air *kuuki* 空気

　hot air *nekki* 熱気

airplane *hikooki* 飛行機

alcoholic beverage *(o)sake (polite with o)* (お)酒

all *zenbu* 全部

　all together *zenbu de* 全部で

　not at all *zenzen (+ negative)* 全然

　all right *daijoobu* 大丈夫

allergy *arerugii* アレルギー

already *moo* もう

also *mo* も

always *itsumo* いつも

amazing *sugoi* すごい

American *amerikajin (person)* アメリカ人

among... *(... no) naka* (〜の)中

amount *ryoo* 量

and *soshite, to, ya* そして、と、や

and then *sorekara, soshite* それから、そして

anemia *hinketsu* 貧血

answer *kotae* 答え

apartment *apaato* アパート

appetite *shokuyoku* 食欲

　have an appetite (to): *shokuyoku ga aru, shokuyoku ga arimasu* 食欲がある、食欲があります

apple *ringo* りんご

application *oobo* 応募

appointment *kiyoo, yoyaku* 起用、予約

　make an appointment (to) *yoyakusuru, yoyakushimasu* 予約する、予約します

approximately *goro, gurai* 頃、ぐらい

April *shigatsu* 四月

arm *ude* 腕

around... *(... no) mawari* (〜の)まわり

arrive (to) *tsuku, tsukimasu* 着く、着きます

arriving... *... chaku* 〜着

　arriving in Naha *naha chaku* 那覇着

as expected *yappari* やっぱり

ask for (to) *onegaisuru, onegaishimasu* お願いする、お願いします

assistant *ashisutanto* アシスタント

at any cost *zehi* 是非

attach (a document) (to) *tenpusuru, tenpushimasu* 添付する、添付します

attend (to) *deru, demasu* 出る、出ます

　attend... (to) *... ni deru* 〜に出る

August *hachigatsu* 八月

autumn *aki* 秋

bad *warui, mazui (taste)* 悪い、まずい

bag *baggu, kaban* バッグ、かばん

ball *booru* ボール

ballpoint pen *boorupen* ボールペン

ballroom dancing *shakoo dansu* 社交ダンス

bank *ginkoo* 銀行

bank clerk *ginkooin* 銀行員

bar *baa* バー

baseball *yakyuu* 野球

basketball *basukettobooru* バスケットボール

bat *batto* バット

bath *ofuro* お風呂

take a bath (to) *ofuro ni hairu, ofuro ni hairimasu* お風呂に入る、お風呂に入ります

bathroom *yokushitsu* 浴室

be (to) *da, desu ; ... de gozaimasu. (polite)* だ、です;〜でございます。

beach *biichi* ビーチ

Beaujolais nouveau *bojoreenuuboo* ボジョレーヌーボー

beautiful *kiree* きれい

beauty salon *biyooin* 美容院

because *node, kara* ので、から

become (to) *naru, narimasu* なる、なります

have become (to) *natte iru, natte imasu* なっている、なっています

bed *beddo* ベッド

bedroom *shinshitsu* 寝室

beef *gyuuniku* 牛肉

beer *biiru* ビール

beer gift coupon *biiru ken* ビール券

before *izen, mae ni, temae* 以前、前に、手前

before going the party *paatii e iku mae ni* パーティーへ行く前に

before the traffic light: *shingoo no temae* 信号の手前

behind ... *(... no) ushiro* (〜の)後ろ

being in charge *tantoo* 担当

a person in charge *tantoo no mono* 担当の者

belly *hara, onaka* 腹、お腹

belong (to) *haitte iru, haitte imasu* 入っている、入っています

best *besuto* ベスト

the best *ichiban ii* 一番いい

You'd better ... *... (ta/da) hoo ga ii desu.* 〜(た/だ)方がいいです。

You'd better not ... *... nai hoo ga ii desu.* 〜ない方がいいです。

between (... and ...) *(... to ... no) aida* (〜と〜の)間

big *ookii* 大きい

big tree *taiboku* 大木

birthday *tanjoobi* 誕生日

bitter *nigai* 苦い

black *kuroi* 黒い

black tea *koocha* 紅茶

blood pressure *ketsuatsu* 血圧

have high blood pressure (to) *ketsuatsu ga takai, ketsuatsu ga takai desu* 血圧が高い、血圧が高いです

have low blood pressure (to) *ketsuatsu ga hikui, ketsuatsu ga hikui desu* 血圧が低い、血圧が低いです

blouse *burausu* ブラウス

blue *aoi (adjective), ao (noun)* 青い、青

body *karada* 体、身体

boiled egg *yudetamago* ゆで卵

boiled fish *nizakana* 煮魚

bone *hone* 骨

break a bone (to) *hone o oru, hone o orimasu* 骨を折る、骨を折ります

bonus *shooyo* 賞与

book *hon* 本

book store *hon-ya* 本屋

boring *tsumaranai* つまらない

borrow (to) *kariru, karimasu* 借りる、借ります

have borrowed (to) *karate iru, karate imasu* 借りている、借りています

both ... and *mo* も

bottle *bin* 瓶

brain *noo* 脳

bread *pan* パン

break a bone (to) *hone o oru, hone o orimasu; kossetsusuru, kossetsushimasu* 骨を折る、骨を折ります;骨折する、骨折します

breakfast *chooshoku (fml.), asagohan (infml.)* 朝食、朝ご飯

bright *akarui* 明るい

bring (to) *tsurete kuru, tsurete kimasu (animate); motte kuru, motte kimasu (inanimate)* 連れて来る、連れて来ます;持って来る、持って来ます

broiled eel on rice *unajuu* うな重

broiled fish *yakizakana* 焼き魚

brown *chairoi (adjective), chairo (noun)* 茶色い、茶色

brunch *buranchi* ブランチ

brush (to) *migaku, migakimasu* 磨く、磨きます

building *tatemono* 建物

high-rise building *biru* ビル

bullet train *shinkansen* 新幹線

bus *basu* バス

bus stop *basutee* バス停

business management *kee-eegaku* 経営学

business report *eegyoo hookokusho* 営業報告書

business trip *shucchoo* 出張

busy *isogashii* 忙しい

but *demo, ga, kedo* でも、が、けど

butter *bataa* バター
buy (to) *kau, kaimasu* 買う、買います
by all means *zehi* 是非
cabbage *kyabetsu* キャベツ
café au lait *kafeore* カフェオレ
cake *keeki* ケーキ
call (to) *yobu, yobimasu* 呼ぶ、呼びます
camera *kamera* カメラ
can do *dekiru, dekimasu* できる、できます
Canada *canada* カナダ
Canadian *kanadajin (person)* カナダ人
cancer *gan* 癌
candle *roosoku* 蝋燭
Cannes *kannu* カンヌ
cap *kyappu* キャップ
cappuccino *kapuchiino* カプチーノ
car *kuruma* 車
card *kaado* カード
　health insurance card *hokenshoo* 保険証
case *ken* 件
cash *genkin* 現金
cat *neko* 猫
catch a cold (to) *kaze o hiku, kaze o hikimasu* 風邪をひく、風邪をひきます
ceiling *tenjoo* 天井
cell phone *keetai (denwa)* 携帯(電話)
cello *chero* チェロ
Certainly. *Kashikomarimashita. (polite)* かしこまりました。
chain *cheen* チェーン
chair *isu* 椅子
chance *chansu, kikai* チャンス、機会
change *otsuri, okaeshi (polite)* お釣り、お返し
change (to) *kawaru, kawarimasu* 変わる、変わります
cheap *yasui* 安い
check *okaikee* お会計
check (to) *miru, mimasu* 診る、診ます
　check one's temperature (to) *netsu o hakaru, netsu o hakarimasu* 熱を測る、熱を測ります
cheese *chiizu* チーズ
chest *mune* 胸
chest of drawers *tansu* たんす
Chicago *shikago* シカゴ
chicken *toriniku* 鶏肉
chicken salad *chikin sarada* チキンサラダ

child *kodomo, kodomosan (somebody else's), okosan (somebody else's)* 子供, 子供さん, お子さん
children *shitee (fml.)* 子弟
three children in a family *sannin kyoodai* 三人兄弟
chill *samuke* 寒気
　have chills (to) *samuke ga suru, samuke ga shimasu* 寒気がする、寒気がします
China *chuugoku* 中国
Chinese *chuugokugo (language), chuugokujin (person)* 中国語、中国人
Chinese characters *kanji* 漢字
chocolate *chokoreeto* チョコレート
chopsticks *hashi* 箸
Christmas *kurisumasu* クリスマス
cigarette *tabako* 煙草
　smoke a cigarette (to) *tabako o suu, tabako o suimasu* 煙草を吸う、煙草を吸います
clarinet *kurarinetto* クラリネット
class *jugyoo, kurasu* 授業、クラス
classical *kurashikku* クラシック
classmate *kurasumeeto* クラスメート
clean *kiree* きれい
clean (to) *soojisuru, soojishimasu* 掃除する、掃除します
clinic *shinryoojo* 診療所
clock *tokee* 時計
close *chikai* 近い
close (to) *shimeru, shimemasu (transitive verb)* 閉める、閉めます
cloudy *kumori* 曇り
　It's cloudy. *Kumori desu.* 曇りです。
club *kurabu* クラブ
coffee *koohii* コーヒー
coffee shop *kissaten* 喫茶店
coincidence *guuzen* 偶然
cold *kaze* 風邪
　catch a cold (to) *kaze o hiku, kaze o hikimasu* 風邪をひく、風邪をひきます
cold *tsumetai (to the touch), samui (weather, room temperature)* 冷たい、寒い
college *daigaku* 大学
college student *daigakusee* 大学生
come (to) *kuru, kimasu; irassharu, irasshaimasu (honorific); mairu, mairimasu (humble)* 来る、来ます; いらっしゃる、いらっしゃいます; 参る、参ります

have come (to) *kite iru, kite imasu* 来ている、来ています

not come readily (to) *nakanaka konai, nakanaka kimasen* なかなか来ない、なかなか来ません

come down (to) *furu, furimasu* 降る、降ります

come home (to) *kaeru, kaerimasu* 帰る、帰ります

company *kaisha* 会社

company employee *kaishain, shain* 会社員、社員

complexion *kaoiro* 顔色

compound ideographic characters *kaii moji* 会意文字

computer *konpyuutaa* コンピューター

concerning *kansuru* 関する

concert *konsaato* コンサート

condominium *manshon* マンション

Congratulations. *Omedetoo gozaimasu.* おめでとうございます。

consult a physician (to) *shinsatsu o ukeru, shinsatsu o ukemasu* 診察を受ける、診察を受けます

contact (to) *renrakusuru, renrakushimasu* 連絡する、連絡します

convenience store *konbini* コンビニ

convenient *benri* 便利

cook (to) *ryoori o suru, ryoori o shimasu* 料理をする、料理をします

cooked rice *gohan* ご飯

cookie *kukkii* クッキー

cooking *ryoori* 料理

cool *suzushii* 涼しい

copy *kopii* コピー

copy (counter for written materials) *bu* 部

copy (to) *kopiisuru, kopiishimasu* コピーする、コピーします

corner *kado* 角

cost *hiyoo* 費用

　at any cost *zehi* 是非

　transportation costs *kootsuuhi* 交通費

cotton *men* 綿

country *kuni* 国

coupon *ken* 券

　beer gift coupon *biiru ken* ビール券

cousin *itoko* 従兄弟

cover (to) *shikyuusuru, shikyuushimasu* 支給する、支給します

credit card *kaado, kurejitto kaado* カード、クレジットカード

croquette *korokke* コロッケ

cross (to) *wataru, watarimasu* 渡る、渡ります

crowded (to be) *konde iru, konde imasu* 混んでいる、混んでいます

　get crowded (to) *komu, komimasu* 混む、混みます

cruise *kuruujingu* クルージング

cucumber *kyuuri* きゅうり

cuisine *ryoori* 料理

curriculum vitae *rirekisho* 履歴書

curry *karee* カレー

customer *kyaku, okyakusan (polite), okyakusama (polite)* 客、お客さん、お客さま

cut (to) *kiru, kirimasu* 切る、切ります

cute *kawaii* かわいい

cutlet *katsu* かつ

cuttlefish *ika* いか

dance, dancing *dansu* ダンス

dance (to) *odoru, odorimasu* 踊る、踊ります

dark *kurai* 暗い

daughter *musume (one's own), musumesan (someone else's), ojoosan (someone else's)* 娘、娘さん、お嬢さん

day *hi* 日

　some other day *gojitsu* 後日

　the day after tomorrow *asatte* あさって

　the day before yesterday *ototoi* おととい

　the first day *ichinichime* 一日目

　the other day *senjitsu* 先日

　day off *yasumi* 休み

　take a day off (to) *yasumu, yasumimasu* 休む、休みます

　take a day off from work (to) *kaisha o yasumu, kaisha o yasumimasu* 会社を休む、会社を休みます

dead (to be) *shinde iru, shinde imasu* 死んでいる、死んでいます

December *juunigatsu* 十二月

decide on ... (to) *... ni suru, ... ni shimasu* ～にする、～にします

degree *do* 度

　38 degrees *sanjuuhachi do* 三十八度

delicious *oishii* おいしい

department store *depaato* デパート

description *setsumee* 説明

design *dezain* デザイン

desk *tsukue* 机

dessert *dezaato* デザート

diarrhea *geri* 下痢
  have a diarrhea (to) *geri o suru, geri o shimasu* 下痢をする、下痢をします
dictionary *jisho* 辞書
die (to) *shinu, shinimasu* 死ぬ、死にます
diesel *diizeru* ディーゼル
difficult *muzukashii* 難しい
dignity *hin* 品
dinner *yuuhan, yuushoku (fml.), yuugohan (infml.)* 夕飯、夕食、夕ご飯
direction *hoo, hookoo* 方、方向
dirty *kitanai* 汚い
disciple *deshi* 弟子
dish eaten with cooked rice *okazu* おかず
dislike (to) *kirai da, kirai desu* 嫌いだ、嫌いです
display *disupurei* ディスプレイ
distribute (to) *kubaru, kubarimasu* 配る、配ります
division manager *buchoo* 部長
dizziness *memai* めまい
do (to) *suru, shimasu; yaru, yarimasu (infml.); itasu, itashimasu (humble); nasaru, nasaimasu (honorific)* する、します; やる、やります; いたす、いたします; なさる、なさいます
  do so *soo suru, soo shimasu* そうする、そうします
  do ... beforehand (to) *... te oku, ... te okimasu* 〜ておく、〜ておきます
  have done ... (to) *... te shimau, ... te shimaimasu; ... koto ga aru, ... koto ga arimasu* 〜てしまう、〜てしまいます; 〜ことがある、〜ことがあります
  Please don't ... *... naide kudasai* 〜ないでください。
dog *inu* 犬
dozen *daasu* ダース
dragon *ryuu* 竜
drawing *e* 絵
dressing *doresshingu* ドレッシング
drink *nomimono* 飲み物
drink (to) *meshiagaru, meshiagarimasu (honorific); itadaku, itadakimasu (humble)* 召し上がる、召し上がります; いただく、いただきます
each *zutsu* ずつ
ear *mimi* 耳
early *hayai, hayaku* 早い、早く
early evening *yuugata* 夕方
earnest *majime* 真面目
(not) easily *nakanaka (+ negative)* なかなか

east side *higashigawa* 東側
easy *kantan, yasashii* 簡単、易しい
eat (to) *taberu, tabemasu; meshiagaru, meshiagarimasu (honorific); itadaku, itadakimasu (humble)* 食べる、食べます; 召し上がる、召し上がります; いただく、いただきます
economics *keezaigaku* 経済学
economy *keezai* 経済
eel *unagi* うなぎ
effect *kooka* 効果
egg *tamago* 卵
eggplant *nasu* なす
eight *hachi, yattsu (native Japanese number)* 八、八つ
eight minutes *hachifun, happun* 八分
eight o'clock *hachiji* 八時
eighteen *juuhachi* 十八
eighth (day of the month) *yooka* 八日
eighty *hachijuu* 八十
electrical engineer *denki gishi* 電気技師
elementary school *shoogakkoo* 小学校
eleven *juuichi* 十一
eleven o'clock *juuichiji* 十一時
e-mail *iimeeru, meeru* イーメール、メール
engine *enjin* エンジン
engineer *enjinia* エンジニア
engineer *gishi* 技師
England *igirisu* イギリス
English *eego (language), igirisujin (person)* 英語、イギリス人
enjoyable *tanoshii* 楽しい
enter (to) *hairu, hairimasu* 入る、入ります
  have entered (to) *haitte iru, haitte imasu* 入っている、入っています
enter school (to) *nyuugakusuru, nyuugakushimasu* 入学する、入学します
entrance hall *genkan* 玄関
error *gobyuu (fml.)* 誤びゅう
especially *toku ni* 特に
evening *ban, yoru* 晩、夜
  early evening *yuugata* 夕方
every day *mainichi* 毎日
every night *maiban* 毎晩
everyday life *seekatsu* 生活
everyone *minna, minasan (polite)* みんな、皆さん
exactly *kichinto, chanto (infml.)* きちんと、ちゃんと
exam *shiken* 試験

examination *kensa* 検査
examine (to) *kensasuru, kensashimasu; miru, mimasu* 検査する、検査します；診る、診ます
Excuse me. *Sumimasen.* すみません。
exercise *undoo* 運動
exercise (to) *undoosuru, undooshimasu* 運動する、運動します
exhaustion *hiroo* 疲労
exist (to) *irassharu, irasshaimasu (honorific); gozaimasu (polite); oru, orimasu (humble)* いらっしゃる、いらっしゃいます；ございます；おる、おります
expense *hiyoo* 費用
expensive *takai* 高い
experience *keeken* 経験
　have an experience of … ing (to) *… koto ga aru, … koto ga arimasu* 〜ことがある、〜ことがあります
export and import business *booeki* 貿易
expression *hyoogen* 表現
eye *me* 目
face *kao* 顔
fall *aki* 秋
fall (to) *furu, furimasu* 降る、降ります
family *(go)kazoku (polite with go)* （ご）家族
　five people in a family *gonin kazoku* 五人家族
　one's family *uchi* 家
famous *yuumee* 有名
far *tooi* 遠い
father *chichi (one's own), otoosan (someone else's)* 父、お父さん
father's day *chichi no hi* 父の日
fathers and eldest sons *fukee (fml.)* 父兄
fatigue *hiroo* 疲労
fax *fakkusu* ファックス
February *nigatsu* 二月
feel dizzy (to) *memai ga suru, memai ga shimasu* めまいがする、めまいがします
feel like vomiting (to) *hakike ga suru, hakike ga shimasu* 吐き気がする、吐き気がします
feel sick (to) *kibun ga warui, kibun ga warui desu* 気分が悪い、気分が悪いです
feeling *kibun* 気分
female *onna* 女
fence *fensu* フェンス
fever *netsu* 熱
　have a fever (to) *netsu ga aru, netsu ga arimasu* 熱がある、熱があります

fifteen *juugo* 十五
fifth (day of the month) *itsuka* 五日
fifth floor *gokai* 五階
fifty *gojuu* 五十
fill out (a form) (to) *kinyuusuru, kinyuushimasu* 記入する、記入します
I'm fine. *Genki desu./Okagesama de. (polite)* 元気です。/おかげさまで。
finish … ing (to) *… te shimau, … te shimaimasu* 〜てしまう、〜てしまいます
Finland *finrando* フィンランド
firefighter *shoobooshi* 消防士
first *hitotsume* 一つ目
　first (day of the month) *tsuitachi* 一日
　first time, for the first time *hajimete* 初めて
　the first day *ichinichime* 一日目
　the first medical consultation *shoshin* 初診
fish *sakana* 魚
　sliced raw fish *sashimi* 刺身
five *go, itsutsu (native Japanese number)* 五、五つ
five minutes *gofun* 五分
five o'clock *goji* 五時
flower *hana* 花
flute *furuuto* フルート
font *fonto* フォント
food *tabemono* 食べ物
foot *ashi* 足
football *futtobooru* フットボール
for a while *shibaraku* しばらく
forest *mori* 森
fork *fooku* フォーク
form (to fill out) *yooshi* 用紙
formerly *katsute* かつて
forty *yonjuu* 四十
fountain pen *mannenhitsu* 万年筆
four *shi, yon, yottsu (native Japanese number)* 四、四、四つ
four minutes *yonfun, yonpun* 四分
four o'clock *yoji* 四時
fourteen *juushi, juuyon* 十四
fourth (day of the month) *yokka* 四日
France *furansu* フランス
free *jiyuu* 自由
　free time *jiyuujikan* 自由時間
free (to be) (having a lot of free time) *hima* 暇
freedom *jiyuu* 自由

Glossary **239**

French *furansugo (language), furansujin (person)* フランス語、フランス人
French cuisine *furansu ryoori* フランス料理
Friday *kin-yoobi* 金曜日
friend *tomodachi, yuujin (fml.)* 友達、友人
from *kara* から
　(sent) from *sooshinsha* 送信者
　from … to … *… kara … made* 〜から〜まで
front desk *uketsuke* 受付
full *ippai* 一杯
fully furnished *kanbi* 完備
fun *tanoshii* 楽しい
furniture *kagu* 家具
future *shoorai* 将来
game *geemu, shiai (of sport)* ゲーム、試合
garden *niwa* 庭
generous *shinsetsu* 親切
gentle *yasashii* 優しい
German *doitsugo (language), doitsujin (person)* ドイツ語、ドイツ人
Germany *doitsu* ドイツ
get off (to) *oriru, orimasu* 降りる、降ります
　have gotten off (to) *orite iru, orite imasu* 降りている、降りています
get on (to) *noru, norimasu* 乗る、乗ります
get up (to) *okiru, okimasu* 起きる、起きます
girlfriend *gaarufurendo* ガールフレンド
give (to) *ageru, agemasu; kureru, kuremasu; yaru, yarimasu (to a plant, an animal); kudasaru, kudasaimasu (honorific); sashiageru, sashiagemasu (humble)* あげる、あげます; くれる、くれます; やる、やります; くださる、くださいます; さしあげる、さしあげます
　give a favor of … ing (to) *… te ageru, … te agemasu; … te kureru, … te kuremasu; … te kudasaru, … te kudasaimasu (honorific); … te sashiageru, … te sashiagemasu (humble)* 〜てあげる、〜てあげます; 〜てくれる、〜てくれます; 〜てくださる、〜てくださいます; 〜てさしあげる、〜てさしあげます
　give an injection (to) *chuushasuru, chuushashimasu* 注射する、注射します
glad to … (to be) *yorokonde …* 喜んで〜
　I'm glad to hear that. *Sore wa yokatta.* それはよかった。
go (to) *iku, ikimasu ; irassharu, irasshaimasu (honorific); mairu, mairimasu (humble)* 行く、行きます; いらっしゃる、いらっしゃいます; 参る、参ります
　have gone (to) *itte iru, itte imasu* 行っている、行っています
go back (to) *kaeru, kaerimasu* 帰る、帰ります
go home (to) *kaeru, kaerimasu* 帰る、帰ります
go out (to) *dekakeru, dekakemasu* 出掛ける、出掛けます
　go out with a camera (to) *kamera o motte dekakemasu* カメラを持って出掛けます
go to sleep (to) *neru, nemasu* 寝る、寝ます
golf *gorufu* ゴルフ
good *ii, yoroshii (polite)* いい、よろしい
　good at *joozu, tokui* 上手、得意
　quite good *nakanaka ii* なかなかいい
Good afternoon. *Konnichi wa.* こんにちは。
Good evening. *Konban wa.* こんばんは。
Good morning. *Ohayoo gozaimasu.* おはようございます。
Good night. *Oyasuminasai.* おやすみなさい。
Goodbye. *Sayoonara./Shitsuree itashimasu. (polite)/Shitsureeshimasu. (polite)* さようなら。/失礼いたします。/失礼します。
(I) got it. *Wakarimashita.* 分かりました。
graduate (to) *sotsugyoosuru, sotsugyooshimasu* 卒業する、卒業します
graduate school *daigakuin* 大学院
graduate school student *daigakuinsee* 大学院生
graduation *sotsugyoo* 卒業
grandfather *sofu (one's own), ojiisan (someone else's)* 祖父、おじいさん
grandmother *sobo (one's own), obaasan (someone else's)* 祖母、おばあさん
green *midori (noun)* 緑
green salad *guriin sarada* グリーンサラダ
grey *guree (noun)* グレー
group presentation *gruupu happyoo* グループ発表
guest *kyaku, okyakusan (polite), okyakusama (polite)* 客、お客さん、お客さま
gun *juu* 銃
hair *ke, kami (on the head), kami no ke (on the head)* 毛、髪、髪の毛
hair dresser *biyooshi* 美容師
hair dye *karaa* カラー
haircut *katto* カット
half *han, hanbun* 半、半分
　for half a year *hantoshikan* 半年間

half a year *hantoshi* 半年
half past the hour *han* 半
hallway *rooka* 廊下
ham *hamu* ハム
hand *te* 手
handkerchief *hankachi* ハンカチ
hard *taihen* 大変
hardware *haadowea* ハードウェア
have (to) *motte iru, motte imasu* 持っている、持っています
　Do you have … ? *aru, arimasu (inanimate); iru, imasu (animate); gozaimasu (polite); omochi desu ka. (polite)* ある、あります；いる、います；ございます；お持ちですか。
have to … (to) *… nakereba ikenai, … nakereba ikemasen; … nakereba naranai, … nakereba narimasen; … nakute wa ikenai, … nakute wa ikemasen; … nakute wa naranai, … nakute wa narimasen* 〜なければいけない、〜なければいけません；〜なければならない、〜なければなりません；〜なくてはいけない、〜なくてはいけません；〜なくてはならない、〜なくてはなりません
he *kare* 彼
headache *zutsuu* 頭痛
　have a headache (to) *atama ga itai, atama ga itai desu; zutsuu ga suru, zutsuu ga shimasu* 頭が痛い、頭が痛いです；頭痛がする、頭痛がします
health insurance card *hokenshoo* 保険証
heart *haato, kokoro, shinzoo* ハート、心、心臓
heavy *omoi* 重い
Hello. *Konnichi wa.; moshi moshi (on the phone)* こんにちは。；もしもし
her *kanojo no* 彼女の
here *koko* ここ
　here (to be) *kite iru, kite imasu* 来ている、来ています
　Here you go. *Doozo.* どうぞ。
high *takai* 高い
high school *kookoo* 高校
high school student *kookoosee* 高校生
high-rise building *biru* ビル
hip *koshi* 腰
hip-hop *hippuhoppu* ヒップホップ
hiragana characters *hiragana* 平仮名
Hiroshima *hiroshima* 広島
his *kare no* 彼の

"his and hers" rice bowl set *meotojawan* 夫婦茶碗
hobby *shumi* 趣味
hold (to) *motsu, mochimasu* 持つ、持ちます
holiday *yasumi* 休み
home (one's) *uchi* 家
　stay home (to) *uchi ni iru, uchi ni imasu* 家にいる、家にいます
hometown *(go)shusshin (polite with go)* (ご)出身
homework *shukudai* 宿題
Hong Kong *honkon* 香港、ホンコン
hospital *byooin* 病院
hospitalized (to be) *nyuuinsuru, nyuuinshimasu* 入院する、入院します
hot *atsui (to the touch), atsui (weather, room temperature)* 熱い、暑い
hot air *nekki* 熱気
hotel *hoteru* ホテル
hour(s) *jikan* 時間
　two hours *nijikan* 二時間
house *ie, uchi* 家
housewife *shufu* 主婦
how *doo, doo yatte, ikaga (polite)* どう、どうやって、いかが
　How about … ? *Doo desu ka.* どうですか。
　How are you? *… wa ikaga desu ka. (polite)* 〜はいかがですか。
　How do you do? *Ogenki desu ka.* お元気ですか。
　How is it? *Hajimemashite.; Doo desu ka.; Ikaga desu ka. (polite)* はじめまして。；どうですか。；いかがですか。
　How was it? *Doo deshita ka.; Ikaga deshita ka. (polite)* どうでしたか。；いかがでしたか。
how long *dono gurai* どのぐらい
how many *(o)ikutsu (polite with o)* (お)いくつ
how much *(o)ikura (polite with o); dono gurai* (お)いくら；どのぐらい
how old *(o)ikutsu (polite with o)* (お)いくつ
however *demo* でも
human resources department *jinjibu* 人事部
hundred *hyaku* 百
　hundred percent *hyakupaasento* 100パーセント
　100% wool *uuru hyakupaasento* ウール100パーセント
husband *otto (one's own), shujin (one's own), goshujin (someone else's)* 夫、主人、ご主人

I *watashi, boku (used only by male speakers)* 私、僕

ice cream *aisukuriimu* アイスクリーム

idea *kangae* 考え

identical *dooitsu* 同一

if *moshi, tara, to* もし、たら、と

  if it's okay, if you like *moshi yokattara, yoroshikattara (polite)* もし良かったら、よろしかったら

ignition *hakka* 発火

illness *byooki* 病気

immediate opening *kyuubo* 急募

impoliteness *shituree* 失礼

important *taisetsu* 大切

in case *moshi* もし

in front of... (*... no) mae* (〜の)前

inch *inchi* インチ

included (to be) *fukumu, fukumimasu* 含む、含みます

inconvenient *fuben* 不便

India *indo* インド

indicative characters *shiji moji* 指示文字

information desk *uketsuke* 受付

inhale (to) *suu, suimasu* 吸う、吸います

injection *chuusha* 注射

injury *kega* 怪我

  get injured (to) *kega o suru, kega o shimasu* 怪我をする、怪我をします

inquire (to) *kiku, kikimasu* 聞く、聞きます

inquiry *(o)toiawase (polite wih o)* (お)問い合わせ

inside... (*... no) naka* (〜の)中

insomnia *fuminshoo* 不眠症

  suffer from insomnia (to) *fuminshoo da, fuminshoo desu* 不眠症だ、不眠症です

insufficient (to be) *tarinai, tarimasen* 足りない、足りません

insurance *hoken* 保険

  social insurance *shakaihoken* 社会保険

interesting *omoshiroi* 面白い

Internet *intaanetto* インターネット

intersection *koosaten* 交差点

interview *mensetsu* 面接

intestine *choo* 腸

it *sore* それ

Italian *itariago (language)* イタリア語

Italian cuisine *itaria ryoori* イタリア料理

Italy *itaria* イタリア

its *sono* その

January *ichigatsu* 一月

Japan *nihon* 日本

Japanese *nihongo (language), nihonjin (person)* 日本語、日本人

Japanese style *wafuu* 和風

jazz *jazu* ジャズ

jeans *jiinzu* ジーンズ

job *o(shigoto) (polite with o)* (お)仕事

job posting *kyuujin (kookoku)* 求人(広告)

jog, jogging *jogingu* ジョギング

join (to) *hairu, hairimasu* 入る、入ります

joint-stock cooperation *kabushikigaisha* 株式会社

judo *juudoo* 柔道

juice *juusu* ジュース

July *shichigatsu* 七月

June *rokugatsu* 六月

junior high school *chuugakkoo* 中学校

katakana characters *katakana* 片仮名

keep (to) *azukaru, azukarimasu* 預かる、預かります

  keep someone waiting (to) *mataseru, matasemasu* 待たせる、待たせます

  I have kept you waiting. *Omatase itashimashita. (polite)* お待たせいたしました。

kendo *kendoo* 剣道

keyboard *kiiboodo* キーボード

kind *shinsetsu, yasashii* 親切、優しい

kindergarten *yoochien* 幼稚園

king *oosama* 王様

kitchen *daidokoro* 台所

knife *naifu* ナイフ

know (to) *shiru, shirimasu* 知る、知ります

  I know *shitteimasu* 知っています

  I don't know *shirimasen* 知りません

Kobe *koobe* 神戸

konnyaku potato *konnyaku* こんにゃく

Korea *kankoku* 韓国

Kyoto *kyooto* 京都

labor conditions *taiguu* 待遇

land *tochi* 土地

language *kotoba* 言葉

last week *senshuu* 先週

last year *kyonen* 去年

late *osoi* 遅い

late (to be) *okureru, okuremasu* 遅れる、遅れます

later *ato de, go, gojitsu* 後で、後、後日

See you later. *Sorede wa mata./Sore ja(a) mata. (infml.)* それではまた。/それじゃ(あ)また。

30 minutes later *sanjuppun go* 三十分後

law *hooritsu* 法律

law firm *hooritsu jimusho* 法律事務所

lawyer *bengoshi* 弁護士

leap *hiyaku* 飛躍

leave (to) *deru, demasu* 出る、出ます

have left (to) *dete iru, dete imasu* 出ている、出ています

leave … (to) *… o deru, … o demasu* 〜を出る、〜を出ます

leave the hospital (to) *taiinsuru, taiinshimasu* 退院する、退院します

leaving… *… hasu* 〜発

leaving Haneda *Haneda hatsu* 羽田発

left *hidari* 左

left side *hidarigawa* 左側

leg *ashi* 脚

lend (to) *kasu, kashimasu* 貸す、貸します

have lent (to) *kashite iru, kashite imasu* 貸している、貸しています

Let me see. *Soo da naa./Soo desu ne.* そうだなあ。/そうですね。

Let's… *… mashoo.* 〜ましょう。

Let's do that! *Soo shimashoo!* そうしましょう！

letter *tegami* 手紙

lettuce *retasu* レタス

library *toshokan* 図書館

lid *futa* 蓋

lie *uso* 嘘

tell a lie (to) *uso o tsuku, uso o tsukimasu* 嘘をつく、嘘をつきます

light *karui (adjective), raito (noun)* 軽い、ライト

light (to) *tsukeru, tsukemasu* 点ける、点けます

like (to) *suki da, suki desu* 好きだ、好きです

like very much (to), like a lot (to) *daisuki da, daisuki desu* 大好きだ、大好きです

I'd like to have… *… o onegaishimasu.* 〜をお願いします。

if you like *moshi yokattara, yoroshikattara (polite)* もし良かったら、よろしかったら

link *rinku* リンク

listen (to) *kiku, kikimasu ; kiku, kikimasu (with focus, such as listening to music)* 聞く、聞きます；聴く、聴きます

literature *bungaku* 文学

lively *nigiyaka* 賑やか

living room *ima* 居間

long *nagai* 長い

Long time no see. *Hisashiburi desu ne.* 久しぶりですね。

long-absence *hisabisa* 久々

look (to) *miru, mimasu* 見る、見ます

look for (to) *goran ni naru, goran ni narimasu (honorific); haikensuru, haikenshimasu (humble)* ご覧になる、ご覧になります；拝見する、拝見します

look forward (to) *sagasu, sagashimasu; tanoshimi ni suru, tanoshimi ni shimasu* 探す、探します；楽しみにする、楽しみにします

look pale (to) *kaoiro ga warui, kaoiro ga warui desu* 顔色が悪い、顔色が悪いです

loud *hade* 派手

low *hikui* 低い

lunch *chuushoku (fml.), hirugohan (infml.)* 昼食、昼ご飯

lung *hai* 肺

magazine *zasshi* 雑誌

mail (to) *yuusoosuru, yuusooshimasu* 郵送する、郵送します

make (to) *tsukuru, tsukurimasu* 作る、作ります

make a phone call (to) *denwasuru, denwashimasu* 電話する、電話します

make a appointment/reservation (to) *yoyakusuru, yoyakushimasu* 予約する、予約します

male *otoko* 男

man *otoko no hito* 男の人

many *ooi, takusan* 多い、たくさん

how many *(o)ikutsu (polite with o)* (お)いくつ

many times *nando mo* 何度も

March *sangatsu* 三月

marketing *maaketingu* マーケティング

married couple *(go)fuufu (polite with go)* (ご)夫婦

mat *matto* マット

match (to) *au, aimasu* 合う、合います

match with jeans (to) *jiinzu ni au* ジーンズに合う

mathematics *suugaku* 数学

matter *ken* 件

May *gogatsu* 五月

may (conjecture) *kamoshirenai, kamoshiremasen* かもしれない、かもしれません

May I ... ? ... *te (mo) ii?;* ... *te (mo) ii desu ka.;* ... *te (mo) ii deshoo ka. (polite);* ... *te (mo) yoroshii desu ka. (polite);* ... *te (mo) yoroshii deshoo ka. (polite)* 〜て(も)いい?；〜て(も)いいですか。；〜て(も)いいでしょうか。；〜て(も)よろしいですか。；〜て(も)よろしいでしょうか。

meal *gohan (infml.), shokuji (fml.)* ご飯、食事

meaning *imi* 意味

measure (to) *hakaru, hakarimasu* 測る、測ります

meat *niku* 肉

medical consultation *shinsatsu* 診察

  the first medical consultation *shoshin* 初診

medical consulting room *shinsatsushitsu* 診察室

medical doctor *isha* 医者

medicine *kusuri* 薬

medium (size) *medium* エム

  medium is okay *emu de ii* エムでいい

meet (to) *au, aimasu; ome ni kakaru, ome ni kakarimasu (humble)* 会う、会います；お目にかかる、お目にかかります

meeting *kaigi, miitingu* 会議、ミーティング

menu *menyuu* メニュー

meter *meetoru* メートル

Mexican *mekishikojin (person)* メキシコ人

Mexican cuisine *mekishiko ryoori* メキシコ料理

Mexico *mekishiko* メキシコ

microwave oven *denshirenji* 電子レンジ

milk *miruku* ミルク

mind (to) *kamau, kamaimasu* 構う、構います

  Do you mind ... ing? ... *te (mo) kamaimasen ka.* 〜て(も)構いませんか。

miso soup *(o)misoshiru (polite with o)* (お)味噌汁

mixed salad *mikkusu sarada* ミックスサラダ

Monday *getsuyoobi* 月曜日

money *okane* お金

monitor *monitaa* モニター

monotonous *ipponjooshi* 一本調子

moon *tsuki* 月

more *motto* もっと

  a little more *moo sukoshi* もう少し

  more than *ijoo* 以上

  more ... than ... ... *yori* 〜 〜より〜

  once more *moo ichido* もう一度

morning *asa, gozen* 朝、午前

  this morning *kesa* 今朝

mosquito *ka* 蚊

(the) most *ichiban* 一番

moth *ga* 蛾

mother (one's own) *haha (one's own), okaasan (someone else's)* 母、お母さん

mountain *yama* 山

mouse *mausu* マウス

mouth *kuchi* 口

move (to a new location) (to) *hikkosu, hikkoshimasu* 引っ越す、引っ越します

movie *eega* 映画

movie theater *eegakan* 映画館

Mr., Ms. *san, sama (polite)* さん、様

Mt. Fuji *fujisan* 富士山

much *ooi, takusan* 多い、たくさん

  how much *(o)ikura (polite with o)* (お)いくら

  not so much *a(n)mari (+ negative)* あ(ん)まり

music *ongaku* 音楽

musical instrument *gakki* 楽器

mussel *muurugai* ムール貝

my *watashi no* 私の

name *(o)namae (polite with o)* (お)名前

  What's your name? *Onamae wa?* お名前は？

narrow *semai* 狭い

nation *kuni* 国

nausea *hakike* 吐き気

nearby *chikaku* 近く

necktie *nekutai* ネクタイ

never *ichido mo (+negative)* 一度も

new *atarashii* 新しい

New York *nyuuyooku* ニューヨーク

newspaper *shinbun* 新聞

next time *kondo* 今度

next to ... (... *no) tonari* (〜の)隣

next week *raishuu* 来週

next year *rainen* 来年

Nice to meet you. *Doozo yoroshiku.* どうぞよろしく。

night *ban, yoru* 晩、夜

  every night *maiban* 毎晩

  two nights *nihaku* 二泊

  two nights three days *nihaku mikka* 二泊三日

nine *ku, kyuu, kokonotsu (native Japanese number)* 九、九、九つ

nine minutes *kyuufun* 九分

nine o'clock *kuji* 九時

nineteen *juuku, juukyuu* 十九

ninety *kyuujuu* 九十

ninth (day of the month) *kokonoka* 九日

no *iie* いいえ

no one *dare mo (+ negative)* 誰も
No, thank you. *Kekkoo desu.* 結構です。
nobody *dare mo (+ negative)* 誰も
noisy *urusai* うるさい
noon *(o)hiru (polite with o)* (お)昼
north side *kitagawa* 北側
nose *hana* 鼻
not at all *zenzen (+ negative)* 全然
not so much *a(n)mari (+ negative)* あ(ん)まり
not so often *a(n)mari (+ negative)* あ(ん)まり
notebook *nooto* ノート
nothing *nani mo (+ negative)* 何も
novel *shoosetsu* 小説
November *juuichigatsu* 十一月
now *ima* 今
nowhere *doko mo (+ negative)* どこも
number one *ichiban* 一番
nurse *kangoshi* 看護師
obstruction *jama* 邪魔
occupation *shokugyoo* 職業
ocean *umi* 海
October *juugatsu* 十月
octopus *tako* たこ
off (to be), have gotten off (to) *orite iru, orite imasu* 降りている、降りています
office *jimusho, ofisu* 事務所、オフィス
office (clerical) work *jimu* 事務
office worker *kaishain* 会社員
often *yoku* よく
not so often *a(n)mari (+ negative)* あ(ん)まり
oh *aa* ああ
okay (good) *ii, yoroshii (polite)* いい、よろしい
if it's okay *moshi yokattara, yoroshikattara (polite)* もし良かったら、よろしかったら
Is it okay? *Yoroshii desu ka. (polite)* よろしいですか。
medium is okay *emu de ii* エムでいい
Okinawa *okinawa* 沖縄
old *furui* 古い
how old *(o)ikutsu (polite with o)* (お)いくつ
older brother *ani (one's own), oniisan (someone else's)* 兄、お兄さん
older sister *ane (one's own), oneesan (someone else's)* 姉、お姉さん
on （... *no) ue* (〜の)上
once *ichido* 一度
once in a while *tamani* たまに
once more *moo ichido* もう一度

once upon a time *mukashimukashi* 昔々
one (number) *ichi, hitotsu (native Japanese number)* 一、一つ
one (indefinite pronoun) *no* の
the American one *amerika no* アメリカの
the one in solid color *muji no* 無地の
one minute *ippun* 一分
one o'clock *ichiji* 一時
one person *hitori* 一人
onion *tamanegi* たまねぎ
only *dake, shika (+ negative)* だけ、しか
only child *hitorikko* 一人っ子
open (to) *akeru, akemasu (transitive verb)* 開ける、開けます
operate (to) *shujutsusuru, shujutsushimasu* 手術する、手術します
operation *shujutsu* 手術
opposite *gyaku* 逆
optional tour *opushonaru tsuaa* オプショナルツアー
or *ka* か
... or something like that ... *demo* 〜でも
coffee or something like that *koohii demo* コーヒーでも
orange *orenji* オレンジ
order *chuumon* 注文
order (to) *chuumonsuru, chuumonshimasu* 注文する、注文します
Osaka *oosaka* 大阪
other *hoka* 他
the other day *senjitsu* 先日
own (to) *motsu, mochimasu* 持つ、持ちます
p.m. *gogo* 午後
painful *itai* 痛い
painting *e* 絵
panda *panda* パンダ
pants *pantsu, zubon* パンツ、ズボン
paper *kami* 紙
Pardon the intrusion. *Ojamashimasu.* お邪魔します。
parents *(go)ryooshin (polite with go)* (ご)両親
park *kooen* 公園
party *paatii* パーティー
passing over a matter *fumon* 不問
patient *kanja* 患者
pay (to) *harau, haraimasu* 払う、払います
payment *(o)shiharai (polite with o)* (お)支払い
pen *pen* ペン

pencil *enpitsu* 鉛筆
pepper *koshoo* 胡椒
perform (to) (music) *ensoosuru, ensooshimasu* 演奏する、演奏します
perhaps *tabun* 多分
perm *paama* パーマ
person *hito* 人
person *mono* (humble), *kata* (polite) 者、方
  a person in charge *tantoo no mono* (humble) 担当の者
  one person *hitori* 一人
  two people *futari, nimeesama* (polite) 二人、二名様
personal computer *pasokon* パソコン
pharmaceutical company *seeyakugaisha* 製薬会社
phonetic-ideographic characters *keesee moji* 形声文字
photograph, photography *shashin* 写真
piano *piano* ピアノ
pictorial characters *shookee moji* 象形文字
pig *buta* 豚
pin *pin* ピン
pink *pinku* (noun) ピンク
pizza *piza* ピザ
place *tokoro* 所
  place of origin *(go)shusshin* (polite with go) (ご)出身
  place of work *kinmuchi* 勤務地
plan *keekaku* 計画
plant (to) *ueru, uemasu* 植える、植えます
plant (to) (seeds) *maku, makimasu* 蒔く、蒔きます
play (to) *asobu, asobimasu* (a game); *fuku, fukimasu* (a wind instruments); *hiku, hikimasu* (piano); *tataku, tatakimasu* (a percussion instrument) 遊ぶ、遊びます;吹く、吹きます;弾く、弾きます; たたく、たたきます
  play sports (to) *suppootsu o suru, supootsu o shimasu* スポーツをする、スポーツをします
Please. *Doozo.* どうぞ。
  Please. (asking for a favor) *Onegaishimasu.* お願いします。
  Please … … *te kudasai.* 〜てください。
  Please don't … … *naide kudasai.* 〜ないでください。
  Please give me … … *o kudasai.* 〜をください。

poison *doku* 毒
police *keesatsu* 警察
police booth *kooban* 交番
police officer *keesatsukan* 警察官
polish (to) *migaku, migakimasu* 磨く、磨きます
pool *puuru* プール
poor at *heta, nigate* 下手、苦手
pop *poppusu* ポップス
popular (to be) *ninki ga aru, ninki ga arimasu* 人気がある、人気があります
popularity *ninki* 人気
pork *butaniku* 豚肉
Portuguese *porutogarugo* (language) ポルトガル語
post office *yuubinkyoku* 郵便局
potato *jagaimo* じゃがいも
practice (to) *renshuusuru, renshuushimasu* 練習する、練習します
prefix meal *teeshoku* 定食
preparation *junbi, yooi* 準備、用意
presentation *happyoo* 発表
  group presentation *gruupu happyoo* グループ発表
president of a company *shachoo* 社長
pretty *kiree* きれい
price *nedan* 値段
  prices (of commodities) *bukka* 物価
  have been priced down (to) *oyasuku natte imasu* (polite) お安くなっています
probably *tabun* 多分
  will probably *daroo, deshoo* だろう、でしょう
problem *mondai* 問題
promotion *kiyoo* 起用
promptly *hayabaya, soosoo* 早々
properly *kichinto, chanto* (infml.) きちんと、ちゃんと
provide (to) *shikyuusuru, shikyuushimasu* 支給する、支給します
psychology *shinrigaku* 心理学
pulse *myaku* 脈
put (to) *oku, okimasu* 置く、置きます
  put into (to) *ireru, iremasu* 入れる、入れます
  put into a salad (to) *sarada ni ireru, sarada ni iremasu* サラダに入れる、サラダに入れます
  put on (to be) *noru, norimasu* 載る、載ります
  have been put on (to) *notte iru, notte imasu* 載っている、載っています
qualification *shikaku* 資格

Essential Japanese

question *shitsumon* 質問
quickly *hayaku* 早く
quiet *shizuka, jimi (color)* 静か、地味
quite *nakanaka* なかなか
  quite good *nakanaka ii* なかなかいい
radio *rajio* ラジオ
rain *ame* 雨
  It's raining. *Ame desu./Ame ga futte imasu.* 雨です。/雨が降っています。
read (to) *yomu, yomimasu* 読む、読みます
  reading books *dokusho* 読書
not readily (in negative) *nakanaka* なかなか
  not come readily *nakanaka konai, nakanaka kimasen* なかなか来ない、なかなか来ません
  Are you ready? *Junbi wa ii desu ka.* 準備はいいですか。
really *hontoo ni* 本当に
  Really? *Hontoo desu ka./Soo desu ka.* 本当ですか。/そうですか。
reason *riyuu* 理由
  for that reason *sorede* それで
receive (to) *morau, moraimasu; itadaku, itadakimasu (humble)* もらう、もらいます; いただく、いただきます
  receive a favor of ... ing (to) *... te morau, ... te moraimasu; ... te itadaku, ... te itadakimasu (humble)* 〜てもらう、〜てもらいます; 〜ていただく、〜ていただきます
recently *saikin* 最近
reception desk *uketsuke* 受付
receptionist *uketsukegakari* 受付係
red *akai (adjective), aka (noun)* 赤い、赤
red wine *aka wain* 赤ワイン
refrigerator *reezooko* 冷蔵庫
regarding *kansuru* 関する
relatives *(go)shinseki (polite with go)* (ご)親戚
relax (to) *rirakkususu, rirakkusushimasu* リラックスする、リラックスします
released from hospital (to be) *taiinsuru, taiinshimasu* 退院する、退院します
replace (a person) (to) *kawaru, kawarimasu* 代わる、代わります
report *repooto* レポート
reservation *yoyaku* 予約
  make a reservation (to) *yoyakusuru, yoyakushimasu* 予約する、予約します
restaurant *resutoran* レストラン
restroom *otearai* お手洗い

resume *rirekisho* 履歴書
return *okaeshi (polite)* お返し
return (to) *kaeru, kaerimasu ; modoru, modorimasu* 帰る、帰ります; 戻る、戻ります
  have returned (to) *kaette iru, kaette imasu; modotte iru, modotte imasu* 帰っている、帰っています; 戻っている、戻っています
reward *shooyo* 賞与
ride (to) *noru, norimasu* 乗る、乗ります
right *migi* 右
  Right? *Soo desu ne. (rising intonation)* そうですね。
  That's right. *Soo desu.; Soo desu ne.; Soo desu yo.* そうです。; そうですね。; そうですよ。
right side *migigawa* 右側
rink *rinku* リンク
river *kawa* 川
road *michi* 道
rock *rokku* ロック
Rome *rooma* ローマ
room *heya* 部屋
rudeness *shitsuree* 失礼
rules *kiyaku* 規約
run (to) *hashiru, hashirimasu* 走る、走ります
sake *nihonshu* 日本酒
salad *sarada* サラダ
  chicken salad *chikin sarada* チキンサラダ
  green salad *guriin sarada* グリーンサラダ
  mixed salad *mikkusu sarada* ミックスサラダ
  seafood salad *shiifuudo sarada* シーフードサラダ
salary *(o)kyuuryoo (polite with o), kyuuyo* (お)給料、給与
  salary increase *shookyuu* 昇給
salt *shio* 塩
salty *shiokarai* 塩辛い
same *onaji* 同じ
Saturday *doyoobi* 土曜日
say (to) *iu, iimasu; moosu, mooshimasu (humble); ossharu, osshaimasu (honorific)* 言う、言います; 申す、申します;おっしゃる、おっしゃいます
scallop *hotate* 帆立
scared (to be) *bikkurisuru, bikkurishimasu* びっくりする、びっくりします
scarf *sukaafu* スカーフ
schedule *sukejuuru* スケジュール
school *gakkoo* 学校

seafood salad *shiifuudo sarada* シーフードサラダ
seasoning *choomiryoo* 調味料
second *futatsume* 二つ目
second (day of the month) *futsuka* 二日
section manager *kachoo* 課長
see (to) *goran ni naru, goran ni narimasu (honorific); haikensuru, haikenshimasu (humble); ome ni kakaru, ome ni kakarimasu (humble)* ご覧になる、ご覧になります; 拝見する、拝見します; お目にかかる、お目にかかります
  I see. *Hee.; Soo desu ka.; Soo ka.* へえ。; そうですか。; そうか。
  See you later/then. *Sorede wa mata./Sore ja(a) mata. (infml.)* それではまた。/それじゃ(あ)また。
  seeing movies *eega kanshoo (lit., movie appreciation)* 映画鑑賞
  seen (to be) *mieru, miemasu* 見える、見えます
seed *tane* 種
selfish *katte* 勝手
seminar *seminaa* セミナー
September *kugatsu* 九月
set (counter for written materials) *bu* 部
seven *nana, shichi, nanatsu (native Japanese number)* 七、七、七つ
seven minutes *nanafun* 七分
seven o'clock *shichiji* 七時
seventeen *juunana, juushichi* 十七
seventh (day of the month) *nanoka* 七日
seventy *nanajuu* 七十
several times *nando ka* 何度か
severe *hidoi* ひどい
shade *sheedo* シェード
Shall we … ? *… mashoo ka.* 〜ましょうか。
she *kanojo* 彼女
shellfish *kai* 貝
Shepherd *shepaado* シェパード
sherbet *shaabetto* シャーベット
shirt *shatsu* シャツ
shoes *kutsu* 靴
shopping *kaimono* 買い物
shopping cart *kaato* カート
short *mijikai* 短い
  short (to be) *tarinai, tarimasen* 足りない、足りません
shortcake *shooto keeki* ショートケーキ
shortly *kondo* 今度
shot *chuusha* 注射

shoulders *kata* 肩
  have stiff shoulders (to) *kata ga kotte iru, kata ga kotte imasu* 肩が凝っている、肩が凝っています
shower *shawaa* シャワー
  take a shower (to) *shawaa o abiru, shawaa o abimasu* シャワーを浴びる、シャワーを浴びます
showy *hade* 派手
shrimp *ebi* えび
shrine *jinja* 神社
siblings *kyoodai (one's own), gokyoodai (someone else's)* 兄弟、ご兄弟
side *hoo* 方
  the side of … *(… no) yoko* (〜の)横
  this side *temae* 手前
sightseeing *kankoo* 観光
simple *kantan* 簡単
since *node* ので
singer *kashu* 歌手
sit down (to) *suwaru, suwarimasu* 座る、座ります
six *roku, muttsu (native Japanese number)* 六、六つ
six minutes *roppun* 六分
six o'clock *rokuji* 六時
sixteen *juuroku* 十六
sixth (day of the month) *muika* 六日
sixty *rokujuu* 六十
size *saizu* サイズ
ski, skiing *sukii* スキー
skillful *joozu* 上手
skirt *sukaato* スカート
sky *sora* 空
sleep *suimin* 睡眠
  get some sleep (to) *suimin o toru, suimin o torimasu* 睡眠をとる、睡眠をとります
sleep (to) *neru, nemasu* 寝る、寝ます
sliced raw fish *sashimi* 刺身
slowly *yukkuri* ゆっくり
small *chiisai* 小さい
smoke a cigarette (to) *tabako o suu, tabako o suimasu* 煙草を吸う、煙草を吸います
snow *yuki* 雪
  It's snowing. *Yuki desu./Yuki ga futte imasu.* 雪です。/雪が降っています。
so *kara (conjunction), sorede (conjunction), soo (pronoun)* から、それで、そう
  do so (to) *soo suru, soo shimasu* そうする、そうします

Is that so? *Soo desu ka.* そうですか。
so-so *maa maa* まあまあ
sober (color) *jimi* 地味
soccer *sakkaa* サッカー
social insurance *shakaihoken* 社会保険
society *shakai* 社会
sofa *sofaa* ソファー
soft drink *juusu* ジュース
software *sofuto, sofutowea* ソフト、ソフトウェア
soil *tsuchi* 土
solid (color) *muji* 無地
some other day *gojitsu* 後日
someone *dare ka* 誰か
something *nani ka* 何か
sometimes *tokidoki* 時々
somewhere *doko ka* どこか
son *musuko* (one's own), *musukosan* (someone else's) 息子、息子さん
Sorry for the trouble. *Sumimasen.* すみません。
　I'm sorry. *Gomennasai./Sumimasen.* ごめんなさい。/すみません。
　I'm very sorry. *Mooshiwake arimasen.* (polite)/*Mooshiwake gozaimasen.* (polite) 申し訳ありません。/申し訳ございません。
sour *suppai* すっぱい
south side *minamigawa* 南側
soy bean paste *miso* 味噌
soy milk *toonyuu* 豆乳
soy sauce *shooyu* 醤油
spacious *hiroi* 広い
spaghetti *supagetti* スパゲッティ
Spain *supein* スペイン
Spanish *supeingo* (language), *supeinjin* (person) スペイン語、スペイン人
Spanish cuisine *supein ryoori* スペイン料理
speak (to) *hanasu, hanashimasu* 話す、話します
special ability/skill *tokugi* 特技
spicy *karai* 辛い
spoon *supuun* スプーン
sport *supootsu* スポーツ
　play sports (to) *suppootsu o suru, supootsu o shimasu* スポーツをする、スポーツをします
sprain *nenza* 捻挫
　have a sprain (to) *nenzasuru, nenzashimasu* 捻挫する、捻挫します
spring *haru* 春
squid *ika* いか
stairs *kaidan* 階段

stand up (to) *tatsu, tachimasu* 立つ、立ちます
station *eki* 駅
stay home (to) *uchi ni iru, uchi ni imasu* 家にいる、家にいます
staying over night *haku* 泊
stiff (to get) *koru, korimasu* 凝る、凝ります
　have stiff shoulders (to) *kata ga kotte iru, kata ga kotte imasu* 肩が凝っている、肩が凝っています
still *mada* まだ
stomach *i* 胃
stomachache *fukutsuu* 腹痛
　have a stomachache (to) *onaka ga itai, onaka ga itai desu* お腹が痛い、お腹が痛いです
store *mise* 店
store clerk *ten-in* 店員
straight *massugu* まっすぐ
strange *myoo* 妙
stream *ogawa* 小川
street *michi* 道
stress *sutoresu* ストレス
　under a lot of stress (to be) *sutoresu ga tamatte iru, sutoresu ga tamatte imasu* ストレスが溜まっている、ストレスが溜まっています
stripes *shima* 縞
stroke (for writing characters) *kaku* 画
　number of strokes *kakusuu* 画数
　stroke order *kakijun* 書き順
strong *tsuyoi* 強い
student *gakusee* 学生
　college student *daigakusee* 大学生
　graduate school student *daigakuinsee* 大学院生
　high school student *kookoosee* 高校生
　teacher and student *shitee* 師弟
study (to) *benkyoosuru, benkyooshimasu* 勉強する、勉強します
　study abroad (to) *ryuugakusuru, ryuugakushimasu* 留学する、留学します
subject (letter, e-mail) *kenmee* 件名
subway *chikatetsu* 地下鉄
sugar *satoo* 砂糖
suitcase *suutsukeesu* スーツケース
summer *natsu* 夏
　summer vacation *natsu yasumi* 夏休み
sumo wrestling *sumoo* 相撲
Sunday *nichiyoobi* 日曜日
sunny *hare* 晴れ

It's sunny. *Hare desu./Harete imasu.* 晴れです。/晴れています。
supermarket *suupaa* スーパー
surgery *shujutsu* 手術
surprised (to be) *bikkurisuru, bikkurishimasu* びっくりする、びっくりします
sushi *sushi* 寿司
sweater *seetaa* セーター
sweet *amai* 甘い
swim (to) *oyogu, oyogimasu* 泳ぐ、泳ぎます
swimming *suiee* 水泳
table *teeburu* テーブル
take (to) *ukeru, ukemasu* 受ける、受けます
  take (photos) (to) *toru, torimasu* 撮る、撮ります
  take (time) (to) *kakaru, kakarimasu* かかる、かかります
  take a bath (to) *ofuro ni hairu, ofuro ni hairimasu* お風呂に入る、お風呂に入ります
  take a day off (to) *yasumu, yasumimasu* 休む、休みます
  take a day off from work (to) *kaisha o yasumu, kaisha o yasumimasu* 会社を休む、会社を休みます
  take a medical consultation (to) *shinsatsu o ukeru, shinsatsu o ukemasu* 診察を受ける、診察を受けます
  take a shower (to) *shawaa o abiru, shawaa o abimasu* シャワーを浴びる、シャワーを浴びます
  take lessons on (to) *narau, naraimasu* 習う、習います
  take off (shoes, clothes) (to) *nugu, nugimasu* 脱ぐ、脱ぎます
  take some rest (to) *yasumu, yasumimasu* 休む、休みます
  take (someone or animal) (to) *tsurete iku, tsurete ikimasu* 連れて行く、連れて行きます
  take (something) (to) *motte iku, motte ikimasu* 持って行く、持って行きます
talk show *tookushoo* トークショー
tall *takai* 高い
taxi *takushii* タクシー
tea (Japanese kind) *ocha* お茶
teach (to) *oshieru, oshiemasu* 教える、教えます
teacher *kyooshi, sensee* 教師、先生
  Prof./Dr. Tanaka *Tanaka sensee* 田中先生
  teacher and student *shitee* 師弟
telephone *(o)denwa (polite with o)* (お)電話

telephone number *(o)denwabangoo (polite with o)* (お)電話番号
television *terebi* テレビ
tell (to) *oshieru, oshiemasu* 教える、教えます
  tell a lie (to) *uso o tsuku, uso o tsukimasu* 嘘をつく、嘘をつきます
(check one's) temperature *netsu o hakaru, netsu o hakarimasu* 熱を測る、熱を測ります
temple *(o)tera (polie with o)* (お)寺
tempura *tenpura* 天ぷら
ten *juu, too (native Japanese number)* 十、十
  ten thousand *ichiman* 一万
  ten thousand yen *ichiman en* 一万円
  ten minutes *juppun* 十分
  ten o'clock *juuji* 十時
tennis *tenisu* テニス
tennis court *tenisu kooto* テニスコート
tenth (day of the month) *tooka* 十日
terrible *hidoi* ひどい
textbook *kyookasho* 教科書
the ... th *... me* ～目
Thank you. *Arigatoo gozaimasu./Arigatoo gozaimashita.* ありがとうございます。/ありがとうございました。
  Thank you very much. *Doomo arigatoo gozaimasu./Doomo arigatoo gozaimashita.* どうもありがとうございます。/どうもありがとうございました。
  No, thank you. *Kekkoo desu.* 結構です。
that (conjunction) *to* と
  that (demonstrative) *sono (far from the speaker but close to the listener)* ; *sore (far from the speaker but close to the listener); ano (far from both the speaker and the listener); are (far from both the speaker and the listener)* その；それ；あの；あれ
  that pen *sono pen (far from the speaker but close to the listener); ano pen (far from both the speaker and the listener)* そのペン；あのペン
  that way *sochira (far from the speaker but close to the listener) (polite); achira (far from both the speaker and the listener) (polite)* そちら；あちら
then *dewa, ja(a) (infml.), sorede wa, sore ja(a) (infml.)* では、じゃ(あ)、それでは、それじゃ(あ)
  and then *sorekara, soshite* それから、そして

See you then. *Sorede wa mata./Sore ja(a) mata. (infml.)* それではまた。/それじゃ(あ)また。

there *asoko (far from both the speaker and the listener) ; soko (far from the speaker but close to the listener)* あそこ;そこ

There is … *aru, arimasu (inanimate); iru, imasu (animate); gozaimasu (polite); irassharu, irasshaimasu (honorific); oru, orimasu (humble)* ある、あります; いる、います; ございます; いらっしゃる、いらっしゃいます; おる、おります

they *karera (people) ; kanojora (people, feminine) ; kanojotachi (people, feminine) ; sorera (inanimate)* 彼ら; 彼女ら;彼女達; それら

thing *koto* こと

think (to) *omou, omoimasu* 思う、思います

third *mittsume* 三つ目

　third (day of the month) *mikka* 三日

thirteen *juusan* 十三

thirty *sanjuu* 三十

　five thirty *goji sanjuppun* 五時三十分

　thirty minutes *sanjuppun* 三十分

this *kore, kono, kochira (polite)* これ、この、こちら

　this morning *kesa* 今朝

　this pen *kono pen* このペン

　this time *kondo* 今度

　this way *kochira (polite)* こちら

　this week *konshuu* 今週

　this weekend *konshuumatsu* 今週末

　this year *kotoshi* 今年

thousand *sen* 千

　ten thousand *ichiman* 一万

　ten thousand yen *ichiman en* 一万円

　thousand yen *sen en* 千円

three *san, mittsu (native Japanese number)* 三、三つ

　three minutes *sanpun* 三分

three o'clock *sanji* 三時

throat *nodo* 喉

　have a sore throat (to) *nodo ga itai, nodo ga itai desu* 喉が痛い、喉が痛いです

Thursday *mokuyoobi* 木曜日

time *jikan* 時間

　this time *kondo* 今度

Times Square *taimuzu sukuea* タイムズスクエア

(sent) to *atesaki* 宛先

　from … to … *… kara … made* 〜から〜まで

tobacco *tabako* 煙草

today *kyoo* 今日

together *issho ni* 一緒に

　all together *zenbu de* 全部で

toilet *toire* トイレ

Tokyo *Tookyoo* 東京

tomato *tomato* トマト

tomorrow *ashita, asu* 明日

　the day after tomorrow *asatte* あさって

tonight *konban* 今晩

too (also) *mo* も

　too, too much *sugiru, sugimasu* すぎる、すぎます

tooth *ha* 歯

tour guide *tenjooin, tsuaagaido* 添乗員、ツアーガイド

town *machi* 町

trade *booeki* 貿易

trading company *booekigaisha* 貿易会社

traffic light *shingoo* 信号

　before the traffic light *shingoo no temae* 信号の手前

train *densha* 電車

transfer (a phone line) (to) *kawaru, kawarimasu* 代わる、代わります

transportation *kootsuu* 交通

　transportation costs *kootsuuhi* 交通費

travel *ryokoo* 旅行

　travel company *ryokoosha* 旅行社

treatment *taiguu* 待遇

tree *ki* 木

　big tree *taiboku* 大木

　tree shadow *kokage* 木陰

true *hontoo* 本当

　Is that true? *Hontoo desu ka.* 本当ですか。

try … ing (to) *… te miru, … te mimasu* 〜てみる、〜てみます

T-shirt *tiishatsu* ティーシャツ（Tシャツ）

Tuesday *kayoobi* 火曜日

tunnel *tonneru* トンネル

turn (to) *magaru, magarimasu* 曲がる、曲がります

twelve *juuni* 十二

　twelve o'clock *juuniji* 十二時

twentieth (day of the month) *hatsuka* 二十日

twenty *nijuu* 二十

two *ni, futatsu (native Japanese number)* 二、二つ

　two minutes *nifun* 二分

Glossary 251

two o'clock *niji* 二時
two people *futari, nimeesama (polite)* 二人、二名様
typhoon *taifuu* 台風
under … *(… no) shita* (〜の)下
  under a lot of stress (to be) *sutoresu ga tamatte iru, sutoresu ga tamatte imasu* ストレスが溜まっている、ストレスが溜まっています
understand (to) *wakaru, wakarimasu* 分かる、分かります
United States (the) *amerika* アメリカ
university *daigaku* 大学
unskillful *heta* 下手
until *made* まで
up to now *ima made ni, kore made ni* 今までに、これまでに
urine *nyoo* 尿
use (to) *tsukau, tsukaimasu* 使う、使います
vacation *yasumi* 休み
  summer vacation *natsu yasumi* 夏休み
van *ban* バン
various *kakushu* 各種
vegetable *yasai* 野菜
very *totemo, taihen* とても、大変
  very much *totemo* とても
vest *besuto* ベスト
vigorous *genki* 元気
violin *baiorin* バイオリン
virtue *toku* 徳
visible (to be) *mieru, miemasu* 見える、見えます
visit (to) *tazuneru, tazunemasu* 訪ねる、訪ねます
vitamin supplement *bitaminzai* ビタミン剤
volleyball *bareebooru* バレーボール
voucher *ken* 券
waist *koshi* 腰
wait (to) *matsu, machimasu* 待つ、待ちます
  I/We will be waiting for you. *Omachishite orimasu. (polite)* お待ちしております。
  Please wait. *Omachi kudasai. (polite)* お待ちください。
waiting room *machiaishitsu* 待合室
waitress *weitoresu* ウエイトレス
wake-to-sleep transition *netsuki* 寝つき
Wales *weeruzu* ウェールズ
walk (to) *aruku, arukimasu* 歩く、歩きます
  five minute walk *aruite gofun* 歩いて五分
want (to) *hoshii, hoshii desu* 欲しい、欲しいです

(Someone) wants *hoshigatte iru, hoshigatte imasu* 欲しがっている、欲しがっています
want to (to) *tai, tai desu* たい、たいです
warm *atatakai* 暖かい
wash (to) *arau, araimasu* 洗う、洗います
washing machine *sentakuki* 洗濯機
watch *tokee* 時計
watch (to) *miru, mimasu; goran ni naru, goran ni narimasu (honorific); haikensuru, haikenshimasu (humble)* 見る、見ます；ご覧になる、ご覧になります；拝見する、拝見します
water *(o) mizu (polite with o)* (お)水
we *watashitachi* 私達
web designer *webudezainaa* ウェブデザイナー
Wednesday *suiyoobi* 水曜日
week *shuu* 週
  a week *isshuukan* 一週間
  last week *senshuu* 先週
  next week *raishuu* 来週
  this week *konshuu* 今週
weekday *heejitsu* 平日
weekend *shuumatsu* 週末
  this weekend *konshuumatsu* 今週末
Welcome. *Yookoso.* ようこそ。
Welcome (to our store). *Irasshaimase.* いらっしゃいませ。
well *yoku* よく
  well … *anoo, etto, hee, uun* あのう、えっと、へえ、ううん
  Well done. *Yoku dekimashita.* よくできました。
west side *nishigawa* 西側
Western style *yoofuu* 洋風
what *nan(i)* 何
  What about … ? *Doo desu ka.* どうですか。
  what kind of *donna* どんな
  what time *nanji* 何時
  What's the matter? *Doo shimashita ka./Doo nasaimashita ka. (polite)* どうしましたか。/どうなさいましたか。
wheat *komugi* 小麦
when *itsu (question); tara, to, toki (conjunction)* いつ；たら、と、時
where *doko, dochira (polite)* どこ、どちら
which (one) *dono* どの
  which one *dore, dochira, dochira no hoo* どれ、どちら、どちらの方
  which pen *dono pen* どのペン
  which way *dochira (polite)* どちら

white *shiroi* 白い
white night *byakuya* 白夜
white wine *shiro wain* 白ワイン
who *dare, donate (polite)* 誰、どなた
why *dooshite, naze, nande (infml.)* どうして、なぜ、なんで
  Why don't we … ? *… masen ka.* 〜ませんか。
wife *kanai (one's own), tsuma (one's own), okusan (someone else's)* 家内、妻、奥さん
wind *kaze* 風
window *mado* 窓
window shopping *windooshoppingu* ウィンドーショッピング
wine *wain* ワイン
  red wine *aka wain* 赤ワイン
  white wine *shiro wain* 白ワイン
winter *fuyu* 冬
with *to* と
woman *onna no hito* 女の人
(I) wonder … *… kana(a)./ … kashira.* 〜かな(あ)。/〜かしら。
woods *hayashi* 林
wool *uuru* ウール
  100% wool *uuru hyakupaasento* ウール100パーセント
word *kotoba* 言葉
word processor *waapuro* ワープロ
work *o(shigoto) (polite with o), kinmu (fml.)* (お)仕事、勤務
  place of work *kinmuchi* 勤務地
  take a day off from work (to) *kaisha o yasumu, kaisha o yasumimasu* 会社を休む、会社を休みます
work (to) *hataraku, hatarakimasu* 働く、働きます
  work overtime (to) *zangyoosuru, zangyooshimasu* 残業する、残業します
Wow. *Hee.* へえ。
write (to) *kaku, kakimasu* 書く、書きます
yard *niwa* 庭
year *nen* 年
  for a year *ichinenkan* 一年間
  next year *rainen* 来年
  this year *kotoshi* 今年
yellow *kiiroi (adjective), kiiro (noun)* 黄色い、黄色
yen *en* 円
  ten thousand yen *ichiman en* 一万円
  thousand yen *sen en* 千円
yes *hai, ee (infml.), un (infml.)* はい、ええ、うん

Yes, it is. *Soo desu ne.* そうですね。
yesterday *kinoo* 昨日
  the day before yesterday *ototoi* おととい
yet *mada (+negative)* まだ
you (subject pronoun) *anata (sg.), anatagata (pl.), anatatachi (pl.)* あなた、あなた方、あなた達
young *wakai* 若い
younger brother *otooto (one's own), otootosan (someone else's)* 弟、弟さん
younger sister *imooto (one's own), imootosan (someone else's)* 妹、妹さん
your (sg.) *anata no* あなたの
zen *zen* 禅
zero *ree, zero* 零、ゼロ